"Revelations of Christ *by Swami Kriyananda comes to us as a 'tour de force' of wisdom. The universality of Christ consciousness as seen through this all-embracing vision rings aloud page after page. Here is truth, not doctrine. Here is peace beyond understanding.*"

—**Roger Montgomery**, Leader, Spirit of Peace Monastic Community, co-author, *The Sacred Light of Healing*

"*Anytime we have a chance to re-look at the man and the message of Jesus Christ we should do so. This history changing message or gospel is as relevant now as it ever was. Yogananda captures the Eternal Truth of the Eternal Christ.*"

—**Rev. Kathianne Lewis**, Center for Spiritual Living, author, *40 Days to Freedom*

"*...Truly inspired writing. The inner meaning of Jesus' teaching is revealed by a writer whose insights come from direct, inner communion with God. Speaking from outside the confines of Christianity, he voices Christian truths from a level, not of dogmatic faith, but of divine realization. While acknowledging the divinity of Jesus, his emphasis is clearly on our privilege, even our duty as children of God, to realize we too are projections of God's consciousness.*"

—**Rev. Robert H. Henderson, DD**, Church of Spiritual Living

"*In its simplicity and practical commonsense it plumbs the depth of the perennial insights that surround every great prophet in history—and especially the figure of Jesus the Christ. There had to be one from outside the official fold of Christendom to undertake the daring task of going straight to the source without the detour of official doctrine....Every reader, whether Christian or not, owes a deep debt of gratitude to Kriyananda, and his master, Yogananda.*"

—**Ervin Laszlo, PhD**, Nominee for Nobel Peace Prize, author, *Science and the Reenchantment of the Cosmos.*

"*I believe that every sincere seeker of truth will benefit from reading this book. I expect it to become a force of illumination for all mankind. I feel myself uplifted even in writing these few words of praise for this truly great work.*"

—**Swami Shankarananda**, Rishikesh, India

Revelations of
CHRIST

Proclaimed by Paramhansa Yogananda,

Presented by his disciple,
Swami Kriyananda

Revelations of
CHRIST

Proclaimed by Paramhansa Yogananda,

**Presented by his disciple,
Swami Kriyananda**

Cover illustration by Dana Lynne Andersen

Crystal Clarity Publishers
Nevada City, California

Cover illustration is a painting by the artist
Dana Lynne Andersen
Commissioned for this book, and titled: *Pearl of Great Price.*

ISBN: 978-1-56589-222-4
Printed in U.S.A.

1 3 5 7 9 10 8 6 4 2
first printing

Crystal Clarity Publishers
14618 Tyler Foote Road
Nevada City, CA 95959-8599
800.424.1055 or 530.478.7600
F: 530.478.7610
clarity@crystalclarity.com
www.crystalclarity.com

Library of Congress Cataloging-in-Publication Data

Kriyananda, Swami.
  Revelations of Christ : Proclaimed by Paramhansa Yogananda /
presented by Swami Kriyananda.
    p. cm.
  Includes index.
  ISBN 978-1-56589-222-4 (hardcover, original commissioned
cover art work)
  1. Jesus Christ—Oriental interpretations. 2. Yogananda,
Paramhansa, 1893-1952. 3. Christianity and yoga. I. Title.

BT304.94.K75 2007
232.9--dc22

                                          2007002920

To Those Sincere Christians
Whose Faith Has Been Shaken

Contents

FOREWORD BY NEALE DONALD WALSCH

TO MY MANY FRIENDS AND SPIRITUAL COMPANIONS AROUND THE WORLD:

Something wonderful has happened. There has been given to humanity a great gift. It is a spiritual treasure to cherish deep in the heart, and to pass on to children for generations. I am speaking of the extraordinary book, *Revelations of Christ.*

For longer than any of us can remember, the words and teachings of the great Master, Jesus, have been guiding lives upon the earth. Yet those words and those teachings have too often been interpreted and understood in ways that may have distorted, however inadvertently, their original meaning. Because the Messages of Jesus are so profoundly important, it is essential that they be embraced with only the deepest love for, and loyalty to, God and truth, not any institution or religious tradition. For spiritual truth lies outside of institutions and traditions and can only reside within the fullness of a human heart that is united with the soul in the purest yearning for the bliss of truly knowing the Divine.

The sadness of some religious institutions and traditions is that, though sincerely motivated, often their own inner political maneuverings and mechanical workings stand in the way of simple, true, and uncompromised religious experience and spiritual knowledge. Now this remarkable and magnificent new book by Swami Kriyananda glides us gently past those maneuverings and workings, bringing us to the doorway of a deeper, richer embracing of Eternal Truth. In a text that is at once crystal clear and wonderfully insightful, we are invited to move through that doorway into a place of gloriously larger views of Jesus and God and of Life Itself than many of us have ever been blessed to behold.

My heart pounded with soft excitement as I turned each page, and now it sings with praise and gratitude to Swami for this astonishing gift to the soul. I believe with all my being that these are the words of Jesus as they were meant to be relayed and understood.

Without adequate words to express my thanks, I am...

NEALE DONALD WALSCH

INTRODUCTION

HOW IS ONE TO UNDERSTAND THE LIFE AND TEACH-
ings of the great master Jesus, whose title
"the Christ" meant the "anointed of God"?
Tradition offers us two approaches: one, the authority of the Church; the other, that of historical analysis, which Christian scholars lately have been applying to certain recently discovered texts.

There is another approach, less widely known but
more reliable than any other: It is to study the writings and sayings of, or better still to live with and
study under, saints who have communed directly, in
deep states of ecstasy, with Christ and God. Such
persons are true spiritual masters. They have lived in
every country, and have belonged to every religion
and every social level. They have taught the Truth
from their own deep realization. When they've been
free to speak out, their impact has been widespread

and profound. Often, unfortunately, freedom of speech has been denied them; they've had to submit to the control of religious superiors, who considered their own authority a supreme right bestowed on them by God.

All true saints—those, in other words, who have reached the highest spiritual attainments—have endorsed the teachings of Jesus Christ either directly or indirectly, by stating the same truth similarly. Christian saints want to support their Church, and usually consider it their duty to sow seeds of harmony, not of dissension. There have, on the other hand, been times in history when a saint was divinely commissioned to correct one or more serious errors.

The difficulty saints have endured under church authority has been due—understandably, but at the same time unfortunately—to officials who were administrators but were rarely, if ever, saints themselves. Such authorities have insisted that their approval was needed before anyone—particularly anyone of real merit—could preach spiritual truth. The very fact of any Christians being also saints has been perceived, at least during their lifetimes, as a threat to institutional authority. For what the authorities want first of all is to ascertain whether some "saintly upstart" is preaching truth or heresy.

Saint Francis of Assisi, whose sanctity was certainly due to his deep love for God and his deep, inner communion with Him, has been acclaimed by the Catholic Church as a true son of the Church, which takes credit for his holiness and attributes it to the saint's humble obedience to Church authority.

Any saint in Christian history who ever spoke, or even hinted at, truths that weren't sanctioned by the Church was punished and, in many cases, excommunicated. An example of one who was excommunicated was Meister Eckhart in Germany, who (fortunately for him) died before notice of this punishment could reach him.

Saint Joseph of Cupertino, to whom even crowned heads in Europe came for inspiration and blessings, was orthodox in everything he said and did. He repeatedly, however, performed the miracle of levitation, an act which embarrassed his less-saintly superiors. After fifteen years of virtual incarceration in an apartment of the Basilica in Assisi, he was carted off—not once, but repeatedly whenever his whereabouts became known publicly—in the dead of night to a succession of small, distant monasteries.

A Claretian monk of my acquaintance in Los Angeles, California, developed a reputation for bilocation (appearing in more than one place at a time). He was quietly transferred to a distant house of the same Order in Spain. Catholics themselves describe this quiet removal as "sending one to prison."

Therese Neumann, the great Catholic stigmatist in Bavaria, Germany, was prohibited for a time by her bishop from even seeing people.

And Padre Pio, in southern Italy, was also for a time forbidden from performing mass in his capacity of priest. Regarding this saint, an Italian friend of mine in Rome once visited him, and, during his confession, stated that he practiced Kriya Yoga (a meditation technique brought to the West by my great Guru, Paramhansa Yogananda).

"Oh, hush!" the saint warned hastily. "You mustn't speak of these things." Then he added, "But you are doing the right thing."

There are two major disadvantages to having a church as the supreme authority. The first is that the churches are committed—necessarily so—to giving priority to their own supremacy as Christ's representatives. Therefore they cannot be objective concerning any concept they perceive as a threat to that supremacy.

The second disadvantage follows from the first: Church authority, if too firmly exercised, reduces religious teachings to a faint echo of the divine truths it proclaims. Water cannot flow higher than its source. When religious institutions appoint themselves as the only source of truth—though in fact, such truths as they utter can only flow *through* them—they block that flow. Of course, they never state that they *are* that source; all of them claim to be representing Christ's Truth. Nevertheless, the teachings they promulgate wane in power from a mighty waterfall to a gurgling rill.

My purpose in writing this book is to present the teachings of Jesus Christ as they were proclaimed by one of the great saints and spiritual masters of our own times, Paramhansa Yogananda, who was sent by God to the West with the commission of restoring the teachings of Jesus Christ to their full and original glory.

There is another, urgent reason why this book is being written. Christendom has come under attack not only from theological dilutions which it has long endured and has at least succeeded in surviving; and not only from those familiar enemies of religion, the materialistic sciences: but also from a new and seemingly formidable (though in fact spiritually toothless) source. For, since the discovery in hidden places of ancient documents, some of which seem to cast doubt on traditional perceptions that have come down from early times, scholars have been attacking the very foundations of Christianity. Works of fiction have, more recently, attacked with false invention some of the basic deeds and utterances of Jesus Christ, which they have twisted out of all recognition.

Only a declaration of certain deep truths in Christ's original divine teachings, proclaimed once again by a truly enlightened spiritual master, can bring the authority that is needed in the world today to counter these bee swarms attacking from all sides. Since the saints in Christendom have been debarred from freely speaking their own perceptions of the Truth, it is urgently important for an enlightened spiritual master to come *from outside Christendom*, and to proclaim once again clearly, forcefully, and unfettered by outside control, speaking from the highest level of perception, the revelations of Christ.

Within the Catholic Church, loyalty to its authority

has always been rewarded. On the other hand, disobedience, disagreement, and disloyalty have been punished as severely as the times permitted. Praise, preferment, and even promotion, both in religion and in the world, were frequently the rewards of loyalty. Therefore people felt an incentive to demonstrate, with ever-increasing fervor, the firmness of their loyalty. Jesus Christ gradually became promoted in people's understanding from the status of a great spiritual master to someone higher than anything even imaginable: the Absolute Master, the "only Son of God."

Few dared to contest this claim. Protests even by sincere Christians were eliminated by the all-powerful Church, and were finally dropped by the writers of Church history. Indeed, it was a foregone conclusion from the start that dogmatism would eventually win out.

Lest anyone think, from what I have written so far, that my own view of Jesus Christ is detached and disinterested, let me affirm unequivocally, here at the outset, that I believe in his divinity with all my heart. I do resist, however, the concept that he was the *only* Son of God, and therefore God's *unique offspring*. I will clarify what I mean by presenting the teachings on this point of Paramhansa Yogananda, whose humble disciple I have the honor to be.

Many subjects will be covered in this book as we proceed, for the teachings I'm giving are Paramhansa Yogananda's, and they address—profoundly and far-reachingly—many of the facets of Christ's teaching.

Part One

THE BASICS

CHAPTER ONE

MAJOR DISADVANTAGES

THERE IS A MAJOR DISADVANTAGE TO KEEPING SPIRI-
tual authority confined in a hierarchy of
prelates. The disadvantage is that institutional hierarchies are composed of human beings,
most of whom have at least a few of the flaws common to mankind, among which must be counted
pride, jealousy, personal prejudice, intolerance, vin-
dictiveness, pettiness, and a tendency to be judg-
mental and unforgiving. Any one of these flaws is
enough to obscure a person's perception of higher
truths. Claims may be (and of course have been)
made that Jesus Christ is guiding his Church to
preserve it from serious error. The Roman Catholic
Church carries this claim to the extent of insisting
that, when the Pope (as the Church's top primate)
speaks "*ex cathedra,*" he is infallible. Other
churches, though lacking historical prece-

dence, insist to varying degrees on their own authority in matters of Christian Truth.

The greatest problem all the churches face is the
simple fact that the majority of their leaders are
only human beings, trapped in ego-centeredness
(rather than souls that are free in God). They are
therefore, and cannot but be, fallible. (Arrogance,
I should add in clarification, is only one of the
manifestations of ego-consciousness, which is a
fundamental human reality.) What, then, is the
ego? It is like a sliver of glass shining in the sunlight. It can reflect the "sun" of God, whose consciousness is the sole reality in existence, but the
ego has no light of its own. Individuality is a universal illusion. It exists wherever creatures have
developed sufficient clarity of awareness to *reflect*
in themselves the light and consciousness of the
infinite Self.

All living beings grow outward from a tiny center: from a seed, or from a first cell created by the
union of sperm and ovum. Creatures grow outward from their own, individual centers. Consciousness of separate individuality is developed
most highly in human beings. Attachment to ego
is the root cause of every human delusion. People's notions of perfection cannot but be limited,
therefore.

High position in a church does not infuse unenlightened ego-centered human beings "out of the
blue" with divine or mystical insights. God can of
course do anything, but the evidence of history

shows that enlightenment comes only to individuals as a result of personal merit. The individual must first seek God personally, and be pure in heart. Enlightenment never comes to people in batches like college diplomas to a "graduating class." Neither—it must be stated also—can belief in "papal infallibility" be viewed impartially as anything but wishful piety. (This dogma is a relatively new development in the Catholic Church, having been declared only in 1869 as, one suspects, an act of desperation to ward off theological challenges from the Protestants.)

All too often, what happens is that high position goes to a "superior's" head. An inflated sense of his own importance draws a thick veil of self-involvement over any ability he might have had to perceive reality, whether mundane or spiritual, clearly. Hence the saying, "Pride goes before a fall."

How shall perfection be defined? In human beings, the root cause of imperfection is ego-centeredness; it conditions one's every perception. In smug self-esteem, and in people's eagerness to be admired by others, they project personal ambition outward, and often assume that institutional promotion raises one automatically to exalted personal importance. Promotion, however, doesn't really change anyone inwardly. What happens all too often is that authority begets arrogance. In church hierarchies, arrogance is followed by ego-boosting attitudes like

self-righteousness, insensitivity, irrational out-
bursts of rage, and indignation (self-defined as
"righteous") at the misbehavior and shortcomings
of others.

Jesus Christ said, **"Be ye therefore perfect,
even as your Father which is in heaven is perfect."** (Matt. 5:48) Translators have not been able
to imagine for human beings a state of absolute
perfection. Often, therefore, they dilute the meaning of that counsel to fit a concept they consider
more universally acceptable, because comprehensible. Translations have appeared with theological dilutions such as, "Be ye therefore good, even
as God is good."

The very idea that human nature can be im-
proved suggests that Christ was teaching us to aspire to greater heights *in ourselves*, and to ever
deeper awareness of God's presence within us.
Not all Christians are equally good, obviously.
Some are better than others; some are worse; and
some manage to be quite a lot worse. All this must
be "perfectly" obvious to everyone.

A further step in this logical progression, however, is not so obvious, and is too seldom considered: namely, that goodness depends on *inner*
standards, and above all on humility and purity of
heart. These qualities are determined much less
by outward behavior than by inner attitudes. They
bear very little relationship, certainly, to a person's rank or position. "God watches the heart" is
a saying that should be kept always in mind.

Divine qualities are certainly not determined by the position one holds in a church. Promotion may come in recognition of personal virtues, but it is not *in itself* any assurance of such virtue, since superiors, being human, can err, and even if they show wisdom in one choice, that choice will never in any case *bestow* wisdom.

Indeed, promotion may also have unfortunate consequences. If the choice, in a church hierarchy, lies between a competent administrator and someone who, although saintly, lacks administrative competence, the selection will certainly go to him who is competent. Thus, clerical hierarchies become almost inevitably top-heavy, in time, with efficient but not particularly saintly administrators.

Administrative types are attracted to others of the same mentality: efficient, executive, interested more in *how* to get things done than in *why* they need to be done in the first place. "Birds of a feather flock together." In religion, the administrative mentality tends toward efficiency, and may even frown on what it considers excessive concern with the lofty spiritual outlook. Administrative types always, therefore, favor others for promotion whom they themselves resemble: people also whom they personally like. If, moreover, a saintly candidate has all the skills required of a good administrator, and someone else is available whose nature is more closely akin to those making the appointment, then it won't matter if this alternate choice lacks saintliness. Indeed, it may help *especially* for him not to be saintly. (Who, after all, wants his own shortcoming to be exposed?) The "bird of the same feather" will almost certainly get the job.

If what I have stated is true—and everyone knows it is true—then it follows that decisions regarding spiritual matters should never be left primarily in the hands of high-ranking prelates. Still less, for that matter—though for a different reason—should they be left in the hands of merely intellectual theologians. Moreover (to conclude my catalogue of spiritual ineptitude), since intellectual learning is often a breeding ground for arrogance, such decisions should never be made by anyone for whom scholarship is his primary credential. The skill of the intellect at distorting reality is notorious. (That is why we have the saying, "Even the Devil quotes scripture.") Indeed, the sharper the intellect, often, the more skillful a person is at distorting truth. As my Guru's guru Swami Sri Yukteswar put it, "Keen intelligence is two-edged. It may be used constructively or destructively like a knife, either to cut the boil of ignorance, or to decapitate one's self. Intelligence is rightly guided only after the mind has acknowledged the inescapability of spiritual law."

Those persons alone are blessed with true spiritual insight who have lived their lives conscientiously by Truth, and who have *done their best (as Christ said) to attain perfection* in themselves.

According to the highest tradition in Christianity—and the tradition exists as well, for that matter, in all true religions—there do exist people who
have actually attained the truths proclaimed in
the Bible. Most of the same truths are, indeed,
proclaimed in every great scripture. The people to
whom I refer have communed inwardly with God;
they have themselves become godly. Deep, inner
experience of the Divine has raised them to the realization of God as the only Truth there is.

For the administrative type, which church hierarchies almost always attract, that divine reality is
a distant consideration. Of more immediate and
even overwhelming concern to them is how to
meet their day-to-day exigencies. Thoughts of
Eternity are, so to speak, "put on a back burner."
Sacred truths are left to take care of themselves!

In their own sphere of influence, church administrators function well enough. Few of them, however, are able at the same time to keep their
hearts' feelings focused on Eternal Truth.

The true custodians of religion, in other words,
are the saints, who alone can speak with full spiritual authority. Whatever his outer position, a
saint's inner consciousness dwells on an exalted
plane, which alone qualifies him to make important pronouncements on any deeply spiritual
matter. Out of the vast variety in human nature,
the saints are a class by themselves: They alone
are the *knowers* of God.

In this sense it must be added, as a balance to

my first criticism, that the Roman Catholic Church, alone among the vast variety of Christian churches, is in a position even today to transmit the true spirit of Jesus Christ. I say this not because the Roman Catholic is the oldest church, nor because the Pope is (as Catholics claim) the successor to St. Peter,* nor because of that purely man-made dogma, "papal infallibility," but because the Catholic Church continues to uphold this highest spiritual tradition: man's ability to achieve direct, inner God-communion, and thereby to be supremely blessed and "anointed" by the Lord.

The Protestant churches on the whole deny this possibility. Even those churches which affirm it reduce its meaning to the lowest common denominator: They claim that *everyone* who professes belief in Jesus Christ is a saint already!

The Christian churches all insist that human perfectibility cannot in any case equal the absolute perfection of Jesus Christ. Indeed, they proclaim man's *inherent sinfulness before God.* Our destiny as souls, they say, is, after death, to suffer eternally in hellfire owing to the original sin committed by our first parents, Adam and Eve. Our only chance for redemption is, according to

---

*This claim determinedly overlooks the numerous gaps in that line of succession, which have occurred in consequence of papal rivalries. Several popes, moreover, have been notorious for their moral and spiritual laxity by expressing which they have dishonored their holy tradition.

them, to accept Jesus Christ as our "only personal Savior."

What have the saints had to say on this subject? Do they speak of man's natural sinfulness? Do they agree that man cannot possibly do anything to save himself? The saints, it must be pointed out to begin with, have decried the spiritually dampening effect of the concept that no man can hope for perfection. St. Teresa of Avila told her nuns that their duty was to strive to *become* saints. All the saints have said that divine grace is for everyone. Paraphrasing them, we may say that grace is like the sunlight on a building: It can enter only into those rooms which have their curtains drawn wide.

Are the saints themselves, then, perfect? This matter will be probed in some depth later on. The groundwork must first be laid, however, for an understanding of the true meaning of spiritual perfection. Let me, for now, emphasize this simple fact: A true saint is as far above the goodness that defines the ordinarily good Christian as is a skyscraper above the humble hut of a peasant. If one is charitable to all, does good works, and shuns vainglory, he deserves admiration as a human being. So long as he remains centered in his consciousness of egoic separateness, however, he should not be considered, in the highest sense of the word, a saint. For in his own eyes it is *he himself* who expresses charity, goodness, and all his other virtues. A true saint, by contrast, allows virtue to *flow through* him. He never sees *himself* as its source. Indeed, most if not all the virtues may be, and have been many times, expressed fully also in the lives of self-declared atheists. Christ's message is much stricter. He told us to transcend ego-consciousness, that we see ourselves, simply, as instruments of God.

In striking corroboration of this statement, I remember one time when Yogananda was praised by someone for his humility. He answered with what might be called a "conversation stopper": "How can there be humility," he asked, "when there is no consciousness of ego?"

The criterion of what it means to be a good Christian has been diluted by what Yogananda called "Churchianity." Nowadays, the usual criterion of a good Christian is someone who merely believes in Jesus Christ, and accepts him as his own "personal" Savior. A person may go regularly to church, be a good neighbor to others, help the needy, and be kind to all, but who tells him that he must also be conscious of his inner need to know God? Spiritual half-heartedness is what Jesus Christ meant when he said, **"Not every one that saith unto me, Lord, Lord, shall enter into the kingdom of heaven; but he that doeth the will of my Father, which is in heaven."** (Matt. 7:21) In the preceding verse he said also, **"By their fruits ye shall know them."**

Is belief in *anything* really enough? People once believed that the world is flat: Did mere belief make it so? Science has demonstrated convincingly that belief is no guarantee of the truth of anything. Because belief has been made the criterion of a good Christian, Christianity has been slowly sinking in popular esteem to the level of a third-rate power.

Belief is only the beginning of the search for knowledge. Belief is the hypothesis. It is needed to provide the incentive for verifying one's hopes and expectations. After hypothesis comes the process of testing. *Proof*, however, will come only after a hypothesis (in this case, a belief) has been fairly tested.

What actual proofs does religion offer? The promise the churches offer is the mere hope of a happy, carefree life in heaven after death. Is that a *proof*? It is only a pious expectation, which invites rather the question: How many have returned from heaven to report their actual arrival there?

Yogananda enjoyed telling a story he'd read in a book about Billy Sunday, the American evangelist. Billy, after death, presented himself at the "Pearly Gates." Knocking loudly, he demanded to be admitted.

Saint Peter appeared, heard Billy's request, and leafed through the Book of Life. "I'm sorry," he announced, "but your name isn't listed here."

"But that's impossible!" expostulated Billy Sunday indignantly. "What about all those people I sent up here?"

St. Peter studied the book once more, then
replied, "You may have sent them, but none have
arrived."

Religious truths can indeed be tested and
proved. The proof consists in the yardstick of experience. If this statement seems simplistic,
please reflect a moment: What does it mean, to
test a spiritual truth? It means to exclude rigidly
from one's life every vestige of ego-motivation. It
means, in time, to realize that God alone *IS*, and
that He alone *DOES* everything. Anyone who
makes this attempt seriously will soon discover in
his seeking that the challenge he faces demands
of him, in fact, a spirit of heroism!

Objective proof of the truth of Christ's teachings
lies in the impersonal love manifested by those of
every religion who have transcended ego-aware-
ness and have, consequently, learned to love all
beings equally. Such persons seek nothing in return, and consider it no sacrifice to retain nothing
for themselves. The definition of impersonal love is
a love that is purely self-giving, that wants nothing for one's self, and that doesn't hold onto anything with attachment.

The alternative way of seeking proof, and the
proof that is usually proposed, is through the syl-
logisms of logic: the analytical, scholarly method.
Truth, however, is not up for election. The modern
mind, educated as people are to trust the proofs of
material science, inclines to view rational scholarship as more objective, and therefore more

valid, than dogmatism. A great fuss, indeed, has been made in recent decades over lately discovered manuscripts that date back to early Christian times. Scholars claim that those documents provide fresh insight into the teachings of Jesus Christ and the origins of Christianity. They have actually announced, on the basis of some of those documents, that Jesus did not die on the cross, but survived his crucifixion and went on to marry Mary Magdalene, the two of them producing a "bloodline" which continues to this day.

Jesus Christ himself, it must be noted, is quoted in the Bible as declaring, **"There be eunuchs, which have made themselves eunuchs for the kingdom of heaven's sake. He that is able to receive it, let him receive it."** (Matt. 19:12) By these words, as well as by the well-known example of his life, Jesus made it clear that he was himself celibate. (Yogananda emphasized that Jesus did not mean, in this passage, that one should castrate himself "for the kingdom of heaven's sake."

("It would deprive you," he told his monk disciples, "of the energy you need to find God.")

Once the authority of the Gospels is challenged on such fundamental points as these, Christianity itself might as well be thrown onto the rubbish heap—or else the Holy Bible preserved in a museum display case of encrusted antiquities, gathering dust. In this case, the religion of our forefathers could not but cease to offer perfection as an ideal to which all can aspire despite what Jesus said, and would deserve rather to be tossed aside as bereft of any divine message. For Christ's message must then be considered as containing nothing but pious platitudes.

Human nature tends to seek the "easy way out." Faced with Jesus Christ's doctrine to "Love thy neighbor," one might find comfort in believing that he is still perfectly free to hate his neighbor's neighbor with frigid fury. Again, faced with the two clear-cut alternatives: heaven or hell after death, he might think, "Well, how could God, being good, condemn me to eternal hell for being—if not perfect, at least *moderately* good?" Gradually, by pursuing this line of reasoning, he might well end up asking himself (as, in fact, many do), "Just how bad can I be and get away with it?"

It has become usual for Christians, in their awareness of claims made by certain "new Christian" scholars that Jesus Christ was "only human," to conclude that it is still possible to be a good Christian and have no spiritual aspirations at all. Alternatively—and this has been claimed also—it would be quite all right simply to dispense with Christianity and "all that religious stuff" altogether, and simply be a normal, decent, well-intentioned human being. And what if self-interest remains a life priority? Well, can't that be said of almost everyone anyway? (And can so many people be wrong? Such may be the usual "take" on that point. It is opposed, however, by the voice of experience, which has repeatedly shown the following to be true: "The majority is always wrong; the minority has at least a possibility of being right.")

I once asked my Guru about someone who was good, kind, honest, and truthful, but who had no interest in seeking God. His reply was surprising: "The road to Hades is paved with good intentions."

The danger of intellectual scholars to religion is not merely theoretical. Surveys of present-day Christians show that a high percentage of them feel shaken in their faith by scholarly claims that challenge the very authenticity of the Gospels. Not a few such claims have been aired, without proper authentication, in works of pure fiction. Others have been made by scholars who, though serious, demonstrate a lamentable absence of spiritual insight. In both cases, the claims to authenticity are based on the supposed antiquity of their sources, supported by a skillful misuse of reasoning.

Man's highest faculty is not his intellect. All human beings possess the power, at least latently, of extrasensory perception. A person might *know*, quite unaccountably (when foreknowledge seems impossible), that something is going to take place, and it happens. Or he may know exactly how to respond fittingly to some unprecedented threat to his person or to his financial security. Again, he may be unaccountably aware of something that will happen in someone else's life, and not even be surprised when it occurs, later. Or again he may, without even a shred of evidence, see behind a person's façade of respectability and recognize in him certain hidden, dishonest intentions.

I offer these examples as commonplace. Such insights are like rents in the veil which separates the majority of people from one another, and from subtler-than-material realities. Yogananda defined intuition, ultimately, as "the soul's power of knowing God."

Consciousness manifests on three levels: subconscious, conscious, and superconscious. Subconsciousness, the first level, depends on external influences to which it reacts instinctively. It is on this level that the lower animals function.

"Man," according to a classical definition, "is a rational animal." Yet man is, in fact, neither entirely rational nor entirely an animal. That definition is a marvel of clarity in the sense that it serves whoever uses it as a premise for pursuing numerous lines of reasoning. It doesn't take into consideration, however, man's irrational moods, his unpredictable whims, his deep-seated prejudices. It gives no recognition, moreover, to the human capacity for developing spiritual insight, and for rising *above* his animal nature altogether. The conscious mind functions through the intellect. It compares things, then analyzes the comparison to achieve a more complete understanding. Usually, understanding that is arrived at by the intellect depends on the perceptions of the senses. This dependence renders the intellect, where higher truth is concerned, more or less incompetent.

Superconsciousness is universally the highest level of cognition. At this level, man transcends his self-limiting human nature and becomes a child of God, forever free in his soul.

One benefit that man has derived from modern science is the realization, intellectually at least, that reality is not confined to what the five senses perceive. Indeed, matter is now known not to have any substance at all: it is a product of innumerable vibrations of energy. Science has greatly expanded our physical and mental horizons, too, with its probes into the vastness of space and into the intricacies of the microcosmic world.

One result of that expansion has been the speed of travel to very distant places. One can even observe scenes now from around the world, flashing instantaneously on his television screen. Almost everyone nowadays is aware of cultures and countries distant and very different from his own. All of us know that the people who live in far-off countries are not essentially different from ourselves or from our near neighbors.

We are also becoming ever more aware that many teachings of other religions are very similar to, and even identical in meaning with our own. Christian theologians, most of whom still cling determinedly to the dogma that Jesus Christ was superior to all others, try constantly to draw their

readers' attention to any *dis*similarities they can
ferret out between Christianity and other religions. The differences, however, are all fairly
superficial. Yogananda described the hidden
motivation behind such scholarly attempts as
"mischievous," for they misrepresent what they
have determined to view as the "opposition."
Where such issues don't arise, it is notably true
that human beings everywhere have basically the
same needs: food, clothing, shelter, as well as the
same basic emotional needs: love, kindness, emotional security, happiness.

People everywhere in the world have also (most
deeply rooted of all) a spiritual dimension, which
the great religions address more or less identi-
cally. No true religion has ever taught people to
hate, or to tell lies, or to inflict pain and harm on
others. All of them urge people to behave in ways
that will expand their ego-identity by including
the realities of others. Every religion, moreover, in-
sists on the need for all men to love unselfishly,
and to develop the virtues of truthfulness, kindness, compassion, forgiveness, and all the rest. No
religion, moreover, recommends the creed of materialists the world over: "Me-firstism."

Nowadays, with increasing awareness that there
may actually be a spiritual dimension in human
life, it would surely show meanness of spirit to
deprecate others' efforts to rise spiritually, each
according to his own capacity and beliefs. Any
teaching that raises human consciousness—for

example, by kindness and unselfish love—can only be good. Why then, in the zeal to convert him, harp on how wrong he is, or on how much he lacks a true teaching? Sympathetic interest in ways different from one's own is becoming increasingly widespread these days. People want to know how others eat, how they dress, how they define gracious living. Given this natural and increasingly universal curiosity, is it not right for people also to be interested in what other people think, in how they define happiness, and in how they approach God?

Dr. Radhakrishnan, who, when I visited him, was the vice president of India (he later became India's president), said to me, "A nation is known by those persons whom its people look upon as great." By that criterion, India is, and has earned the right to be, known as the most spiritual country on earth. For people elsewhere mostly define greatness by political, literary, or—God help us!— "sports hero" and "movie star" criteria. India's principal standard, by contrast, has always been its spiritual giants: its saints.

I was once asked by a Christian missionary in India, "What do you mean when you use the word, 'saint'?"

"My reference," I replied, "is to the Sanskrit word, *sant*, from which our word 'saint' is derived." (Thus did I nip in the bud a blossoming theological challenge!)

The great figures in India's past have always

been men and women of Self-realization. Emperors, warriors, political leaders and other worldly figures in history, though admired and respected, have always been given a secondary status. Wisdom, moreover, has not been confused in India with scholarship or with intellectual brilliance. True wisdom is determined by a person's inner experience of God and by his consequent understanding of the true meaning of life. The great masters of that country have seldom been theologians or philosophers: in other words, men addicted to learning, each with his own carefully pondered theory on Meaning. Superconscious realization has given the wise of India keen intellects, but what most distinguishes them is their *mental clarity*. They *live* the high truths they preach. Superconscious experience has given them a uniform perception of what is and is not real. Their deep insights, based on direct experience, could never have come to people who had only keen intellects.

Declarations by the great masters in all religions, though not always exactly coinciding, have shown a remarkable unanimity with respect to the highest truths. Any differences, in other words, between the statements of a Self-realized saint in one religion and those of another saint in some other religion are due simply to differences of culture and environment and to people's temporal needs.

So great, on the other hand, is their agreement

concerning spiritual truths that when Christian missionaries first came to India, and encountered there a quite unanticipated corroboration of Christ's teachings in the teachings of Krishna in the Bhagavad Gita (India's favorite scripture), they decided that Krishna's teachings must have been borrowed from Jesus Christ. According to indigenous tradition in India, however, the "Gita" (as people fondly call it) is much older.

When you really get down to it, the only essential difference between Christianity and, let us say, Buddhism lies in the names of their founders. The differences in teaching can easily be explained by the different cultural exigencies encountered by those two great masters. Without what is claimed as the "uniquely saving grace" of their own masters, the teachings themselves are basically the same.

The following pages will offer Christian truths (eternal and universal) from a new point of view. This book will be completely orthodox in its adherence to Christianity, but its orthodoxy will not always correspond to what is taught by Christian sects. It will not always conform, in other words, to "Churchianity."

I submit this humble effort, as I stated in the Introduction, in the hope of helping to reinstate Christianity on its fully deserved plateau as a foremost among the great religions of the world (though not as the *only* great religion). I am writing in the sincere conviction that what I have to say, which I learned from my Guru, Paramhansa Yogananda, is universally true. For truth is one and eternal. This book is a humble offering to you, the reader, of explanations given by Paramhansa Yogananda, who opened the teachings of Jesus Christ to the world. I write in the conviction that, though it may always be possible to imagine new *facts*, one can never create a *new* truth. Truth does, however, assume *ever-new expressions*, like the leaves of a tree which are generically all the same, though every leaf is unique and different from all its fellows. Even so, differing *expressions* of the timeless truth are only outer sheaths for the one and only, changeless and eternal Truth, which pervades the whole universe.

CHAPTER TWO

A NAME FOR TRUTH

SANAATAN DHARMA IS A SANSKRIT TERM MEANING, "The Eternal Religion." *Sanaatan Dharma* has for long ages been the accepted name in India for the universal Truth: God, Creator and Sustainer of the universe, every atom of which, being a conscious projection, is destined eventually to merge back consciously into the Supreme Spirit.

"Hinduism," the popular name for India's ancient religion, was imposed on that country, by foreigners, in relatively recent times. "Hinduism" is actually a misnomer. For one thing, *Sanaatan Dharma* belongs not only to India, for it is the eternal Truth underlying all manifested existence. The religion it proclaims is universal, and must be considered to be as essential for some planet in a distant galaxy as for our own Earth. *Sanaatan*

Dharma is basic to every true religion of man.

It should therefore be understood that Divine Truth has nothing to do with separative or sectarian beliefs. *Sanaatan Dharma* is not a man-made religion, but explains, rather, how God brought all things into manifestation and how every soul, each one a "Prodigal Son," can return and merge back into Him.

Sanaatan Dharma is not in itself a revelation, for it has to be expressed verbally, and words can be misleading. Rather, the Eternal Religion is the *fruit* of revelation, for it shows people how to achieve for themselves the inner revelation of the highest truth. The fundamental truths of *Sanaatan Dharma* can be perceived by everyone who has the willingness to offer himself up completely to God, in deep humility and devotion.

Sanaatan Dharma, then, concerns that divine revelation which all true saints have described: Infinite Light, Sound, Love, Bliss, Power, Calmness, and Wisdom. They have described it also as St. Paul did when he spoke of **"the peace of God, which passeth all understanding."** (Phil. 4:7)

When St. Teresa of Avila announced once to her priestly confessor that she'd had a vision of "the formless Christ," the priest, who until then had been her staunchest defender, began to doubt her. His faith, however, in her deep spirituality impelled him to research the matter, and he was led at last to discover, in the writings of St. Thomas Aquinas, a surprising truth: Visions of Christ

without form, he learned, are indeed higher than
any vision with form.

Paramhansa Yogananda often cited this story.
What can St. Teresa of Avila, and later on Yogananda have meant when they spoke of "the
formless Christ"?

If we think of the material universe as compris-
ing the vast number of galaxies science claims—
over one hundred billion of them!—the question
must arise in the minds of even the most devoutly
orthodox Christian: "How can God be like the popular image of an old man with a long, white
beard?" Another question follows naturally: "How
can Jesus Christ himself really have been God's
only Son?" Surely those concepts can be viewed
only as quaint archaicisms. No form, however
vast, could have projected the universe as we now
know it to be.

Of course, no anthropomorphic God could have
projected a universe even the size people thought
it to be when Jesus was alive. The earth they
knew then was relatively tiny, but even at that it
was also infinitely complex, with countless flora
and fauna; with populous nations; with a relatively vast territory; with innumerable, unex-
plained stars in the heavens; with shifting seasons, winds, and climates in constant flux and
repetition; and with the changing but constantly
repeating positions of the constellations. The list
might be stretched out indefinitely. Enough variety, however, has been suggested here already to

show that the reality behind everything could not possibly be some individual brain, however divine. It would have, if anything, to be a formless consciousness.

I remember when I crossed the Atlantic Ocean with my family by ship, a thing we did nine times during my childhood, back and forth between Europe and America. My father must surely have explained to me the phenomenon I observed, though I don't recall whether it was before or after my observation. (Probably it was before.) I do clearly remember noting, however, that other ships, as they approached us from a distance, didn't begin as tiny dots on the horizon that grew in size gradually on drawing nearer. What first appeared was the tips of their masts, which slowly rose out of the ocean instead of merely increasing gradually in size. Next, the whole ship rose slowly out of the water, until it became fully visible. The explanation for that almost abrupt appearance was, of course, the curvature of the earth. I can only believe that this phenomenon had to have been observed thousands of times before me, and long before people realized that the earth is round. Why didn't the people in the days of Jesus Christ, and for centuries thereafter, ask themselves the reason for this sudden appearance?

The waxing and waning moon is something every human being with eyes to see has observed for thousands of years. How is it that *no one*, until recent times, related it to reflected light from the sun? Today, the solution seems to us obvious.

Why didn't anybody give reasonable thought to why the sun rises through the seasons at different points on the horizon—always repeating the same directions of change, and always in the same sequence throughout the year? After all, brilliant men lived in those days. We today have no monopoly on intellectual acumen.

I'll discuss in a later chapter the strange fact that a veil of varying opacity seems to obscure even brilliant minds. Could it be that man simply wasn't ready to perceive certain realities which, to us nowadays, seem so obvious? People for countless centuries were also aware of the mold that appeared on bread, but it wasn't until the 1920s that penicillin was discovered in that mold, and only in the 1940s did its use become widespread.

The same may be said of countless other discoveries: the facts may have stared all humanity in the face, yet man wasn't ready to understand them, and perhaps wasn't even ready to observe them. Were people not sufficiently developed intellectually in those times to ask the right questions? Or did they make new discoveries simply because the facts themselves had piled up high enough to be noticeable, thereby making the questions inevitable?

Whatever the case, another interesting phenomenon obtrudes itself also: Many scientific discoveries have been made simultaneously by two or more people, sometimes at a distance from one another. I have read (though other research I've done suggests otherwise) that if Charles Darwin had waited one week before announcing his *On the Origin of Species by Means of Natural Selection*, Alfred Russel Wallace would have published a similar theory before him. From a religious point of view, Darwin's "win by a nose" was perhaps unfortunate, for Wallace's outlook was more spiritual; he also believed in things less purely material: for example, in psychic phenomena.

Lobachevsky and Bolyai, in Russia and in Hungary respectively, discovered spherical geometry simultaneously, and were ridiculed for a time as crazy, after they first announced their finding.

One is at least free to suspect that inspiration either passes from brain to brain, or is perhaps dropped by divine, possibly angelic, beings into minds that are prepared and receptive.

As I said, I'll pursue the curious phenomenon later of man's varying levels of understanding during different historic eras. It is fascinating to think that ability may advance and decline cyclically, almost like the seasons, though in different rhythms. For now, however, my theme must be limited to the fact that it is only recently—indeed, in my own lifetime—that people have come to know enough to realize how vast the material universe is, and therefore to understand how utterly impossible it would be for any anthropomorphic being to have created it.

We'll have, as we proceed, to discuss how God

could have created anything at all. In doing so, we'll confront the fundamental scientific dogma of our own times, namely, that consciousness springs only from brain activity, which is to say that nothing is really conscious, and inert matter is the bedrock reality of everything.

Let us consider that last question first: Is consciousness really something each of us "produces" by what scientists describe as a "movement of electrons through a circuit of nerves"?

Some aspects of awareness in human nature, it must be admitted, are universally true and therefore cannot be individually created. A happy baby has no need to learn how to smile. When it is distressed, moreover, it knows perfectly well, on its own, how to cry. These are very simple examples, but they show at least that certain tendencies in human nature are innate. Even dogs *seem*, at least, to be smiling when they wag their tails happily, and manage to *look* ferocious when they are angry. Any child knows, surely, that when a dog is wagging its tail it is being friendly.

Many comparisons might be submitted to show how states of consciousness express themselves uniformly everywhere. When a person feels some positive emotion such as happiness, he experiences a corresponding rise of energy in the body and in the spine, accompanied by outward signs of that upliftment: he sits up straight, looks naturally upward, and curves the corners of his mouth upward in a smile.

When, on the other hand, a person feels a negative emotion such as unhappiness, he experiences a corresponding lowering of energy in the body and the spine. Accompanying that "sinking feeling" is a tendency to slump forward, to look down, to let the shoulders sag—even to walk heavily.

Human bodies all have basically the same features and attributes. Tastes in the mouth are, it is fairly safe to say, more or less the same in all bodies. Sourness puckers the lips of everyone. And sweetness is all-but-universally pleasurable.

"Man," Jean Paul Sartre declared, "is radically free." His declaration forces the question: Free from *what*? All human beings are born "equipped" with the same nervous system. They respond in ways that are basically uniform. The same things soothe or irritate their nerves.

It has been scientifically demonstrated that electric wires react to stimuli in ways very similar to stimulation of the nerves. In *Out of the Labyrinth*, a book I wrote many years ago, I showed that even morality is rooted in certain universal realities of human nature. Why, for instance, are the words of Jesus Christ, quoted by St. Paul in Acts, universally true? **"Remember,"** Paul wrote, **"the words of the Lord Jesus, how he said, It is more blessed to give than to receive."** (Acts 20:35)

Is this statement founded in actual human experience, or is it simply a matter of blind belief? Experience shows, in fact, that the statement is

universally true. One does indeed feel "blessed"—
in other words, happy, and perhaps even blissful—when his consciousness and feelings expand
to include others in his reality. On the other hand,
when one excludes others from that reality, his
feelings withdraw into himself, and his sensitivity
to objective reality shrinks.

The issue of consciousness is not limited merely
to that abstraction, "consciousness," itself. It includes feeling also. Indeed, our feelings are more
important to most of us than is our ability to reason. It is stated that computers will someday be
sophisticated enough to be conscious. The humble earthworm, however, is as simple a creature
as can easily be observed, and the earthworm is
obviously conscious. It is also *self*-conscious: If it
is pricked, it tries to squirm away. Feeling, on the
other hand, is intimately connected with the sense
of self, whereas rational progressions are more or
less mechanical, and can be performed by mere
computers.

Consciousness, obviously, is not a *product* in
any case of brain activity. It *precedes* the ability
to think and reason. Allied to consciousness are
two things which transcend even the ability to
reason: *feeling*, and *self-awareness*.

Sanaatan Dharma declares that the essence of
the Supreme Spirit is *Satchidananda*: Ever-existing, Ever-conscious, Ever-*new* Bliss, as
Paramhansa Yogananda translated the term.
When the question was posed in that ancient

teaching, "*Why* did God create the universe?" the answer given was, "He created it so that He might enjoy Himself through many."

What is the essence of that enjoyment—of bliss? It is calm, limitless, unmoving yet ever-thrilling enjoyment of the essence of one's own Being, ever-changing yet essentially changeless, ever-new yet eternally unaffected, Self-existent, uncaused, the Supreme Source of everything manifested, Absolute Perfection, a fulfillment of perfect "enjoyment beyond imagination of expectancy."* Pure Bliss is the fulfillment of selfless Love for the Infinite Self. God created the universe not merely out of His own consciousness, but out of His perfect love for the manifestations of Infinite Bliss in all beings.

These are thoughts which science would never dare even to contemplate. They reveal the deep need of human beings for more than "Just the facts, please." We all *need* religion, if only because it stresses love above the countless scattered bits and pieces of intellectual knowledge.

Why should we ever imagine that anyone else is radically different from ourselves? The same desire for love, leading to perfect bliss, is inherent in every human being. It could not be otherwise, for we all emerged like the Prodigal Son at the beginning of our roaming in foreign lands far from that one Bliss-God. *How* did God create us? That im-

*From the poem "*Samadhi*," by Paramhansa Yogananda, quoted in *Autobiography of a Yogi*.

portant question will be addressed in a later chapter, but what He did essentially was project us as His superconscious "dream" from Infinite Consciousness.

Jesus Christ was sent to earth to proclaim the Heavenly Father's love for us all, and to awaken love in our hearts for Him. Science has shown us, however, a universe too vast to have been created by any human Father figure. Science's view too, however, is limited. Whatever, or Whoever, brought everything into existence created also human beings with human feelings, and with individual appreciation for parental love, filial love, romantic and friendly love. If that Infinite One is omniscient, then He certainly knows our innermost feelings, no matter how often science, with its dry, factual outlook on reality, scoffs at the idea of a Being infinitely superior to the scientists themselves, far beyond their intellectual games, lambent with tenderest feelings of love for us all, unceasingly forgiving, and awaiting only our love in return to bring us back to Himself.

A scientist once said to Paramhansa Yogananda, "The universe is nothing but an aggregate of protons and electrons."

"Granted," that great sage responded. "Those protons and electrons are what we might call the building blocks of creation. But if you dumped a pile of bricks onto an open field, would they form themselves into a building? Don't you see? It takes intelligent design to build buildings with whatever materials are at hand. And it takes Cosmic Intelligence to form the vast universe, with its infinite complexity at every level of manifestation."

How much more wonderful, this view of a universe vibrant with compassion and with Cosmic Love, rooted in Infinite Bliss. Yes, of course there is pain and suffering also for us, "Prodigal Sons" all. It is because in some way or another we have flouted the perfect harmony of our own being. Man's first reaction to suffering is often to harden his heart against pain by telling himself, for example, "I'll never love again." Bitterness may ensue. It is a distortion, merely, of essential feeling. Or else one may try simply to deaden his ability to feel any emotion, in which case he becomes hardly more than a living corpse. For what is consciousness itself, without feeling? It can produce no more than mechanisms. Such people were described by Jesus when he said—well, let me repeat the story:

"And another of his disciples said unto him, Lord, suffer me first to go and bury my father.

"But Jesus said unto him, Follow me; and let the dead bury their dead." (Matt. 8:21,22)

How much more perceptive is that prodigal wanderer who says to himself, "What I tried didn't work. Let me now try some other way." Constantly seeking a positive solution, he comes at last to realize that, after every disappointment, he has withdrawn into himself to "regroup." And the thought comes to him at last: "Maybe my answer lies, not 'out there,' but in myself!" He returns at last, then, to his "Father's house," and rejoices finally in his Father's love and eternal welcome.

Yes, *of course* there is more to life than an endless, dry desert, barren of any life, of any love because all the plants have been pulled up out of the ground, dissected, and set aside for further analysis.

"Intelligent design" has become a hot issue nowadays in the schools. I think the problem may lie with how the term itself is defined. Surely it ought not even to be a matter for debate whether the universe manifests conscious intelligence. The very fact that it takes considerable human intelligence even to demonstrate that the universe has no intelligence must itself be considered the undoing of that whole argument!

A woman informed me somewhat proudly the other day, "Women are more intelligent than men." She wouldn't hear any further discussion on the matter, so I was happy to leave the subject as she'd stated it. In this book, however, since I'm in control, I can say what I would have liked to tell her: "It all depends on how you define intelligence!" A long life has convinced me that women are indeed, in certain respects, more intelligent than men, and that men, in other respects, are more intelligent than women. Both types of intelligence are needed. Only thus can mankind form a more complete picture of reality.

A man and a woman may be walking down the

street. The woman says, "What did you think of those shoes?"

The man answers, "What shoes?"

"On the lower shelf of that window we just passed," replies the woman, "to the left, toward the front."

"What window?" the man asks.

We need particulars; we also need abstractions. We need those things and concepts which appeal to our feelings; we also need to understand the *what* and the *why* of things. We need both feeling and reason, in other words. We need enjoyment as well as understanding. Both are necessary. As Yogananda said, "Feeling must be kept in a state of reason; otherwise it becomes fanatical." Either aspect of our nature without the other would leave us incomplete.

The question of "intelligent design" can be settled quite simply by deciding, first, what we mean by "intelligent." George Gaylord Simpson, the eminent biologist, when discussing intelligent evolution according to his own definition of the term, considered anomalies of design in certain creatures as faulty from an engineering standpoint, and wrote (this is a paraphrase), "Would it not be impious to impute such fumbling to the Creator?" Well, the answer is that his definition of "intelligent design" is altogether simplistic. (So also, for that matter, are the typical explanations advanced by many religious "fundamentalists.")

Let us assume something that human arrogance usually rejects out of hand: an intelligence infinitely wiser than man's. God is both infinite and infinitesimal. The fact that omniscience can embrace the vast universe in no way precludes it from embracing also every individual atom. And if omniscience can embrace the atom, why not embrace also the *feelings* of—well, if feelings can't be visualized as existing on an atomic level, then at least the feelings of human beings?

Why is it so difficult to believe that God, in His love for mankind, should incarnate among men as a man, himself? Jesus Christ himself described his inner consciousness as infinite. He said, **"Where two or three are gathered together in my name, there am I in the midst of them."** (Matt. 18:20) He didn't say he'd get to all of them in time. He said, "There *am* I." Christians "sell short" the very man they think of and pray to as their Savior. Jesus was, and *is*, the Christ. These are, I grant you, deep waters. We'll explore them further as we proceed. For now, let me present Yogananda's explanation: Jesus was not only a man: he was also God. And, as God, he dwells forever in the hearts of all men.

Another question raises its serpent hood, ready to inject us with the mental poison of doubt if we neglect to address it honestly. The question becomes more pressing, the farther back in time science pushes history: Did God really wait all those *millennia* before deciding to bring to mankind His supreme revelation through the teachings of

Jesus Christ? If so, how can one fail to ask, Was it quite fair of God? For in this case, countless generations passed before man could be given "a true teaching" on how to reach heaven (which Jesus equated, as we shall see later, with God). Is this a true dogma? If so, doesn't the dogma contradict any claim of divine compassion?

Christ's revelation was, above everything else, that God loves each one of us, His children. If God does really love us, why did He wait so long to tell us so? For it is now evident that human history didn't begin a few centuries, merely, before the Christian era. Archaeologists have pushed human history back many, many thousands of years. Indeed, a discovery was made in the twentieth century of the imprint of a sandal in sandstone, dating back—one assumes—millions of years. Another astonishing discovery was a nail found not long ago in America, embedded in a block of coal. That block was formed many millions of years ago; yet within it was a man-made nail. Is all this, as certain fundamentalist Christians would have us believe, merely the "work of Satan" to confuse us? Surely, if we want to achieve any insight into God's ways, we must at least try to use what intelligence He has given us!

Many Christians convince themselves that when the members of other religions express devotion to God, or when they speak of God's love for man, they express sentiments quite different from those felt by devout Christians. "Pagans," we are told, cannot experience "Christian love." Well, do they think love for Kali or Krishna has in some way to be different from "true" Christian devotion to Mary or Jesus?

After Yogananda's visit to Therese Neumann (the story is presented in *Autobiography of a Yogi*) he described having beheld also, through her eyes, the vision she received of the Passion of Christ. An article in a Catholic magazine, which appeared several years later, sneered, "As if a Hindu yogi could have a true Catholic vision!"

The truth is that even the bodily experiences aroused by deep yoga practice—a science related to universal human realities, discovered in India millennia ago—correspond exactly to human nature everywhere. The upliftment of consciousness in the deeply meditating yogi is exactly the same as the ecstasies of St. Francis of Assisi and St. Teresa of Avila. Sincere truth seekers in every age have loved and communed with God. It simply cannot be that Jesus Christ brought a completely new and unique revelation to mankind. Had he done so, indeed, his very teaching ought to be suspect. For Truth is *Sanaatan*: Eternal.

Christian theologians notoriously rush in with the caveat that "Christian grace" is somehow special and quite different from anything "pagan," which, according to them, is merely physical and not the result of divine grace. "Mischievous" is the word Yogananda used to describe such attempts to denigrate other religions.

As scientists in Germany, America, China, and India work with universal material realities, which never change from country to country, and would not change even from planet to planet, the Truth also, taught by Jesus Christ, Krishna, and Buddha, is universal and should be heard and studied everywhere with equal trust and confidence. It is a travesty to treat forms of truth that seem different from one's own like shop merchandise which a salesman, eager to secure a sale, compares with other products to their disadvantage.

Perceptive is he who, when considering a new spiritual teaching, asks himself first, "Is this teaching *realistic* in terms of my own experience of life?" If he is perceptive, he will next ask himself, "Does it conform to the high Truths taught through the ages by people of true wisdom?" If it fails on both counts, it should be tossed aside as scripturally worthless.

If, on the other hand, it at least conforms to actual experience, even though it is not true to the eternal verities, it may be considered from a point of view, at any rate, of how *helpfully* it relates to actual human needs. If one is seeking true wisdom and isn't able to estimate the truth of a teaching from his own or from wiser experience, he should consider it cautiously. Probably, it is a merely human invention.

For as the electron (the ultimate "building block" of material creation) is basically the same everywhere, so life, aspiration, love, and fulfillment are the same in all creatures, albeit more consciously so in human beings. The truths of consciousness everywhere must be universally the same, then, and—given all that we know of life—must also be eternal.

CHAPTER THREE

TRUE, VS. FALSE, RELIGIONS: PART ONE

PEOPLE OVER MANY YEARS HAVE SOMETIMES ASKED me my opinion of a certain well-known book, published some years ago, which claims to be based on true revelation. Even on my first perusal of this book I observed that it lacked at least three of the vital ingredients of true scripture. First, its words conveyed no vibration of divine power. Second, I found in it little corroboration with my own life experiences. Third, it failed in basic respects to correspond with the universal teachings of the ages, declared by every great scripture in the world. For these reasons I have never considered the book a genuine scripture, and when people have asked me, have stated my opinion.

"Ah," some have protested, "but it speaks so beautifully of God's love and compassion!"

"Well," I've replied, "couldn't any good poet write of those blessings as beautifully? The issue is, Do those words convey the *conviction* born of personal experience? To me, they do not."

Any statement of divine truth must also contain a certain sternness, almost an aloofness, of self-abnegation and non-attachment, indicative of complete inner freedom. It should seem almost to say, "This truth is something that should not be trifled with." God loves us all, and is unstintingly compassionate, but His outpouring of grace is not for the faint-hearted. Rather it is, as the Bible puts it, a "refining fire." One who deeply wants to receive God's love must first be purified of every selfish desire—indeed, of every self-definition except that of belonging utterly, completely, and forever to God alone.

Any spiritual statement that falls short of this highest truth—for example, by diluting it to make it more palatable to the average person's taste (which is something that book does), is either catering to people's ego-defenses or is in flat contradiction of the Truth. If, for example, it says that man is *inherently* evil, that statement is simply false. Man, in his soul, is inherently divine, for he is a manifestation of Divine Consciousness. It is of course true that man can *express* evil, but that is another matter and depends also, first, on how we define evil.

Dilution comes when a teaching is too accepting of the ego as the central fact of human existence,

instead of trying to get people to follow determinedly the upward path to freedom from all egoic
limitation. Flat contradiction comes, moreover,
when a so-called scripture states an untruth: for
example, that evil doesn't exist, or (as some have
averred) that "God does not know evil." Evil or
Satan is, as we shall see later on, a cosmic reality.
Final salvation is, however, for all—yes, even, eventually, for Satan himself—who, as he merges back
into the Supreme Spirit, ceases to be satanic and
becomes divine.

Another teaching that flatly contradicts spiritual
truth is a claim, which one hears sometimes, that
the soul has a limited number of opportunities to
be redeemed, after which it is destroyed forever.
The fatal flaw in this teaching is that the soul,
being a part of God, cannot *ever* be destroyed. As
my Guru said to me when I queried him somewhat fearfully on this point, "How can you destroy
God?"

A very great error occurs when people insist—as
some have done—that *any* personal effort to commune inwardly with God is fraught with spiritual
danger, for it leads to self-deception. This error is
allied to the belief that divine communion—which
is, certainly, a grace of God—is in no way the result of human effort. Were this really true, no
scripture need ever have been written. As well
might one say that nothing can be done to bring
sunlight into a room, when the only obstruction to
it is the fact that all the window curtains have

been drawn shut. God *certainly* wants us to commune with Him. It is we who shut Him out by our restlessness, material desires, and dull indifference. Meditation is, in fact, the best way of removing all mental obstacles.

Fundamental to the error concerned here is the mistaken belief that meditation induces a sort of self-hypnosis. The difference between prayer and meditation, however, can be clarified very simply: *Prayer means talking to God; meditation means **listening silently for His answer**.*

Is it possible to delude oneself that he is receiving answers when in fact he is merely imagining them? Well, *of course* it is! The human mind houses a veritable factory of fantasies, produced in the workroom of the subconscious. Certain tests can help to determine whether one is receiving true or false inspiration and guidance. Christian tradition—especially the Greek Orthodox, on the subject of *prelest*—contains many excellent pointers. I suggest the sincere seeker study and apply them. This subject cannot be addressed deeply here; it would detract from my main theme. I will list a few such tests, however, fully confident that anyone who is sincere will not remain in delusion for very long, for *God Himself will lead all "by the hand" who seek Him with full sincerity.*

"Seek," said Jesus, **"and ye shall find."** (Luke 11:9) Be not afraid. The very fear of possible confusion due to meditation is placed in the heart by Satan himself, usually suggested in the first place

by church organizations in their desire to gather
everyone under their protective wings, wholly dependent on official, carefully crafted dogmas.

One very important test can be suggested here:
See whether inner meditative experience brings
you greater mental clarity, or progressive
dullness. A spiritually advanced disciple of
Paramhansa Yogananda's declared, "Your religion is tested in the cold light of day." If meditation awakens in you a tendency to approach the
challenges of daily life vaguely, with a diminishing sense of responsibility, this is a sign that,
during meditation, you are drifting about in
clouds of subconsciously induced images, instead of rising into the clear skies of superconsciousness. If you have visions that are cloudy
and lack brilliance, especially if they bring you
no heightening of awareness, you may know that
you've been allowing imagination to draw you
down into a passive state. There's no harm done,
but in this case try to inject more will power into
your efforts at achieving inner calmness. Imagination is a diversion people sometimes encounter
on their way to Superconsciousness. Whenever
you find your thoughts drifting, recall them
calmly (not agitatedly), and mentally gird your
loins to dive deeper, ever deeper into the ocean
of inner peace.

A chant my Guru wrote begins with these words:

Without meditation, mind,
Hither, thither wanderest thou.

Indeed there are false as well as true experiences in meditation. To avoid meditating from fear of the false ones would be like refusing to go out of doors from fear of being hit by a truck. In meditation, take care that your efforts to surrender the ego to God involve openness to *higher awareness*, not the false "openness" of a blank mind. Never, moreover, surrender *passively* to stray thoughts and fantasies. Inner surrender should be upward, toward the superconscious, not downward into subconsciousness.

The clearest proof that you are meditating properly is when you find existing cobwebs in the mind being cleared away.

Years ago, in my quest for God but before I found Paramhansa Yogananda, I read the diary of the great Russian ballet dancer, Nijinsky. You might like, if you can find that book—it is, however, quite rare—to read excerpts from it at least. It affords a very clear example of false, hallucinatory guidance. The author's indiscriminate acceptance of every whim that chanced to enter his mind shows that he was not consulting reason or common sense. His submission to vague guidance from the subconscious clearly pointed to his own gradual disintegration, which ended in madness.

Divine grace is essential, certainly, to true inner communion. Nothing man can do will ever *oblige* God to respond. On the other hand, even trying to bring about divine communion by will power alone is a sign of egotistical presumption, not of the

humility that comes with true openness of heart
and mind. Most of the warnings against meditation, especially (in the West) against *yoga* meditation, are based on the thought that meditation implies presumption. The warnings are either
mischievous or simply ignorant.

I have read statements to the effect that the
bliss experienced in meditation is "addictive"—as
if meditation were a kind of mental drug! Is it
really possible to become "addicted" to wisdom?
Whatever false euphoria one might experience in
meditation, it would certainly not be wisdom. Nor
could it be bliss, which itself bestows wisdom of
the highest order.

Hallucinogenic drugs—cocaine, LSD, and the
like—are indeed, to varying degrees, addictive, for
they dull the mind and reduce one's ability to cope
with down-to-earth, daily realities. Worst of all,
perhaps, they have a debilitating effect on the will.
Drugs like these may induce a delusive euphoria,
but I have personally observed people under their
influence, and unable to relate to anyone whose
mind was not drifting about in similar euphoric
clouds. The "universal love" some of them claimed
to feel had nothing to do with anyone else's actual
feelings. They might have felt just as "inspired" by
the "beautiful" red blood on the vest of a person
who had just been stabbed.

Superconscious bliss has nothing in common
with ego-separative, subconsciously induced "euphoria." Without the practice of meditation, more-

over, the mind will remain forever restless and incapable of receiving true inspiration from God.

It is, then, *an absolute fallacy* to insist that meditation leads to self-deception. Meditation is in fact the best way of testing one's religion. It is scientific, for it offers the test of actual experience.

Imagination, however, is not in itself a bad thing. The ability to visualize something clearly is in fact helpful as a means of opening the mind to higher perceptions. To avoid "flights of fancy," however, it's necessary to submit those perceptions to the tests of objective experience and common sense.

During Yogananda's early years in America, he was approached one day by a man who informed him, "I go frequently into cosmic consciousness."

We all know the saying, "It takes one to know one." Yogananda knew at once that this man only had an unusually vivid imagination. He also perceived, however, that it would not help the man to be told he was only hallucinating. He therefore invited the person to come up to his hotel room.

In the room he asked his guest to be seated. He then said, "Now, please go into 'cosmic consciousness' for me." The man sat with flickering eyelids—a sure indication of mental restlessness—and began his visualization. Anyone observing him would have seen that he was far from being uplifted into any exalted state.

Finally the meditator could stand the suspense

no longer. "Why don't you ask me where I am?" he inquired.

"Very well then, where are you?"

"On top of the dome of the Taj Mahal!" called the man as if hallooing from a great distance.

"There must be something the matter with your own dome," commented the Master. "I see you sitting here right before me."

"All right, all right," conceded the visitor. "Test me again."

"If you are able to go so far away as the Taj Mahal, in India," the Master said, "what about going somewhere we can verify easily? Why not go downstairs to the restaurant in this hotel, and tell me what you see there?"

The man closed his eyes again. A moment later he said, "I see a piano to the left of the door as you enter from the lobby. The restaurant is empty, but two customers have just entered through the street door."

Yogananda countered, "There is no piano in the room at all; three people are seated near the lobby entrance. No one is entering from the street, but there are people seated at two more tables in the center of the room."

They at once went downstairs together. The scene the man had described bore no resemblance to the reality. What Yogananda had described was what they actually saw.

"You see," our Guru commented to us, "that man really believed he was seeing whatever he visualized. I had to propose an objective test, which would show the lack of validity in his visualization."

The man had to accept the testimony of his own eyes. In this way, he became convinced. Experience was the "reality check" that he needed, which finally convinced him.

Many indeed are the ways of misrepresenting the Truth. The most important thing always to keep in mind is that all Creation comes from God, and that all beings must eventually merge back into Him no matter how long it takes. The ultimate destiny of all men is to realize God's bliss as their own true nature. He has hidden that Bliss in us all; it is what endlessly impels us to seek fulfillment, like Prodigal Sons, until we tire of wandering in this "foreign land" of delusion, and determine earnestly to return again at last to our true home in God.

There are also other ways to test the genuineness of a teaching. If, for example, it states, "God gave us our bodies for us to enjoy them," we may know at once that the teaching is false—not because God doesn't want us to enjoy this world, but because He wants us to enjoy it *in the right way*: without ego-consciousness, and in a spirit of sharing our enjoyment with Him. Refined, spiritual enjoyment is possible only when the ego is completely surrendered to the Lord.

The opposite concept—that we should hate our bodies—is equally false. The problem with both these concepts is that they are oversimplified and one-sided. The solution is to enjoy everything *without attachment.* Hatred, on the other hand, is a negative emotion which pulls the energy in the body downward, to one's lower nature. There is much groundwork I must lay, however, before clarifying this truth more fully.

God certainly wants us to enjoy His creation. He doesn't want us, however, to identify ourselves, by either attraction or repulsion, with any part of it. All emotional reactions, whether positive or negative, must be neutralized by offering them up to inner soul-freedom in God. Even evil—which must be strictly avoided for the spiritual disease it is—should be rejected *in principle* only, not hated.

God wants us to enjoy life *in the right way:* not for ego-gratification, that is, but with *His* joy. The question may occur to some minds: "But does God really *want* anything?" This, however, is a mere quibble. There are two kinds of desire: the one a contractive shrinking inward into one's self; the other, an expansive, outward sharing with all. The second is called a "desireless desire," for it is self-liberating and is born of the nature of pure joy, which seeks in everything reflections of the higher Self. Divine joy is self-expansive. The reason we should offer up all our enjoyments to God is that, if we do not, egoic self-indulgence will lead to the very opposite of enjoyment: satiety, disgust, boredom, and, yes, suffering. In everything pertaining to the ego, duality is the ruler. There cannot be pleasure without its corresponding opposite: pain.

In an important book, *The Essence of the Bhagavad Gita Explained by Paramhansa Yogananda*, Yogananda is quoted as telling a story (evidently a true one) about a man who wrote something he wanted people to accept as a genuine scripture. He buried it under a tree, then left it untouched in the hope that, with age, it would acquire a certain patina of antiquity. Years later that man, claiming to be acting under the guidance of angels, returned to the tree, and there, to everyone's amazement, "discovered" buried underneath it a "divinely revealed scripture."

The main problem with this document, something few people have taken into account, was that it failed in many ways to correspond to the timeless truths God has revealed through the ages to mankind. Its novelty, which believers took as a sign that it contained true revelations, constituted in fact its major flaw.

Novelty is attractive to many people. The times we live in are filled with newness and excitement. People want to keep on getting the latest "news." Where divine truths are concerned, however, there is no room for ephemeral stimulation. Truth is eternal. It is more fundamental and enduring than the very laws of physics. How could God ever declare truth once only, or through only one great master? And how could He, later on, contradict Himself through any other true master?

Would it have been possible for that miraculous discovery beneath a tree to be genuine? It would, admittedly, be a marvel: the sort of thing people might *like* to see happen. Besides, God can do anything, even if He has never done it before. It wasn't the novelty of the event itself, however, that condemned it. What did the condemning were the teachings that "miraculous" document contained.

I should mention in passing, moreover, that "angelic guidance" is far less trustworthy than the teachings of a great spiritual master whom God has sent down to earth. Redemption comes through divine *human* channels, not through angels. (Nor, it may be added, does any divinely new revelation come through visitors from other planets. I say this because books have been published in modern times that claim to make such "revelations.")

As for that miraculously discovered book, the acid test of the truths it proclaimed would have been whether it corresponded to the eternal, Divine Truths that have been handed down through the ages by great masters to mankind. The validity of true teachings has been *demonstrated conclusively* by the uplifting influence they've had on sincere spiritual seekers who, the world over, devoted years to their practice. In the above case, it is evident that this manuscript failed to meet the supreme test of spiritual truth. No doubt the manuscript said "good things," and spoke truths— such as, "Love others, and be generous to them"—

that are recognized and accepted by all. Many of the claims it made, however, were actually *antithetic* to *Sanaatan Dharma*.

Truth is either knowable or not knowable. If thousands of otherwise truthful, reliable persons—saints and masters—who have been accepted through time as great, have stated *from their own experience* that a certain reality is fundamentally true to God's ways and to the way the universe was made; and if this teaching, moreover, or something in harmony with it, has been expressed by true saints everywhere: then it must follow that anyone who contradicts that teaching is either mistaken, or else needs very strong arguments to bolster his contradiction. The act of discovering a manuscript that has lain buried— how? when? by whom?—under a tree doesn't come under any such heading as "a strong argument."

Truth can of course be variously presented, like the facets of a diamond. A true statement may be phrased in such a way as to meet the needs of one particular society, but be differently phrased for the needs of another society. One particular (and true) scripture may, for instance, lay special emphasis on the supremacy of divine Law, and another, perhaps written for a society that is overdependent on religious legalities, may insist on the transforming power of divine love and grace. True teachings all agree, however, on the fundamentals of *Sanaatan Dharma*, the Eternal

Religion, as represented in every great religion. Were anyone solemnly to declare, for example, that God loves this group but hates that one, the declaration would contradict an eternal truth: namely, that God loves all equally. It *is* true, however, that the magnetism of true devotion can elicit a greater *expression* of God's love.

Divine Love is impersonal and impartial. The seemingly conflicting belief that the Jews are "God's chosen people" was clarified by Yogananda in these words: "God chooses those who choose Him."

Some aspects of true religion are almost universally accepted. Who, indeed, would deny them? Were anyone to declare that Jesus Christ's real meaning in the verse, **"Except ye . . . become as little children, ye shall not enter into the kingdom of heaven"** (Matt. 18:3), was that we should all put on rompers and play on the beach with spades and buckets, he would be merely laughed at. To be *childlike* is not the same thing at all as to be *childish*.

Most followers of every religion fail, in certain basic respects, to understand what their founders really meant to convey. Many Buddhists, for example, insist that the Buddha denied the existence of God, because he spoke of the goal of life as the state of *nirvana*. That attainment, for most of his followers, means utter and permanent extinction of everything—even of consciousness: in other words, eternal nothingness. Nothingness is, however, so my Guru asserted, by no means what the Buddha meant his followers to accept as the goal of life. Belief in unconsciousness as the highest truth—and this has to be what total nothingness means—is simply an error. How could anything come out of *nothing*? How could the very compassion of the Buddha have sprung out of no feelings at all? Consciousness, so far from manifesting essential unconsciousness, is the one abiding reality underlying the entire universe. Consciousness cannot even create, in the human sense of the word: it can only *manifest* Itself. The well-known compassion of the Buddha, to repeat, could never have arisen out of a total lack of feeling. The atheism asserted by Buddhists is simply a misunderstanding of their founder's teachings.

This misunderstanding exemplifies a host of errors that appear in every religion, simply because fallible human beings "get their paws" on a truth and twist it in fumbling blindness. Thus, religion becomes corroded in time by the acid influence of ignorance.

In the case of Buddhism, the reason the Buddha did not speak of God was that his mission was to emphasize man's need—a concept that was falling into desuetude—to make a spiritual effort individually, rather than merely performing Vedic ceremonies and waiting passively for divine blessings. In this respect, Yogananda once, in my hearing, urged a disciple to overcome a particular tendency in himself. The disciple replied, "I *want* to change, Master, but how can I do so without your blessings?"

"Well, my blessings are there already," said the Guru. "God's blessings are there. It is *your* blessings that are lacking!"

Nirvana doesn't mean a total cessation of consciousness. It only means the end of delusive desires and of self-limiting egoism. From initial emptiness which, Yogananda said, ensues after the soul wins final release from egoic bondage, there follows complete, eternal attainment of and absorption in Absolute Bliss.

Swami Shankara, several centuries after Buddha, was sent by God to correct this misunderstanding. Shankara defined divine absorption as *Satchidananda*: "Ever-existing, Ever-conscious, Ever-new Bliss."

CHAPTER FOUR

TRUE, VS. FALSE, RELIGIONS: PART TWO

Spiritual masters are repeatedly sent by God to correct human misunderstandings. For it is man alone, not the saints, who obscures Truth. No true master would ever deny a deep truth declared by any other master who ever lived. Divine realization is not a triumph of the intellect. Divine Truth, moreover, is, figuratively speaking, as much higher than the comprehension of mere theologians as the Himalayan peaks soar above the Gangetic plain. Truth can be grasped only by clear spiritual insight, which is to say, by divine intuition.

Science, in its declarations concerning material reality, changes its mind every few years on fundamental issues. That vacillation demonstrates the limitations of the intellect, never completely satisfied with any conclusion, and never completely certain of anything. True saints, who have found God, and have shown themselves to be great and wise human beings, have (by contrast) never contradicted or disagreed with one another on *any* basic issue.

Thus it was that, when Paramhansa Yogananda visited Therese Neumann, the great Catholic stigmatist of Konnersreuth, Germany, she at once recognized his spiritual stature and sent a message, "Though the bishop has asked me to see no one without his permission, I will receive the man of God from India."

In the vision of God there can never be anything but agreement. The only possible alternative would be, of course, that the vision of God is not possible for mankind, and that everyone who claims to have seen Him is simply hallucinating. True saints respect and honor one another. Instead of crowding forward, moreover, like children zealous for acclaim as the finders of a "new" truth, they themselves bow before the Truth itself, for they recognize that it alone *is.* Jesus Christ stated during his Sermon on the Mount, **"Think not that I am come to destroy the law, or the prophets: I am not come to destroy, but to fulfill."** (Matt. 5:17)

Sanaatan Dharma would be as true if man had never discovered it—even as the billions of galaxies predated their discovery by man. *Sanaatan Dharma* is, however, very different from the dry facts that masquerade as truth in the material sciences. What *Sanaatan Dharma* describes is the truth *behind* all appearances, whether gross or subtle. This is why one feels joy even in the contemplation of eternal truths. People who seek to probe only the mysteries of material reality feel alternations of ego-satisfying exaltation and ego-drenching disappointment.

The ultimate goal of all seeking is Bliss-Consciousness, which resides at the calm, unmoving center of all existence. This Reality is ever-conscious, omniscient, and self-aware. It is loving in both a personal and an impersonal, universal way: impersonal, because it seeks nothing for itself; personal, because it seeks supernal blessing, eventually, for every living creature.

A fundamental aspect of Divine Truth is that all creatures are motivated *from within themselves*, whether consciously or unconsciously, to seek changeless, eternal bliss, which is the very essence of perfect Self-awareness. Bliss itself is Self-aware, which explains why the divine Self is customarily written with a capital "S." People who seek fulfillment through the senses are really, however mistakenly, seeking divine bliss.

That Bliss, being Self-aware, filters down consciously into human beings. It becomes restricted, in the process, by ego-consciousness. Sometimes, when an urgent need exists among men, Cosmic Bliss takes birth in the world as a savior. God has indeed, through the aeons of time, descended many times and lived as a human being among men in order to bring His children to eternal safety from all sorrow. Never does God descend, however, in "full power and glory" as if to overwhelm mankind with His majesty. Rather, He descends humbly, letting Divine Love and Bliss be the magnets to draw people. God comes dressed in the human reality of human masters who overcame that "reality" at some time in the past, rising above every human limitation and attaining perfection in God. Such souls know from personal memory what it means to live in ego-limitation, for they have lived in delusion themselves. They therefore appreciate *from their own experience* the effort needed to attain enlightenment. Eternally free souls remember their own past mistakes, and the suffering that was consequent upon those mistakes. What draws them back to earth is the "desireless desire" to uplift humanity. Their divine mission is not ever to proclaim their own greatness, but only to convince people of *man's own potential spiritual greatness.* All human beings are equally children of God, manifestations of the Supreme Consciousness even if they are themselves, at present, barely conscious of that divinity.

Thus, Jesus Christ, Krishna, Buddha, and many other great, liberated beings have returned to earth again and again for the upliftment and salvation of mankind. Other people who, over incarnations, have become spiritually refined enough to recognize a true, divine manifestation, and to receive his expanded consciousness in their hearts, attain salvation. For God is able, through His divine messengers, to free from their ego-prisons all those who lovingly call for help.

The heavenly message is always essentially the same, for the Truth never changes. Only its outer forms assume new clothing from time to time, to conform to the fluctuating needs of mankind.

None of those great messengers has ever been God's unique creation, even if their followers have often made this claim, or similar ones. Christian dogma defines Jesus Christ as the "only Son of God," but it is *Christ* who is the Son of God, not Jesus the man. Jesus himself is quoted in the book of Revelation as saying: **"To him that overcometh will I grant to sit with me in my throne, *even as I also overcame*, and am set down with my Father in his throne."** (Rev. 3:21) This statement raises the important question: How, and what, had he overcome? I will explain Paramhansa Yogananda's answer to this all-important question, later on.

There is a further problem, which has to do with the many wrong interpretations that have been made of true scriptures. Man is easily bewildered when he confronts unfamiliar abstractions, which he finds utterly beyond anything he has experienced in daily life. Bewilderment pervades religion everywhere. As Yogananda put it, "Ignorance, both East and West, is fifty-fifty."

Let us consider these few examples from the New Testament:

It is a dogma in Christianity, as I've stated and as everyone knows, that Jesus is "the only Son of God." Paramhansa Yogananda declared this to be a truth. He also said, however, that it is a deeply *esoteric* truth, and applies as much to the foundation of the universe as to that divine human being who was born in Bethlehem.

God could never *in essence*, of course, be anthropomorphic; that is to say, He could never, in essence, possess a human form. It is inconceivable that the Creator of a hundred billion galaxies, each with its own innumerable stars and planets, could have any intrinsic form at all. It is even more inconceivable that such a God, needing help in getting His "job" done on earth, could have created one human being as His "only son." Paramhansa Yogananda stated that the dogma that Christ is God's "only Son" is true only if we understand it in the deeper sense expressed in the Eternal Truth, *Sanaatan Dharma.*

The Star of Bethlehem is another example of people's widespread misunderstanding of a deep truth. Could any star in the heavens really "stand over" a particular building? Were we to go behind that building we would see it standing over some other building, or over a tree, or above the crest of a hill. This tradition, too, conceals a deep teaching, one that has been misunderstood because people lack familiarity with spiritual truths.

The whole message of the Christmas story is

deeply inspiring, and was intended to convey the subtle message that Jesus had indeed descended from the highest realms of divine consciousness, charged by God with a divine mission. The "Star of Bethlehem" was not a comet or any other celestial phenomenon. This subject, along with the other examples I am giving here, will be explored later in this book.

A final example may be offered. Jesus Christ said, **"And as Moses lifted up the serpent in the wilderness, even so must the Son of man be lifted up:**

"That whosoever believeth in him should not perish, but have eternal life." (John 3:14,15)

The words, "lifted up," are interpreted by theologians as a veiled prophecy that Jesus would, in future, be "lifted up" on the cross to be crucified. These words convey, however, a much deeper and richer meaning. This too is a passage (there are many others) which tradition has utterly misconstrued.

A pressing need exists among Christians today for a fresh outlook on the holy mission and teachings of Jesus Christ. Too long have his supposed representatives—"authorities" in the churches, and scholarly theologians—offered pale platitudes as substitutes for the Truth. Christian belief has become centered ever-increasingly in concepts that are rooted in ordinary human understanding, and not in spiritual insight. It is urgent nowadays for Christ's message to be proclaimed once again in its thrillingly deep, radiantly beautiful, and eternal Truth.

It was partly for this purpose that Paramhansa Yogananda was sent by his line of great gurus and by God to the West. They commissioned him to "bring back the original yoga teachings of Krishna in the Bhagavad Gita, and the original teachings of Jesus Christ in the Bible."

Yogananda would sometimes remark wryly, "Jesus Christ was crucified once, but his teachings have been crucified daily for the past two thousand years by persons who lack spiritual understanding."

Much has been made by scholars recently of the Gnostic teachings. Indeed, from everything Paramhansa Yogananda said and wrote on the subject, there were Gnostics who did come much closer than the churches to the original teachings of Jesus Christ to his disciples. Those truths comprised what Yogananda called "original Christianity."

Not long after the death of Jesus, however, the Church perceived a need for resolving theological controversies in unanimous agreement. The Gnostics claimed they were seeking (indeed, some of them claimed to have attained) direct, inner communion with God. Certain Gnostics said they had been initiated into these truths through a line of direct succession from Apostolic times. They insisted, moreover—and Yogananda endorsed their statement—that Jesus Christ's emphasis had been on seeking personal verification by direct, inner experience of God.

There was always a problem, however. It concerned which, out of many claims, to believe. For there were also inconsistencies and contradictions among the Gnostics. Some of those who made the claims were—reason itself suggests it—self-deluded. Valid tests can be applied to their claim that they experienced higher-than-ordinary perceptions. I've already listed a few of those tests. Chief among them is whether those making the claims seemed lacking in any ego-motivation.

It is, of course, possible for ordinary people to be fooled. A man lying by the roadside in a seemingly unconsciousness state might be asleep; he might be drunk; or he might be a saint absorbed in divine ecstasy. How is one to know? A church investigating committee would usually lack the qualification for determining his actual mental state. That is why committees inquiring into a person's sanctity make such a big issue of miracles, thinking (quite mistakenly) that miraculous powers are proof of a person's holiness. Miracles alone, however, are insufficient for that purpose.

I'll tell a story later about Sadhu Haridas, a wonder-worker who lived in India several centuries ago, whom some people considered a saint. There still remained for him, however, important spiritual lessons to be learned.

A conscientious investigating committee, if in fact one is needed at all, has a need to be skeptical.

Skepticism, however, is an aspect of intellection which judges everything on a basis of external observation alone. The intellect might easily attribute that recumbent man's mental state, for example, to catalepsy.

The best person to judge whether he was in fact a saint would be another saint. A church would consider it necessary first, however, to appoint a committee to determine the sanctity also of this judge. The whole process would become in the end so laborious, expensive, and for all that uncertain, that the authorities might well ask themselves, "Is it worth it?" Perhaps the best "way out" for them would be simply to drop the whole matter and let the committee members return to their normal lives.

The solution that evolved in India suggested this last decision. There, investigating committees in religion were never appointed in the first place. It was easy to avoid creating them, since there never existed, in India, a ruling body of prelates to do the appointing!

Early Western missionaries were amazed to find so little organized religion in India. E. Stanley Jones, a famous Protestant missionary from America, wrote of an occasion when he was speaking about Jesus Christ to a crowd in Benares (the new name for which is Varanasi). A pundit (priestly scholar) in the crowd, who had been fidgeting restlessly, finally rose and approached Jones. He placed a *tilak* (spiritual mark) on his forehead, then, before returning to his seat, declared with satisfaction, "Now you are a Hindu. I can listen to you with a clear conscience."

It does happen, and has indeed happened repeatedly, that some spiritual mountebank presents false teachings that to many seem credible. The mass of evidence, however, accumulated over millennia as to the real teachings of *Sanaatan Dharma*, has established such a firm tradition that false teachings, and false saints, are in time weeded out of that garden. Often, a merely understated smile by a true saint suffices to make the point so clearly that he doesn't need to say anything.

One who teaches Tantra Yoga as a path to enlightenment, but who recommends gleeful indulgence in the pleasures of the senses instead of calm inner detachment from all pleasure, is soon discredited, and before long is forgotten. People look at his followers; they see in their eyes a depletion of spiritual power. After a time, everyone simply loses interest. It should be added that those teachers of Tantra who teach the deliberate enjoyment of sensual pleasure without attachment are suggesting not only a dangerous path, but a false one. Mental non-attachment during moments of pleasure is at least a right teaching, for it is realistic; people will seek sensory enjoyment, anyway. The idea here, then, is, Why not tell them how to escape, at least relatively unscathed, from the clutches of sense infatuation?

This is, nevertheless, a lower teaching, one that is easily misunderstood, and one, therefore, that is not recommended by true sages. Most people, taking this teaching as their path to God, would only experience a spiritual fall.

The Christian churches don't trust their own members to sift truth from error. (So much for the quality of their teaching!) The problem with not doing so is that when adults are treated like children, they find it difficult to grow up, spiritually. Richard Wurmbrand, a Protestant pastor who, because of his religion, was imprisoned in communist Romania, wrote impressive examples of how clearly people understood Biblical truths when they no longer, under that repressive regime, had pastors whom they could trust for spiritual guidance. Even a child who hears nothing but, "NO! NO!" may at last rebel and become unmanageable.

Nature's way is prolific. It would be absurd for any committee to try to limit austerely how she should behave. An oak tree drops numerous acorns, of which only a few sprout and become trees. Were a "nature committee" to be assigned the task of choosing which acorns should be allowed to grow, the committee might end up allowing an entire forest to die, for the seeds it selected might all turn out to be barren.

One might even say then, of India, that pure religion flourishes there exactly *because* India has allowed human nature simply to take its course. In that country, no priestly authorities meddle in people's spiritual lives. Perhaps the process of stern selection is partly what Jesus referred to when he said, **"Judge not, that ye be not judged."** (Matt. 7:1)

Going back to the Gnostics: It should be clear enough that, as all sorts of people live on earth—a few of them wise, most of them foolish—so also there must have been all sorts of Gnostics. Not everyone who picks up a paintbrush, after all, becomes a great artist. And not everyone who claims true spiritual insight can speak from superconscious wisdom.

The insights of a few Gnostics, however, must surely have been valid. Jesus himself said, **"And I say unto you, Ask, and it shall be given you; seek, and ye shall find; knock, and it shall be opened unto you."** (Luke 11:9) No one could seek God for many years with full sincerity and not find *anything*!

Many Gnostics also, however—or so one suspects—were spiritual duds: well meaning, but wandering still through fogs of delusion. It can hardly be doubted, moreover, that the self-proclaimed truths uttered by certain Gnostics were born of imagination. Indeed, it must surely be ceded, in favor of the anxious churchmen of those days, that there was a need at that time for at least *some* criterion to determine who was what. India's religious traditions were, like India herself, very ancient. Valid tradition from long ages past had set down deep roots in that millennial soil.

Christianity, unlike India's heredity of *Sanaatan Dharma*, was for many people a new teaching. It wasn't really new, of course, for what Jesus taught were eternal truths. Nevertheless, to his followers it seemed new, and especially so after orthodox Jewry had condemned Christianity and had driven its adherents out of their synagogues. There arose in the perceptions of Christians, therefore, a need to get organized.

Slowly there emerged an authoritarian Church, centralized and all-powerful. As soon as the Church was in a position to do so, it declared a need for fixed definitions—that is to say, dogmas—to protect Christ's teachings from numerous ideological assaults. Dogmas were seen by the church authorities as the obvious solution, because dogmatic definitions offered a safe and easy way of "refuting" error.

In spite of everything, however, the wisest and best choice has always been to consult the wisdom of true saints. How to find such saints, then, in a church that feared (and still fears) the possibility that the saints might feel inspired to utter an inconvenient revelation? Not everyone whom the Church has declared a saint has been such in the highest sense of the word, though it seems safe to say that all of them have been spiritually dedicated and sincere. It is best in any case to look even to lesser saints for right understanding of the revelations of Christ than to seek the highest guidance from ordinary priests, pastors, and ministers. At least those who live deeply dedicated lives *inwardly* speak from some level of personal experience, rather than from established policy, and may have wisdom to offer that is never attained by intellectual theologians and administrators whose knowledge is formed almost entirely by book learning and institutional precedents.

Paramhansa Yogananda belonged in a different category altogether from those who have been declared saints by the Catholic Church. First of all, he was not a member of any Christian church, but came from outside the Christian "fold" altogether. Yogananda loved Jesus Christ deeply and reverently. Moreover, he, too, participated in the wisdom that has been attained by the greatest Christian saints, for he, too, had attained their level of divine, inner communion. Coming from outside the fenced enclosure of "Churchianity," Yogananda was free, as the saints within the church have never been, to speak the truth from his own realization. He had no need, moreover, to submit what he taught to church dignitaries for approval. He lived in, and could speak from, God-consciousness.

Christians who sincerely wanted to understand the true message of Jesus Christ were drawn to Yogananda wherever he went. Some of them came to him after receiving superconscious visions which told them to go to him. Others were attracted by the radiant example of his life. And still others responded because every word he uttered

rang with divine truth. Yogananda's divinely revealed insights into the teachings of Christ converted many thousands also who had been, until
then, hardened skeptics.

Once, during his first year in America, he received an unsigned letter criticizing him for "promoting" Jesus Christ (as the writer put it) in the
West. "Don't you realize," the letter stated, "that
Jesus Christ never lived? He is a myth created to
bring people under the control of religious authority." The letter was unsigned, as I've said. The
young missionary from India—a true Christian
missionary, indeed, though a "missionary" to a
Christian land!—prayed that God would lead him
to the writer.

Several days later, Yogananda entered the
Boston Public Library, where he sometimes went
to do research. As he entered, he saw a stranger
seated under a window on a bench, and, going
over, sat on the bench beside him.

"Why did you write me that letter?" he inquired.

"Wh-what letter?" the man demanded in amazement.

"The one in which you told me that Jesus Christ
never lived."

"But—how did you know I wrote it?"

"Never mind how," the Indian yogi replied with
a quiet smile. "I have my ways. The reason I've
come to you is to tell you that the same power of
God's which enabled me to find you has also
shown me that Jesus Christ did live, and that

he was everything the Bible says about him.'"

More than once my Guru told us of a wonderful vision he'd once had. "As I was writing my commentaries on the Bible," he said, "I prayed to Jesus for confirmation: Was what I had written true to his actual meaning? Jesus Christ then appeared to me, after which the Holy Grail also appeared, touched his lips, then descended and touched my lips. Jesus declared, 'The cup from which I drink, thou dost drink.'"

During worship services on Sunday mornings, Yogananda would proclaim deep truths, first, from the Bible, then compare those truths with the sayings of Krishna in the Bhagavad Gita. He also wrote a long series of articles called, "The Second Coming of Christ," which appeared for many years in the magazine put out by Self-Realization Fellowship (SRF), the organization he'd founded to disseminate his teachings. His discussion of Biblical truths during those services, and the articles he wrote for the magazine, were published—heavily edited, unfortunately—in a compendium of two volumes titled, *The Second Coming of Christ*. I do recommend to the reader that he read that book, though I have felt to add that caveat to be prepared for cumbersome editing.

I have also written a work comparing passages from the Bible and the Bhagavad Gita. It is called, *The Promise of Immortality*.

The present book is not intended to replace that first, much larger work. What I say here will be

limited to the essence of what Paramhansa Yogananda taught. I have come to feel, however, that
there is a growing need today for my Guru's teachings on this subject, restated simply and clearly
as he himself gave them.

There is, as I've said, an urgent need for a fresh
and authoritative commentary on the true meanings of Christ's teachings. I shall try to present the
insights my Guru proclaimed, with his simplicity
and clarity. My hope for this book is that it will
bring understanding to many who are Christians,
but who feel ready to understand Jesus Christ's
teachings more deeply.

I myself am a direct disciple of Paramhansa Yogananda. I came to him in 1948, nearly sixty
years ago, lived with him until he left his body in
1952, and have followed and practiced his teachings ever since. During the time I spent with him,
he told me that my work would include editing his
writings and authoring books to explain and present his teachings. He also told me to lecture
widely in his name.

I worked with him in 1950 at his desert retreat,
where I helped him with the editing of two commentaries especially: one, on the Bhagavad Gita,
and the other on a work which he declared is a
true scripture: *The Rubaiyat of Omar Khayyam.*

He told me he wanted me to work on another of
his commentaries also: his explanations of the
teachings of Jesus Christ. Unfortunately, during
the time I was with him we had less of an oppor-

tunity than I would have liked to discuss his Bible commentaries. During lengthy conversations that we had at the desert, however, he gave me many insights into these teachings also. And he appointed me a minister in his organization, within which it was my privilege to be active for many years, presenting his teachings to the public.

It is without presumption, therefore, that I offer my version of his Bible commentaries. I do so out of deep dedication to what he himself commissioned me to do, which was to transmit his teachings far and wide throughout the world.

CHAPTER FIVE

THE PURPOSE OF RELIGION

MOST PEOPLE THE WORLD OVER, IF THEY TAKE their religion seriously, treat it even at that as if it were more a social than a spiritual activity. They believe in God and worship Him, but always their belief is in the broader context of their normal lives. If they go regularly to church, synagogue, temple, mosque, or vihara, and make customary devotional offerings of prayer, chanting, *arati*, or other pious acts, even so the main focus of their lives is on their own private affairs. Apart from formal acts of worship, when they address God in the second person— usually to beg favors of Him—they almost always think of Him in the third person.

This much "faith" the Christian must grant people in other religions also. With such a tepid approach to religion, there cannot really be any dif-

ference between one religion and another. Every
religion teaches people to be honest, truthful,
kind, and serviceful. No religion teaches them to
be selfish or grasping. Nor do any of them tell people to ignore God while haggling in the market-
place.

The basic virtues are much the same, in other
words, and perhaps even identical, everywhere. In
Western countries one hears the term, "Christian
humility." Why Christian? Humility is esteemed in
every religion. Another term one reads in Western
religious writings is "Christian grace." Again, why
Christian? The concept of grace was common to
humanity long before Jesus Christ came to earth;
his word for grace wasn't the first time that concept was ever mentioned. To claim otherwise
would be to show almost wilful ignorance. The ancient teachings of India contain a perfectly good
word for grace, one that is very often used in that
country, and in the same sense (though I have
read theological works in which the writers have
insisted that the concept is absent from Hinduism). The word is *kripa.*

Most people in all religions feel a certain distaste
for fanatics. The majority of Christians wince at
least inwardly if, for example, some zealot sings
hymns loudly in public places, obviously intent on
drawing attention to himself, or if he informs
everyone he meets, lugubriously, that that person
is destined to eternal hellfire for his sins; or if, to
show how holy he is, he sighs openly for the sins

of others. No one likes the poseur. Jesus Christ put it well:

"And when thou prayest, thou shalt not be as the hypocrites are: for they love to pray standing in the synagogues and in the corners of the streets, that they may be seen of men. Verily I say unto you, They have their reward." (Matt. 6:5)

Incidentally, I have always enjoyed the humor in that last sentence. According to Christian tradition, Jesus was **"a man of sorrows, and acquainted with grief."** (Isaiah 53:3) His sense of humor, however, shows repeatedly in the Gospels, usually (as here) by sly innuendo.

Certain characteristics of the fanatic are worth noting. Have you ever met a fanatic with a sense of humor? I haven't—not kindly humor, at least. His body, especially his jaw, is tense, indicating the inward strain on his nerves. He can hardly converse on any subject other than his own personal obsession. He demonstrates little or no sensitivity to the feelings and needs of others. And he is intolerant of opinions that don't agree with his own.

Most well-balanced people define the "good" Christian, Jew, Buddhist, Moslem, or Hindu as someone who minds his own business, wishes harm to no one, has good will toward some, and is a responsible and useful member of society. The average person cannot imagine that God would want more of him than this (as he considers it) exemplary life. The heroic efforts that a few men and women have made through the ages to find God, and to achieve higher states of consciousness may seem to him strange, perhaps even excessive in their piety—bordering on fanaticism. If he thinks about such people at all, however, he must notice that these seeming "overachievers" are at least inoffensive, and that they actually show enviable qualities such as humility, compassion, non-judgmentalness toward others, and even sympathy for them, and—well, yes, one supposes, wisdom. We are, of course, referring to those persons whom many religions describe as saints.

Most people have little or no contact with saints. If they happen to hear of them, they may question whether they really exist.

Protestant Christians, who lack the tradition of sainthood, often protest quite seriously, "Why, we're *all* saints!" A popular Protestant hymn begins with the words, "Oh, when the saints go marching in"—giving thereby the impression that every sincerely believing Christian is already a saint. (The other images suggested by these lines are so patently *unsaintly* as to invite only smiles.)

There come times in everyone's life, however, when tragedy strikes: A baby is born blind, or dead; a young mother dies while giving birth; a family wage-earner is unjustly fired from work, or contracts a fatal illness; people whom one has trusted betray that trust cruelly. There are many kinds of suffering, but come suffering must to everyone sooner or later, in one form or another.

In the life of Buddha, a woman once approached him with the lament that her only son had just died. Would the Buddha, man of great spiritual power that he was, bring her child back to life?

The Buddha, after expressing deep sympathy, replied, "If I am to do anything, I shall need a special kind of oil." (He specified which kind.) The woman, filled with hope, was on the point of leaving when Buddha called to her and added this caution: "The oil must come from a home that has not seen death."

"That's easy!" she thought. A week later, however, she returned still mourning. "I have not," she announced, "been able to find a single home that has not seen death!"

"My daughter," the Buddha gazed commiseratingly at her, "now do you understand? Death is the lot of every being. Whether it come early in life or late, come it *must*. The *Dharma* (Divine Way) I have brought to humanity cannot save people from death. What it can do is help to prepare them for every vicissitude, so that when death or any unexpected loss comes, they can face it calmly and acceptingly."

How much suffering people experience in this world! So long as a person is healthy and prosperous, lives in a happy family, owns a nice home, and is respected by others he is seldom concerned over other people's tragedies. Yet tragedy awaits him, also. Relentlessly it stalks his trail. It may lurk just around the next corner, or over the next hill. How strange, that when people find themselves plunged suddenly into a sea of suffering it isn't long before they cannot imagine ever emerging from those waters again. Grief, to them, seems their eternal reality. Yet when their hearts again soar in happiness, they very soon can't see themselves ever weeping again. Life's fulfillments and disappointments, however, rise and fall constantly, like waves on the ocean.

Everyone alternates repeatedly between grief and happiness. He lives between tears and laughter, every joy being an interval between two sorrows; every sorrow being an interval between two joys. The trough of every wave of sorrow rises ever and again in relief, crests in glad fulfillment, then crashes again toward the next moment in grief. Experiencing these unceasing ups and downs in life, there piles up a growing burden of painful memories in his subconscious.

Christianity officially rejects the doctrine of reincarnation. Many Christians privately, however, recognize reincarnation as a truth, and, after thinking about it, realize that the Gospels in several places, far from rejecting this doctrine, actually seem to suggest it. Many Jews in those days, apart from Jesus himself, seem to have accepted it. I mentioned earlier this passage in Revelation:

"To him that overcometh will I grant to sit with me in my throne, even as I also overcame, and am set down with my Father in his

throne." (3:21) Is not this sentence very suggestive?

And then we read a few verses earlier:

"Him that overcometh will I make a pillar in the temple of my God, and *he shall go no more out*." (Rev. 3:12)

There is also the famous passage in the Gospel of St. Matthew, where Jesus asked his disciples, **"Whom do men say that I the Son of man am? And they said, some say that thou art John the Baptist: some, Elias; and others, Jeremias, or one of the prophets."** (Matt. 16:13,14)

Obviously, if there were people in those times who said Jesus might have been one of the ancient prophets, they clearly meant that he might be their *reincarnation.*

In another passage the Bible states, **"And as Jesus passed by, he saw a man which was blind from his birth. And his disciples asked him, saying, Master, who did sin, this man, or his parents, that he was born blind?"** (John 9:1,2)

Whether philosophically or theologically, this was an important question for any disciple to ask his teacher. It begged to be answered in a way that would apply generically to all similar misfortunes. The fact that John's Gospel describes Jesus as responding only to this particular case is puzzling. What he said, in effect, was, "This man was born blind so that I might later heal him with a miracle." I find this reply quite unsatisfactory. Indeed, it seems to suggest that a claim made by modern scholars may have some merit. They claim the Gospels were tampered with, later, to bring them into line with what the scribes thought should have happened. And I ask myself, did that poor fellow really have to suffer from blindness all the way to manhood, meeting Jesus at an indeterminate age after that, just so that he might at last receive a miraculous cure? (And who knows how much longer he still had to live? Perhaps he died only a few years later, balancing—let us say—twenty-five years of blindness against only ten of miraculously gained vision.)

It is difficult to believe that this passage is stated just the way that event happened. Another example like it occurs when Jesus is reported to have said: **"Whosoever will come after me, let him deny himself, *and take up his cross*, and follow me."** (Mark 8:34) At the time Jesus spoke those words, his audience would have been utterly baffled. What did he mean by "taking up his cross"? The Crucifixion was an event still way "beyond the horizon." Jesus may have used a *similar* expression, such as, "accept every hardship that comes." For a scribe in later years to change such an expression to, "take up his cross," would not really have been presumptuous, for it would have given the same message, and might have seemed to the scribe, assuming he did make such a change, stronger and quite fitting.

A more serious question concerns that man's blindness. I can't imagine the person who, in later years, prepared this gospel for dissemination would actually have changed anything. I *can* imagine him, however, *omitting* something that the church had already decided against: the teaching of reincarnation. We'll see, later, that an entire section had to have been omitted from the Bible: the "lost years" between Jesus as a boy of twelve and later at the age of thirty, when he began his mission.

Would Jesus, however, have simply passed lightly over his disciple's question? We are told he said, **"Neither hath this man sinned, nor his parents: but that the works of God should be made manifest in him."** (John 9:3) I am willing to admit the possibility, since I can't really believe any later scribe would have been so bold as to add even that one word, "Neither." Still, I have lived with a great spiritual master myself, and to me this answer, given in those circumstances, carries an aura of unreality, even of unbelievability. The question those disciples posed clearly points to the issue of reincarnation, of course. Maybe Jesus had indicated agreement with that doctrine enough times not to feel a need to say anything more. The omission would have been especially noteworthy had the question been based on a spiritual error. Still, it is striking that the quoted reply says nothing whatever on the subject.

Many babies are born blind, after all, without the slightest karmic anticipation of a miraculous cure. A human being, as opposed to a master, might see the answer to this very far-reaching question in terms of one individual, but the wisdom of a master would surely view even this situation as a doorway also to a more universal explanation. No wise spiritual teacher, with a duty to instruct his disciples in universal truths, could overlook the broader issues in a case like this. If the disciples who asked him that question were wrong in suggesting that that man might have sinned before he was born, Jesus would have had a duty to correct that fallacy immediately. And if the disciples were touching on a teaching that had already been explained by Jesus, Jesus would surely have acknowledged the fact (rather than sidestepping the issue completely) before passing on to this particular case.

From all evidence, reincarnation was at least discussed among the Jews of those days, and believed in by some even if denied by others. Elsewhere in the Bible, after the transfiguration of Jesus on Mount Tabor, the disciples asked him, **"Why then say the scribes that Elias must first come?"** Jesus answered, **"Elias truly shall first come, and restore all things. But I say unto you, That Elias is come already, and they knew him not. . . . Then the disciples understood that he spake unto them of John the Baptist."** (Matt. 17:10–13)

Again, Jesus said elsewhere, **"For all the prophets and the law prophesied until John. And if ye will receive it, this is Elias, which was**

for to come. He that hath ears to hear, let him hear." (Matt. 11:13–15)

It was not my intention in this chapter to write at such length on reincarnation. This subject deserves to be treated as a separate issue. My book, *The Path*, devotes a whole chapter to this subject, and contains much more information than I've given here. I recommend to the interested reader that he study that chapter. I might also mention one more passage here, in passing, which shows the subtlety of insight Yogananda himself brought to bear on the sayings of Jesus in the Gospels.

At the outset of Chapter Four in the Gospel of St. John, the words appear, **"He [Jesus] left Judaea, and departed again into Galilee. And he must needs go through Samaria."** (John 4:3,4) This seems a perfectly simple and straightforward statement based on the fact that Samaria did actually lie between Judaea and Galilee. Yogananda stated, however, that the words, "And he must needs go," referred to a hidden truth also, one which the disciples of Jesus may have missed altogether. (Masters don't often disclose the deeper reasons for much of what they do.) Jesus also (Yogananda explained) had a particular reason for visiting Samaria. He knew that a fallen disciple of his from former incarnations lived there. This was the woman known simply through this account as "the woman of Samaria."

Jesus posed several tests to prove her sincerity and her readiness to receive his teaching again.

He asked her for water, then hinted that he had "living water" to give her. He then said, **"Go, call thy husband, and come hither."** She answered him truthfully that she had no husband. In fact, Jesus told her, she had had five husbands, and the man she lived with at present was not even her husband. It was only after she'd given him a correct answer, and truthfully admitted to an embarrassing reality, that Jesus decided to accept her once again as a disciple.

The soul goes through countless experiences before it wins its way to final release, when it is free from ego-bondage and able at last to merge back into God. A simple glimpse at any crowd should suffice to show, clearly written upon those variegated faces, the buried memories and tendencies of many lifetimes. The personality, through its many incarnations, endures countless ups and downs, victories and disappointments, joys and sufferings. In the life of one who has reached the point at last where he yearns for release, it suffices to experience even a touch of suffering for the thought to arise in his mind, "Must this process drag on *forever?*"

Waves of hopeful expectation and painful disappointment rise and fall, continuously. Life assumes at last an aspect, as Yogananda described it, of "anguishing monotony." The subconscious memory of repeated sufferings, added to even a slight touch of pain in the present life, awakens in the heart an intense desire for release and eternal freedom in God.

The doctrine of reincarnation is traditionally rejected in Christianity. The Gospels, however, as we have seen, give a number of clear hints (of which I've named but a few) that Jesus Christ, and also many Jews of his time, accepted this teaching. Surveys have shown that many Christians today accept reincarnation privately as a truth, or at least as a perfectly reasonable explanation. For one thing, the doctrine explains what must otherwise seem a great injustice, and quite inexplicable if one posits only one lifetime on earth. Is not suffering, indeed, something universally experienced by all? Anyone who longs for spiritual understanding cannot but ponder that fact and ask himself first, "Why?" And then, if he is thoughtful, he wonders, "Who, then, is safe?"

Buddha's destiny had been foretold when he was born: He would be either a mighty king, or a mighty teacher of Truth and a great renunciate of all worldly glory. His royal father did his best to influence the child to accept his royal destiny, and to prevent him—especially after the child became a youth—from beholding any instance of death and suffering. The king surrounded his son, therefore, with every luxury and with only people who were in the glow of youth.

The young prince, in spite of everything his father had done, discovered his alternate destiny, which was to seek enlightenment. What awakened these buried memories in his consciousness was, first, the chance sight of an old man. Later, he beheld a man who was ill. Finally, he beheld a corpse. These three encounters sufficed to awaken in him the keenest awareness of three inescapable truths of life. All men are subject to extremes of calamity. Understanding dawned on the young man; it became his absolute imperative to find a truth by which all mankind would be enabled to escape suffering forever.

Buddha lived two thousand five hundred years ago. For many people today, his anguish may seem remote; some people might even consider it irrelevant to "modern" life. Yet millions of people everywhere experience the same calamities every day—by no means less so, nowadays, than millennia ago. History affords countless examples of men and women, also, who turned to God all the more urgently because of the suffering they beheld around them, or endured in their own lives. Such dedicated souls were by no means "fanatics." Nor can I recall that any of them became (an adolescent reaction) bitter or cynical. They were realists who never doubted that God is basically good. What they came to understand, however, was that worldly *desires and attachments* are bound to plunge everyone, sooner or later, into what Yogananda described as life's "ocean of suffering and misery."

Many Christians — Protestants particularly, whose doctrines leave no room for a beatitude higher than simple, "Christian" goodness—dismiss

as exaggerated the urgency with which saints have
sought direct communion with God.

Let me become personal for a moment, that
what I write may have more immediacy for the
reader. I myself received a good, normal, Protestant Christian upbringing. My mother was a devout Episcopalian. My parents sent me from Romania, where my father's work caused us to live,
to a Quaker School in England. With the outbreak
of World War II in 1939, we moved back to our
own country, America. There I was sent to Kent
School in Connecticut, an institution run by Episcopalian monks of the Order of the Holy Cross.
When I returned home on vacations, I attended
church on Sunday mornings with my mother, and
participated in many church activities. The first
college I went to was, again, Christian: the Quaker
institution known as Haverford College, outside
Philadelphia.

It is customary for many people, when they've
grown old, to describe themselves when young as
"gay blades." In my youth, it must be admitted, I
was basically quite serious and not frivolous at all.
I had a certain aptitude for athletics, for I was a
fast runner, and I also loved an occasional "good
time." I also hungered deeply, however, to know
the truth. And I felt I was not getting the truth I
sought at church, nor in my scholastic studies. I
cannot remember a time when I was not constantly, and with increasing urgency, asking of
Life that ancient question: "*Why?*" My growing

hunger for answers was forever left unanswered.

My mother did believe in the saints. She tried to get me interested in them also. In this attempt she was, perhaps unfortunately, unsuccessful. I didn't believe in the miracles of which she spoke so devoutly; I lacked the devotion to feel inspiration in their works of piety. I was, I told myself, seeking truth, not sweet sentiments.

For several years my search took me far afield. At first I sought it through the sciences, thinking (at the age of thirteen) to become an astronomer. Then I decided that truth for human beings had to have a more human reality. I gave deep thought to political solutions, and sought answers that might help everyone, not only myself. In time, I discarded this direction also as I came to understand that no system can ever make anyone better than he is, in himself. Realizing, then, that the truth I sought was something that would *inspire*, and not merely inform or impose changes from without, I decided to seek truth in the arts—particularly in music and literature, for both of which I had some flair. I hoped by these means to inspire people with an understanding of truth. This aspiration, too, I forsook when I realized that, not knowing the truth myself, I would only be flooding the world with my own ignorance if I imposed my "art" on others.

My upbringing might have led me to seek Truth in the churches. Unfortunately, what I'd found in them was not inspiration, but self-righteousness,

which only starved me for actual answers to my
own burning desire for true, universal rightness.

Early in my search I reached the conclusion that
what I sought must provide satisfaction for the
heart. Truth had to be deeper than mere facts. I
discarded both science and social theory, therefore, as incapable in themselves of bringing anyone true happiness. At last it dawned on me that
what I really wanted, and what everyone wanted,
really, was happiness—indeed, more than happiness (which is forever fragile and uncertain), but
joy, expansive joy, an inspiration that was eternal. This ideal became, for me, the very essence
of everything I was seeking.

It was only after reaching this decision that I
began to find myself veering toward a truth which
(I was forced to admit at last) soared up to embrace spiritual dimensions. Could there really be,
I asked myself, a God, Creator of all things? People sometimes ask this question casually. In my
case, the question was urgent. My answer held
the only possibility of purpose and meaning that
I could imagine in Life.

I had been brought up in a well-to-do home,
surrounded by a loving family and many friends.
I had lived in a succession of good neighborhoods.
And I'd had held up before me all the dreams most
people cherish: a comfortable home of my own, a
loving and supportive wife, an interesting and
well-paying job, happy children, good neighbors.

It was with growing desperation, however, that I

listened when people described these goals. I saw no alternative to them, yet my heart rejected them all as empty of real meaning. Life, I thought, simply *had* to offer more than this pale substitute for the ideals I cherished in my heart.

Gradually, I came to realize that there *is* only one worthwhile goal in life. That goal is to find God. Was this, I asked myself, a sign that I was becoming a fanatic? My companions thought me much too serious, but I at least kept my sense of humor, and tried always to see things in a broad perspective. I accepted that others had goals that, for them at least, seemed valid. Often, indeed, I wished I could be more like them, rather than forever tortured in my own seeking. Inwardly, however, I was becoming increasingly convinced that life could never hold any meaning for me unless it brought me closer to God. God I defined in my heart as that final perfection which all men seek.

To make a long story short, I finally came upon Paramhansa Yogananda's great book, *Autobiography of a Yogi*. I read it avidly, then took a bus almost the next day and traveled across the American continent to meet him. My first words at that meeting expressed something I had never imagined myself addressing to anybody. I said, "I want to be your disciple." It was at that meeting that he accepted me.

Through him I came to understand that I had been too mental in my searching. I'd imagined truth as something I could find by thinking my way to it. I'd been over-intellectual. Paramhansa Yogananda showed me that the way to God is through the heart. Devotion is heartfelt yearning for Infinity. Devotional love is the selfless enjoyment of that aspiration.

In time I found that everything I had thought of as Christ's message was utterly shallow. I had thought that Jesus wanted people to be ordinarily good, ordinarily kind to others, and to hold ordinary expectations of life. Those "Christian" expectations had been, I saw, but a scratch on the surface of the deep, inspiring love and eternal wisdom of that great divine Teacher and eternal Savior of men.

CHAPTER SIX

A QUESTION OF DEGREES

D ID JESUS CHRIST SAY THAT LIFE HAS A SPECIFIC purpose? or did he perhaps say (as if anticipating the modern, "fair-minded" professor) that life has ("Hmm, yes, I imagine we should say") several purposes? Of the statements attributed to Jesus, some of them are quite unequivocal.

"Seek ye first the kingdom of God, and his righteousness; and all these things shall be added unto you." (Matt. 6:33)

This statement is surely a powerful one. It denotes an absolute purpose. What do most orthodox Christians make of it? Well, given the outwardness of their own comprehension of religion, the only thing they could possibly make of it would have an outward direction also. The kingdom of God to which most of them look forward is a visible, tangible, three-dimensional place. (When I was a child, I theorized that world—three-dimensional as I visualized it—as being perhaps located on the planet Saturn because of its beautiful "halo.")

Most Christians think of the kingdom of God as a place of heavenly beauty where souls go who have lived a good life. In heaven, they visualize themselves inhabiting bodies much like the ones they have now, enjoying beatific happiness forever. What they think Jesus meant was that, after living as we should on earth, we'll be admitted into his "kingdom" after death and live there "forever after" amid surroundings where "cool breezes blow evermore," stroll serenely through peaceful, shadowed woods, sit in undisturbed comfort beside gently rippling streams, and wander calmly through gay, flowery meadows in the blessed company of angels. Perhaps, like them, we shall have wings.

Salvation for most Christians means living eternally in a body, amid surroundings very different from what Jesus Christ himself described elsewhere in the Bible:

"The kingdom of God," he said, **"cometh not with observation: Neither shall they say, Lo here! or, lo there! for, behold, *the kingdom of God is within you.*"** (Luke 17:20,21)

This passage is, for most Christians, quite incomprehensible. It is one they keep, therefore, as if in a drawer, out of sight (and out of mind).

Instead, the words of that Christian hymn, "Oh, when the saints go marching in," suggest something closer to the popular perception: that after a good life on earth the "saint" is shown a place into which he will be able (perhaps literally) to "march."

Entry into heaven means above all, for most Christians, that one is saved. And what is one saved *from*? According to them, from the terrors of eternal hell. Damnation is, in fact, proclaimed as the soul's inevitable destiny, in consequence of the Original Sin committed by Adam and Eve when they ate "the forbidden fruit" and thereby disobeyed God. It was because of that act that they were driven from the Garden of Eden. We have inherited their legacy—so we've been taught—of sinful disobedience.

The orthodox dogma—clearly specified by many churches—is that mankind is therefore *naturally* sinful, and doomed to hell.

There is a "but" here, however: We can be redeemed by special grace if we "receive" Christ, who sacrificed his life for us on the cross. Christians are encouraged to think of Jesus Christ, through that penitential offering, as their "personal Savior." Receiving him has always been understood as the essence of true Christianity because of those words in St. John's Gospel: **"As many as received him, to them gave he power to become the sons of God."** (John 1:12)

That word "received," however, demands extra-cautious attention. Does "receiving him" mean simply formal baptism—followed years later by equally formal confirmation? Does it mean instead, perhaps, a single ardent act of self-offering before the altar in a church? Considering any one of these explanations as a hypothesis, we should submit it to the test of experience. Do people really emerge from the first ceremony, or at least from the second one, purged and *permanently* changed? Is it enough even to make a single, emotion-charged *self*-submission? Again, thinking of Christ's sacrifice as having been made for all men, did human nature everywhere undergo a radical transformation after his crucifixion?

In answer to the first question, I submit once more my own experience. I was a babe in arms when I was baptized; I don't imagine I had the slightest idea why they were splashing me at that baptismal font in Ploeşti. The question of my consent can be written off, therefore, as a clear *nolle prosequi*. It was, of course, sweet of my parents to offer me up to Christ at such an early age, but as far as my own will was concerned the event cannot have had my willing consent. My baptism had to have been an imposition on my free will, since my own part in that ceremony could, at best, have been only to struggle and cry in outrage at the indignity of the whole proceedings.

Later, at the age of thirteen, I was confirmed by the bishop at our Church of St. James the Less in Scarsdale, N.Y. What this meant was that my baptismal dedication to Christ received episcopal confirmation, lest any doubt existed in my mind that I belonged to him. Again, this happened years before I reached the legal age of consent. Was it the purpose of my Confirmation ceremony to catch me before I could register intelligent protest? (Only years later would I be deemed mature enough to get a driver's license, to vote in elections, or to pledge myself to another person in marriage.) Did these sacraments constitute, in any sense but the liturgical, "receiving Christ"? Surely not!

Does "receiving him" mean, then, some emotional or even intellectual acceptance? The meaning must go deeper. Belief alone is not enough. Consider this: We may believe in someone, but does our belief in any way guarantee his trustworthiness?

As for a single emotional conversion—popular among Fundamentalists—again, the Epistle of Paul to Titus states, **"Not by works of righteousness which we have done, but according to his mercy he saved us, *by the washing of regeneration, and renewing of the Holy Ghost.*"** (Titus 3:5) The implication here is *continued* "washing," and repeated *"renewing."*

What about humanity as a whole? Judging at least from the gloating sadism of the mobs at the Roman Colosseum, where gladiators did their best to disembowel one another, one must conclude that the Crucifixion was not followed by any notable mass upliftment.

Well then, what about the great and growing body of Christian worshipers in those days? Did Christ die to save at least *them*? Any heroism they showed in facing martyrdom calmly was followed, long years after the persecutions, by shameless bickering and dissension among the prelates. It all may be perfectly understandable, and even excusable, but by no stretch of the imagination may we say of the Christians in those days that they comported themselves like "sons of God."

Paramhansa Yogananda stated that to "receive" Christ means to receive Christ's presence consciously and inwardly, on a soul level, which is to say, in a deep state of ecstasy. Anything less than that is superficial and should not be taken seriously, since it produces no real or lasting change in a person's consciousness and no increase of spiritual power (such as one would expect of a "Son of God").

The Pope, some time ago, described what the Roman Catholic Church has to offer. He referred to it as, "the mystery of salvation." Mm-yes. A mystery. I suppose it would have to be something like that.

Dogmatism apart, ask yourself this question: *Are* most Christians notably different from other religionists around the world? An unbiased gaze forces the answer: No, by no means do they seem notably so.

What about those words I quoted in an earlier

chapter, **"Be ye therefore perfect, even as your Father which is in heaven is perfect"**? This commandment makes a seemingly impossible demand of human nature. Who, then, can be considered a really good Christian? What Christ's call to perfection demands of us is that we try to become like God! No wonder this saying is seldom, if ever, mentioned in any Sunday sermon in the churches.

Omitted also from most sermons are other key statements, like the one Jesus repeated from Deuteronomy 6:5: **"Thou shalt love the Lord thy God with all thine heart, and with all thy soul, and with all thy might."** The Gospel of St. Mark (12:30) quotes the same statement, adding, **"[Love God] . . . with all thy mind. . . . this is the first commandment."**

Frank Laubach, the great Christian missionary, once launched a campaign to get more ministers and preachers in America simply to *mention* God in their Sunday sermons.

What, then (to repeat my question), *is* the kingdom of God? Where is it? How, moreover, can we be expected utterly to love Someone we've never seen, and of whose presence we've never had even an inkling? Obviously, devotion grows from experience at least of some kind.

There are a number of other sayings attributed to Jesus that suggest truths too lofty for inclusion in the usual Sunday morning sermon, and too demanding to be urged upon the average Christian (lukewarm as he is in both his beliefs and his practices). Yet those truths form, in fact, the basis of Christ's teachings. They comprise also part of the ancient teachings of *Sanaatan Dharma.*

Sukdeva, a great saint of ancient India, stated, "All time is wasted that is not spent in seeking God."

Will Christians say that their own religion falls short of the heights achieved by the ancient teachings of India? If they are honest with themselves, they must at least admit that their experience of Christ's teachings has not yet plumbed their depths.

In fact, Christ's true teachings are as lofty as anything ever taught in any religion. Jesus Christ fully expressed the Truth, which is to say, therefore, that no teaching can (or ever could) be higher than his. To speak of relative heights would in fact be absurd, for God is Absolute. If truth is indeed one and eternal, the question is not even debatable: The message of Jesus Christ must be, and by every reasonable test is, as lofty as Eternal Truth itself.

Can there be relativities in the exposition of that truth? Here the answer must be, "Yes, of course there can. How could there *not* be?" Even to state a truth in words is to bring it down from Absolute Perfection into the world of relativity. For one thing, the meaning of every dogma (a word formula) depends partly on people's varying ability to understand it. The effort of dogmatists to define with exquisite precision what they think to be an "absolute truth" must still depend on their own human understanding, and on their human capacity, therefore, for *mis*understanding. And, let's face it, that capacity seems, sometimes, to amount almost to genius! The formulators of those dogmas, being only men, lived under the very human misconception that it is possible to nail down a truth "absolutely" by encapsulating it in some mere formula.

Abstractions are, necessarily, elusive. *Love*, as a word, means different things to different people. It covers a wide spectrum of meaning, from brutish lust to the absolute purity of oneness implied in the Sanskrit word, *prem*.

Peace, too, has many subjective meanings, all the way from a temporary cessation of conflict to the **"peace of God, which passeth all understanding"** (Phil. 4:7)—a condition possible only in inner communion with the Lord.

Joy also, finally, can mean many things depending on a person's own experience of life. Some people equate joy with winning the lottery. Saints equate it with the soul's immersion in God.

Truth is absolute, but man's understanding of it is relative. Therefore is it said, "Even the Devil quotes the scriptures."

It is important to realize that people's understanding of religion is limited everywhere by the narrowness of their *capacity* for understanding. Their comprehension even of objective reality was,

during the era of Jesus Christ's life, narrowly
circumscribed. For most people, it was simply impossible in those days to have any concept of universal realities, even on the material plane. Aris-
totle, wise though he was, declared that the air we
breathe is—because we can't see it—nothing at
all. The earth (flat, of course) was located in men's
minds at the center of a comfortably small cosmos. Matter was considered solid and substantial.
Our Earth's age was computed at a very few thousands of years. And human history was estimated
in the hundreds of years.

Civilization is still considered, even today, a relatively recent development. For most of Christian
history, reality was more or less limited to what
we now think of as the Western world. Truth itself
was thought capable of encapsulation in short,
pithy dogmas. Other religions were looked upon
as pagan, and only Christianity was believed (by
Christians, of course) to be based on divine revelation. Indeed, this last belief is still waved by theologians like a flag, though the ship they travel in
is now foundering on the rocky coast of inconvenient discoveries, made as man becomes growingly
aware of other religions.

During the early Christian era, it was simply not
possible to imagine a scheme of things that embraced timelessness and infinity: a cosmic reality
in which we human beings might seem to have
hardly more significance, objectively speaking,
than that of any of the other fauna on Earth.

Were it not for the fact of suffering, mankind might continue in "relative" ease to stroll through life satisfied with common fulfillments, and seeking nothing more from life than self-gratification, until death draws its final curtain over the whole scene. There might be no problem, moreover, with happily awaiting eternity in heaven after death, even if the regrettable alternative to that beatitude were the possibility of eternal life in hell (which, of course, no one wants). But somehow the question, "How bad can I be and get away with it?" keeps people hoping for the best, since anticipation of either heaven or hell comprises so minuscule a part of their present reality.

The smug satisfaction they feel in contemplating this scheme of things is undermined constantly, however, by life's very present uncertainties, disappointments, failures, and miseries. Suffering makes people question the justice of it all. Misery plunges them into a sort of mental darkness. These stark realities keep people from ever becoming too smug in their happiness.

For everyone who is satisfied with life, there are countless others who hurl at religion the mocking challenge: "What about suffering? Can God really love man, when He permits so many people to suffer? Is there even a way out? If you believe that, tell your hopes to the sufferers!"

A cosmic view of truth, however, allows even for suffering, just as a broad view of the ocean includes all the many moods that pass over it, each of them only temporary and perhaps, therefore, interesting. A narrowly human view, on the other hand, forces the question, "Why *me*? Why must *I* be the one to suffer? And how is it that others seem prosperous and happy?" There is little visible correspondence between how good (or bad) people are and the punishments and rewards to which they are subjected on earth. The common explanation—the *only* one, really—is that God's ways are inscrutable. Resignation is easier to achieve during prosperity than during suffering.

Modern science has provided us with a cosmic view. Many orthodox Christians, even today, find it difficult to adapt to that view, even though, of course, they now accept that the world is round; that there are other religions with relatively lofty concepts, which contain at least some portion of "Christian" truth; that our Earth is by no means central in the great scheme of things; that the universe is inconceivably vast; that there may well be life elsewhere in it. They accept facts, at least, that have been scientifically proved. Still, they find it difficult to reconcile those facts with the teachings of Jesus Christ. Christianity retains, in their view, its erstwhile anthropomorphic concepts: a Heavenly Father seated on a throne in heaven, His "only begotten Son" seated to His right.

Little effort, if any, is devoted to reconciling the dichotomy between anthropomorphic images and abstract truths. Facts that have been scientifically proved are no longer denied, but they can be, and still are, kept immaculately separate from people's religious beliefs, which people confine still, as most other religionists do, within high-walled enclosures, even if those walls need constantly to be raised in order to protect religious belief from desecration by the ever-new discoveries science makes.

Religiously inclined Christians still think of God as their Heavenly Father. Hindus still prefer to think of Him as Krishna or Rama, whom they, too, think of as divine beings like Jesus, and whose beloved presence they keep in their hearts. Religious groups tend to think of their own teachings as God's only true revelation to mankind. It is becoming increasingly difficult, however, to believe that one group of people alone is in possession of the only divine revelation.

If ever orthodox Christians succeed in breaking out of their mental limitations, which persuade them that their faith is the only truth, they will find both inspiration and understanding in the fact that those same truths are declared elsewhere. Narrow-minded Christians are naturally reluctant to accept the dogmas of other religions, many of which claim (with equal bigotry) that Jesus was less enlightened than their own great founders. What, however, if unbiased investigation were to show them that the teachings of Jesus Christ were *much broader and more profound* than anything Christians themselves ever imagined: that it was simply their own understanding that was limited?

Indeed, the purpose of this book is to offer a glorious truth, deeply inspiring to anyone who really wants to know the truth:

"If ye continue in my word, then are ye my disciples indeed;

"And ye shall know the truth, and the truth shall make you free." (John 8:31,32)

That Truth is wonderful to contemplate. It is, indeed, life changing. It is also, moreover, soul-liberating. Who indeed would say, merely because people's understanding of reality was once narrowly circumscribed, that Jesus himself therefore taught that narrow view, and nothing more exalted? Preposterous!

The churches are, as I have said, centered in their institutional commitment. They cannot easily even speak of the vastness of infinite Truth. Scholars, who are also in their way seeking truth, are limited by their notion that truth must be sought by a process of analysis and reasoning. Only people with spiritual vision are clearly aware that the intellect, though adept at forming and defining ideas, lacks the ability, born of *direct inner experience*, actually to *know* Truth and God.

Christian saints have labored under the disadvantage of church control. The authorities in any church, moreover, few of whom have had deep spiritual experience, cannot be relied upon to promote those deeper truths, even though the truths are clearly stated in Jesus Christ's message.

India has had one definite advantage: Its religion has never been formally organized in an institutional sense. There *are*, of course, certain formal beliefs in Hinduism, but there has never been a central authority to enforce them, nor any person in a position to dictate how those beliefs must be stated.

Had a board of scientists been appointed to determine which scientific discoveries were acceptable, and which ones should be rejected, the scientific way-showers—men like Galileo, Newton, Albert Einstein, and a host of others—would undoubtedly have been declared heretics by the establishment. Einstein's Law of Relativity was so abstruse that, when he first announced it, there were hardly ten scientists in the world who could understand it. Fortunately, they were the right ten: highly qualified men of science with already-established reputations in the eyes of their fellows. Only because these ten men accepted Einstein's thesis was it hailed everywhere, eventually to revolutionize not only science, but many other aspects of modern thought as well.

The greatest Christian saints have been not merely pious, kindly, charitable, honest, and scrupulously truthful—the sort of persons, in short, whom most people would think worthy of emulation. What particularly distinguished them was the depth of their love for God, and of their absorption in Him.

What of the inner communion of those saints? Could it be verified? Many tests could be applied, both subjectively and objectively. I've already proposed a few of them, which were designed to show, first, that the inner, divine communion of saints has demonstrated almost palpably their overwhelming love, bliss, and expanded understanding. They have given outward evidence of being utterly fulfilled, inwardly. Every true saint has declared, of his experience of God, that there remains in him no desire for anything else. They have in common an intense focus on God's love and joy. And all of them agree that finding God is the only truly worthwhile goal of life.

Physically, during their state of ecstasy, saints have been observed without breath, sometimes without heartbeat, and with little or no outward awareness of what is going on around them. Far from being mentally dysfunctional, however, as a result even of months of inner withdrawal from their surroundings, they always return from that state greatly recharged both physically and mentally.

The testimony of the saints regarding their uplifted state of joy, and their greater sense of reality in that joy, is universal. Truth, as we've already stated, is universal; it is "one without a second," and cannot be fragmented. Truth alone is also *Sanaatan*: Eternal.

That this is the true goal of life is explained in the Bhagavad Gita, where life's goal is declared to be the soul's merging into God. The great Christian saints—whose lives have been completely transformed by divine ecstasy—have also declared the same truth. Many Christian saints have described divine union as "marriage with God." All of them have asserted that the true goal of life is *complete absorption in the Lord.*

Saints in the Roman Catholic Church would have been excommunicated had they openly revealed everything they knew. And even assuming that some of them might have not been affected personally by that punishment, they would no longer have been in a position to serve others openly. The majority of them, therefore, have been careful not to contradict church dogmas.

Persecution has been inflicted on those also who have performed miracles. Indeed, persecution has come even to those who were only outstandingly holy, and hasn't ended until they were safely dead. It is never convenient for an institution which relies on self-perpetuation through dogma to admit the possibility of an anomaly to its carefully and precisely framed formulae.

One can see this matter from the point of view of the clerical authorities. Priests are all supposed to be equally ordained by "Mother Church." What to do, then, when someone—and a priest, at that—appears on the scene who is obviously *more* ordained than others? Priests cannot afford to have their congregations drifting off to some other, more divinely ordained priest. What to do about saintly priests, then, who seem to have received some kind of "extra-curricular" ordination? In the case of that Los Angeles priest whom I mentioned earlier, worshipers from other congregations were forsaking their churches on Sunday mornings and flocking to his services. What then—to repeat the question—are the authorities to do about it? The line of reasoning they followed was, in their eyes, the only practical course: They banished this priestly embarrassment to the distant clime of Spain, hoping that his reputation for sanctity had not preceded him.

Thus it befell, as I said earlier, in the case of St. Joseph of Cupertino. This saint's inconvenient "habit" of levitating (by no means a unique phenomenon among saints) was causing serious concern among the authorities in Rome. Persons highly placed in society were traveling great distances to visit him. One highly placed visitor simply took St. Joseph by the hand while the saint was praying, and both of them rose high up into the air! Joseph's superiors, as we saw earlier, felt they simply had to intervene.

Therefore did Padre Pio, in the name of discretion, enjoin my friend to silence. Indeed, Padre Pio had been reprimanded already by the Church, and several attempts were made during his lifetime to silence him. (His staunch supporters, peasants brandishing pitchforks, loyally "rescued" him.)

Although the Catholic Church usually, during the lifetime of those saints, made it a practice to persecute them, it did at least canonize them once they were safely dead. The Protestant churches, by contrast, have never considered even posthumous recognition.

The mission of Jesus Christ has proved too powerful to be destroyed, although scientific challenges have been raised against it from all sides for centuries, and attacks have also come, more recently, from scholars, novelists, and anyone else who found it profitable to jump on the bandwagon. The more Jesus Christ's message has come under attack, however, the more it shows its intrinsic power to stand firm.

Nevertheless, many *Christians* have found themselves not standing so firm. Their faith has been shaken, and their perception of reality, confused. The churches today are in a state of serious crisis. For these reasons, there is an urgent need today to bring to the attention of Christians everywhere the thrilling and insightful commentaries of Paramhansa Yogananda. Because his deep insights have come from *outside* the normal orthodox enclosure, they carry a freshness and a clarity which have been somewhat dimmed by centuries of theological debate, rendering it very hard to achieve understanding within the "fold" of Christianity.

Paramhansa Yogananda pointed out that there is in many ways an opposition between *Christianity* and *Churchianity*. To be a Christian means to adhere to the true teachings of Jesus Christ. *True* Christianity cannot be shaken, since its precepts are based on eternal Truths. *Churchianity*, how-ever, was created in the minds of men, by no means all of whom were wise. The churches have long trembled before the onslaughts of science, even if centuries of warding off those attacks have given them a certain fortitude. Christendom is now being destabilized once more by many of the new claims of scholarly research. Finally, it has also come under attack most recently from novel-ists, whose fantasies, though lacking in valid scholarship, have nevertheless by their pretense of scholarship shaken the faith of many Chris-tians. The Christian religion, resting as it does on *realized* wisdom, can never be destroyed. What Yogananda urged, however, is becoming now a desperate need. As I stated earlier, he urged a gen-eral return to *original Christianity*.

My aspiration in this book is to help Christians to recognize and understand the true depth of Jesus Christ's teachings. Thus alone, I believe, will they develop the new and deepened faith they need today, more than ever, in his true and ever sublime teachings, which are their centuried heritage.

CHAPTER SEVEN

RELIGION AND THE HEART

DESPITE RATIONAL ATTACKS ON RELIGIOUS ORTHO-doxy, and the inability of orthodoxy to re-spond with needed clarity, there remains a vitally important aspect of religion which reason alone can never touch. These are the feelings of the heart, feelings much deeper than mere senti-ment. Devotional feelings are evoked by religious belief, and are then strengthened by religious *ex-perience*. Without the quality of feeling, it may be seriously questioned whether one would be even conscious. Certainly, one could not be deeply de-vout.

I remember accompanying a Catholic priest—a dear friend of mine who later asked me to initiate him into Kriya Yoga—to the deathbed of an old woman. She spoke to us of the joy she felt while receiving holy communion. When she discovered that I was not a Roman Catholic, she looked at me with deep concern and said, "Oh, you don't know what you're missing!"

I sincerely appreciated the depth of her feeling, and would never have dreamed of offering an alternative to it. Her loving statement did not tempt me, however, to change my practices. The devotional upliftment she felt in the Eucharist was something I too experienced in Kriya Yoga, and in my other spiritual practices.

The sad longing for God expressed in the Gregorian chants is uplifting and heart-purifying. So also is the joyful utterance of *mahamantra,* the Vaishnava chant to Krishna and Rama. Self-uplifting devotion can be experienced in many ways. Sometimes it expresses what my Guru called the "romance of religion," which is more an upward-flowing mood of exaltation than a deep, inward commitment. Beyond even the sweetest emotion, however, lies the actual experience of divine states of love, joy, soul-expansion, and bliss.

It is a pity that Christians generally deride as idolatrous the devotion of Hindus for their spiritual images. In fact, those images are not *idols* in the true sense of the word. They are personifications, rather, of the *ideals* people hold concerning God and higher aspects of truth. Instead of idol worship, then, the practice deserves to be named "ideal worship." Without devotion, no one can find God. And without concepts of some sort, few could progress beyond the fixed dogmas of orthodoxy to a state of transcendent awareness, and (for that matter) beyond form to formlessness. Images of Krishna are no more idolatrous than images of Jesus Christ on the cross, which every Christian sees as a reminder of Jesus Christ's love for us. Those who think of Christ as verily present on the altar and in the Eucharist are not at all idolatrous, either. The consciousness of Christ is omnipresent, so why not focalize him in something tangible, in which omnipresence dwells also, that can remind one of him?

Images of Kali, Ganesha, Saraswati, and the numerous other divine forms visualized in Hinduism are equally meant, simply, as focal points of devotion. Ram Proshad, a great saint in Bengal over two hundred years ago, was an exalted devotee of God as the Divine Mother in the form of Kali. Yet in one of his most beautiful songs to Her he said, "Thousands of scriptures declare my Mother is beyond all form and infinite. Nevertheless, it is in this form that I choose to adore You." After the great pujas, or seasons of worship, moreover, the images of Kali, Durga, etc., are immersed in the Ganges to keep devotees aware that the forms they worship are only fancied, transient images of the Infinite, portrayed in human form to make them more comprehensible, and to help people to direct their ultimate devotion to God alone.

God is Absolute Love. Very few people, however, would be capable of understanding divine love if it were austerely divorced from everything they know already: the love they have for their mothers, for example, their fathers, their friends, or for other people beloved by them.

Who will say, then, that the Hindu's love for Vishnu, Lakshmi, Shiva, Krishna, and Rama is less truly meaningful than the love that old, dying woman felt for Jesus in the Eucharist? Deep devotion is a gift, in every religion, of divine grace. No outward form can ever encapsulate it, for the Divine Consciousness is infinite.

Someone once asked Yogananda if there is any end to evolution. "No end," he replied. "You go on until you achieve endlessness." Why have forms, if grace does it all anyway? Because grace is like milk poured out from the breast of the Divine Mother. One's cup of expectation must be held up to receive it. Human longing for God receives that grace of love, and becomes true devotion (instead of ego-inspired pleading for divine favors).

No sincere truth seeker would ever deprecate anyone's sincere devotion, whatever the form it takes. Our images of God can assume numerous forms. Whatever uplifts our heart's feelings is sacred. To make my point even clearer, fanatical emotion does *not* uplift the heart's feelings: It narrows them, first, then lowers them owing to its deprecation of others. Even sentimental devotion may lead the heart outward, rather than upward. The direction of energy-flow from the heart is an all-important issue.

Although skeptics, excessively dependent on

reasoning, may be willing to wound people's faith in religion, and fanatics may gloat as they denounce any beliefs different from their own, true devotion, being experienced in the heart, is discerned inwardly as a flow of energy rising from that point. True religious feeling cannot be affected by any outer influence.

Truth also is perceived by the heart, and cannot be destroyed by intellectual doubt so long as the heart is clear in its upward aspiration. It should be added, however, that sincere devotion may be driven into the defensive mode, which can force the energy to flow downward and resurface, later, as fanaticism. In this age, indeed, the apologists for religion tend sometimes to express themselves fanatically. They shout their belief loudly, as if to silence the voice of reason, and even persecute those who disapprove of their excessive religious zeal. Thus, dry scientific investigation, and over-intellectual but spiritually ignorant scholarship, have damaged many people's grasp on religious truth even if they try to defend it.

The most dependable defense of religion comes therefore not from devotional ardor, but from direct, inner communion with God. It is this inner communion which has made the saints in every religion the true custodians of high truth. What ardent believer, regardless of his faith, comes even close to matching the calm, unshakable conviction of those who have achieved inner communion with, in the case of Christians, Jesus Christ? Saint Augustine said, "Lord, Thou hast made us for Thyself, and our hearts are restless until they find their rest in Thee." Could even a sincerely devout, but in human terms quite ordinary, Baptist or Presbyterian come close to making a similar statement from his own inner experience?

Saint Jean Vianney, a much-loved priest in France, once remarked, "If you *knew* how much God loves you, you would *die* for joy!" How many Christians, regardless of their sectarian affiliations, could utter such words with anything like as deep fervor?

It is surely time, and long past time, for someone to speak up from outside the confines of Christianity: to voice Christian truths from a level, not of dogmatic faith, but of divine realization. Once again the fact needs to be emphasized: Jesus Christ's teachings embraced *the whole of cosmic reality*—far beyond even the discoveries of modern science. It is time for his words to be proclaimed in the fullness of their true meaning, which embraces all that modern science declares and much, much more besides. It is also very much time that someone of divine insight put a stop to the nonsense being spouted by so many modern scholars who are without superconscious insight, and by novelists and others who lack even respect, but treat religion and its followers as if they were fair game for any pot shot they may feel like taking. All these spiritual outsiders claim that they are offering new information on what *really* happened during and after Jesus Christ's life on earth.

It is time, in short, that serious religious errors, too long expounded by the ignorant, be shown up at last for what they really are: spiritually speaking, the babbling of mere "idiot savants"!

CHAPTER EIGHT

WHENCE THE CORRECTION?

I HAVE SAID REPEATEDLY THAT THE SAINTS EVERYWHERE are the true custodians of religion. What is to be done, however, when those saints are muzzled by their own church? when they are ostracized and excommunicated by it? when a vast number of Christians scoff at the very need to listen to them? In Christianity as it is officially practiced, sainthood is not, so to speak, "in the driver's seat." Its authority is reined in, obstructed, and, as frequently as not, denied by church authorities and, perhaps, by the majority of Christians also.

Great saints have indeed lived on earth, appearing in every country, in every age, and in every religion. There are such saints on earth, true spiritual masters, even in these materialistic times. But how much are they able to say when people turn away from them with comments like, "Your *opinions* seem sincere, but our experience of life is our own. Why should we listen to what you have to say?" People of true wisdom never try to *impose* their insights on others. As Jesus Christ counseled, **"Give not that which is holy unto dogs, neither cast ye your pearls before swine."** (Matt. 7:6)

(And Christian tradition, again, accords Jesus no sense of humor!)

What follows is the voice of common sense as well as of wisdom. The true author of the following commentaries, for whom I am (as I have already said) only a mouthpiece, was Paramhansa Yogananda. For nearly sixty years I have been his disciple. He showed himself to me convincingly as the greatest human being I had ever, or *have* ever met. Yogananda more than once told us who lived with him why he had been sent by his great spiritual teachers to the West.

"The first in my line of gurus," he told us, "Babaji, a great master in the Himalayas, recounted the following event to his chief disciple Lahiri Mahasaya [Yogananda's spiritual grandfather, so to speak]. Babaji stated that Jesus Christ had appeared to him and declared, 'What has happened to my religion? My followers are doing good works, but too many of them have forgotten the essence of my message of direct, inner communion with God. Let us together send again to the West the secrets for achieving that communion.' Babaji then told Lahiri Mahasaya, 'What Jesus meant was the technique of Kriya Yoga, which helps the sincere seeker to unite his soul with God.'"

Jesus Christ promised to send, through a disciple of Lahiri Mahasaya's, a yogi for special training. That disciple, Babaji said, would disseminate once again in the West the true message of Jesus Christ to the world.

Swami Sri Yukteswar, Yogananda's own guru, declared to him (as stated in *Autobiography of a Yogi*), "You, my son, are the one Jesus promised to send for training."

Yogananda's message, as he often told us, was to bring back "original Christianity." His further message was to make the public once more aware of "original Hindu yoga, as taught by Krishna." Babaji himself declared to Lahiri Mahasaya—as was conveyed to his disciples, and as Paramhansa Yogananda conveyed to us—that he himself was the reincarnation of Lord Krishna, the divine expounder of the Bhagavad Gita.

I was with Yogananda when he finished his commentaries on the Bhagavad Gita. He declared to me personally, "A new scripture has been born! Millions will find God through this work. Not just thousands: *millions*. I have seen it. I *know!*"

There has always been a subtle link between the *Sanaatan Dharma* in India and the line of great Judaic prophets of whom Jesus himself declared himself to be a representative.* I myself have

---

*"**Think not that I am come to destroy the law, or the prophets. I am not come to destroy, but to fulfill.**" (Matt. 5:17)

sometimes wondered—perhaps not altogether fancifully—whether an etymological connection may not be drawn between the Biblical name, Abraham, and the Hindu concept of Brahma.

Less than a month after I met Yogananda and was accepted by him as a disciple, he invited me to join him at his desert retreat at Twenty-Nine Palms, California. There, he dictated a few lessons for his yoga correspondence course. One evening, to my amazement, he included the following information: "The three wise men who came to honor the Christ Child after his birth were the line of gurus who later sent me to the West: Babaji, Lahiri Mahasaya, and Swami Sri Yukteswar."

Yogananda emphasized at the same time the basic oneness of all true religions. The fact that he placed particular emphasis on Hinduism and Christianity was not intended by him in any sense to imply exclusivity. I think he selected (or, rather, was commissioned to concentrate on) these two because there exists a subtle link especially between these religions. Hinduism and Christianity have remained the purest of the mighty streams of truth that God has sent to mankind.

Of the Semitic religions (Judaism, Christianity, and Islam), Christianity is the purest in the sense that its spiritual traditions still include the saints, and the saints—the truest representatives of Christian truth—have always emphasized the importance of direct, inner communion with God as the path to liberation in the Infinite.

Of the great Eastern religions (Hinduism and its several offshoots, which include Buddhism, Jainism, and Sikhism), the *Sanaatan Dharma* in Hinduism has been most emphatic regarding the need for inner, direct communion. Indeed—and most importantly—it alone of all religions has emphasized the highest possible attainment, the reality referred to almost always by Jesus Christ when he spoke of heaven and of the Kingdom of God: *Kaivalya Moksha*, complete soul-liberation and eternal union with God, the Infinite and Supreme Lord. Indeed, every true religion (one that is not merely man-made, in other words) leads to *Kaivalya Moksha*, though few Hindus, even, are aware that this final, absolute destiny awaits them at the end of their long journey through the numerous by-ways of ignorance.

That certain religions are not valid in the highest sense should go without saying, for human beings naturally try to figure out for themselves the meaning of life, death, and eternity. It seems eminently improbable, however, that God should have waited thousands of years—the length of time that civilizations, as is now believed, have been active on earth—before sending a true revelation. Indeed, any claim Christians advance as "proof" that what Jesus Christ brought was the one true *revelation*, whereas what all the great teachers of other religion taught before him was merely the fruit of deep philosophical thought, is undone by the fact that many of those teachers, and the religions they founded, meet every test one can apply to Jesus Christ.

Miracles? In the eighteenth century, a holy man in India, Sadhu Haridas, was rowing a boat on a lake. His passenger was a Christian missionary. The missionary wanted to convert him to the Christian religion. Haridas suddenly challenged him: "Is there any miracle your Jesus performed that others could not perform also?"

The fact that they were in a boat, surrounded by water, inspired the missionary to offer, as proof, the story of how Jesus walked on the water of the sea of Galilee.

"Is that all?" Sadhu Haridas retorted. He stepped out onto the water forthwith, and walked on it. Wherever he went (thus my Guru told me the story), the boat followed behind him.

Miracles are not in themselves any proof of saintliness, however. Certain yogis in the East have been known to possess amazing powers, yet have not been truly deep in a spiritual sense. Haridas himself later fell, my Guru told me—albeit temporarily only—from his spiritual attainments.

The true proofs of spirituality are ecstatic absorption in the Divine, and selfless, impersonal love. Such spirituality is evidenced outwardly, as I stated earlier, by complete non-attachment to all things worldly, by unselfish love for all, by unfailing kindness, calmness, and forgiveness, and by the outward manifestation of unshakable inner bliss.

Differences of national outlook must also be borne in mind. Indians, for example, are more contemplative by nature. Americans are more inventive and practical. Julius Caesar once, commenting on the different peoples of Europe, made a few fascinating observations: the Teutons (the Germans of those days) were, he said, highly capable and intelligent, and therefore rose rapidly to the top in comparison to other nations. They always failed in the end, however, because they became ensuingly proud of their accomplishments. Thus, they fell from those heights. Even today, after two thousand years, the same assessment might be made.

Of the Gauls (the modern-day French) Caesar said, "If five of them happen to be together, and four of them agree on some point, the fifth will disagree *on principle.*" Amusingly, that assessment seems rather true of the French even today.

Of the Romans, Caesar said, "They are fickle in their loyalties, and never cling long to anything or anyone." That, too, was a fair assessment which might be applied as well to Romans even today.

There is a story related of a group from different countries who were assigned the task of writing about the camel. The American flew straight to Cairo, stayed in an expensive hotel, and went out casually to observe a few camels in the streets. He also saw one camel striding along in the desert. Returning home, he wrote his paper based on that direct, but superficial, experience.

The Englishman, more careful with his money, visited the London zoo and there observed one or two camels. He based his paper on that slightly more careful observation.

The German went to the nearest library, studied whatever facts he could dig up about camels, then wrote a learned treatise, complete with footnotes, but without ever seeing an actual camel.

The Indian returned to his room, pulled down the blinds, sat in the lotus pose on the floor, and prayed that God would drop a well-composed paper on his lap.

This amusing story was told me, I should add, by a Hindu friend from Calcutta, India.

There is certainly some truth in the comments one hears about the differences in national characteristics. One should, indeed, be grateful that the differences exist. They lend a certain interesting variety—"spice," so to speak—to the panorama of life.

There is one such difference between the various nations that has been widely noted, and seems also to be generally true. The outlook of Western countries is basically more materialistic and outward, whereas, in the East and especially in India, it seems to be more mystical and spiritual, in an inward sense.

The Eastern view of religion—especially the Hindu—is also inclined to be more impersonal. This view somewhat affects people in their own lives as well. When affliction comes to people everywhere on earth, their tendency is to think, "Why *me*?" In the East, however, and especially (again) in India, this thought is followed more naturally by the thought, "Ah, well—light and darkness, pleasure and pain, joy and suffering: such contrasts are the very nature of reality."

In the West, the natural reaction, after the thought "Why *me*?" is to decide, "Something has to be done about it!" A Westerner may universalize his reaction also, as people do more typically in the East, but in his case his way of doing so may be to add (and by no means resignedly), "What can be done?"—or, better still, "What can *I myself* do to improve matters?"

The Western temperament is by nature executive and more inclined to assume responsibility; the Eastern is more naturally open and accommodating. These two attitudes should be balanced, ideally speaking, for balance is what leads to perfection.

It should be pointed out, however, that Jesus Christ was, essentially, an Easterner. His teachings contain definite undertones of what has been called "Eastern fatalism." Consider his counsel, for example:

"Therefore take no thought, saying, What shall we eat? or, What shall we drink? or, Wherewithal shall we be clothed?

"(For after all these things do the Gentiles seek:) for your heavenly Father knoweth that ye have need of all these things. . . .

"Take therefore no thought for the morrow, for the morrow shall take thought for the things of itself. Sufficient unto the day is the evil thereof." (Matt. 6:31,32,34)

(Incidentally, that last sentence is another example of his wry wit. One can see him expressing it with a slight smile.)

This counsel, be it noted, is very different from what one would expect from an American chief executive (in other words, a "Gentile"!).

Thus, I suggest again that a study of Eastern religions may provide even Christians with a new, and perhaps deeper insight into their own religion. The Eastern view—perhaps particularly that which is known as Hinduism—tends especially, because of its impersonality, to be particularly receptive to the discoveries of modern science. Indians have had no discernible difficulty with the discovery of the vastness of the universe; with the great spans of cosmic time; with the relative insignificance of our planet Earth; and with man's apparent unimportance in the great scheme of things. These relatively new scientific discoveries have not been the challenge to the Eastern—and perhaps especially, again, to the Hindu—perception of reality that they have been to the Christian churches.

The Hindu scriptures, particularly, have always described vast aeons of cosmic time. The statement by modern astronomers that the material universe is billions of years old was fully anticipated in

India, whose ancient seers held that a "Day of Brahma" (the time-span of one cosmic manifestation) lasts billions of years, and is followed by an equally long "Night of Brahma." According to those teachings, these cosmic "Days and Nights" have recurred in endless succession. If we compare that claim with the Biblical account of Creation, in which God created everything in six days (ending with a seventh day of "rest"), it soon becomes evident why Hindus may, with their view of reality, have found it easier than Christians to accept the actual age of the universe.

A corresponding belief in Hinduism, which many Christians have rejected, is the doctrine of reincarnation. Most Hindus take this doctrine for granted. It fits comfortably into their perception of vast periods of time. (Is it not perfectly possible, in that vast scheme of things, that the duration of our own existence is comparably vast?) Christian "authorities" formally insist that reincarnation is not a Christian teaching. We have already seen, however, that some of Christ's statements do suggest this doctrine.

One basic difference between the Western and the Eastern view of reality is the way each views cosmic creation. The executive side of human nature acts upon things from without. In this mode, human beings mold or sculpt a statue; they create a painting by placing lines and layers of color on a canvas; they make motors by molding pieces of metal, then screwing or welding them together.

Life, by contrast, always grows *outward from within*. The Eastern view is more naturally inclined to think of creation as a process of becoming.

Consider how a human being is formed: first, by the union of two cells, the sperm and the ovum, which then subdivide, ultimately to produce the body. Plants grow from little seeds. Life, in other words, manifests altogether differently from the objects man produces. As the American poet Joyce Kilmer wrote, "Only God can make a tree."

The Indian view of life accommodates itself more naturally to the concept that all things are formed from within, rather than imposed on Nature from without. Ancient wisdom claims that God *dreamed* the universe into existence. In other words, He *became* the universe—without ever changing, even slightly, His own aloof, ever-watchful nature.

Christians have imagined God producing the universe as if out of a hat, like a stage magician. Nowhere, to my knowledge, has the process of Creation been deeply pondered. "He just made it. What more do we need to know?" These words describe most people's way of explaining it all. The Hindu teachings, however, and (if you think about it) the New Testament also, give a virtually identical explanation for cosmic beginnings. The first verses of the Gospel of St. John describe God as *becoming* the universe:

"In the beginning was the Word, and the Word

was with God, and the Word was God.

"The same was in the beginning with God.

"All things were made by him; and without him was not any thing made that was made.

"In him was life; and the life was the light of men. . . . And the Word was made flesh, and dwelt among us." (John 1:1–4,14)

These verses contain much food for thought. Although St. John seems, at first glance (because of those words, ". . . and dwelt amongst us"), to be referring only to Jesus Christ, everything *was*, in fact, "made" that way: the vibration (word) of God's consciousness which manifested the universe *became* it. It didn't mold it: It may be said, indeed, to have *become* it.

I'll give Paramhansa Yogananda's explanation more fully in a later chapter. For now, let us contemplate an even more urgent question: What is God?

CHAPTER NINE

WHAT IS GOD?

MANY CHRISTIANS, IT IS SAID, VISUALIZE GOD AS the venerable old man Michelangelo depicted on the ceiling of the Sistine Chapel at the Vatican. That famous work shows the Lord manifesting Adam, the first man, by pointing a forefinger in his direction. (Of incidental interest is the shape of one of Adam's lower legs, the knee raised in an attitude of relaxation. Clearly suggested here is the body of a woman, Adam's wife, her breasts evident in two natural-seeming bulges on the knee; her body artfully suggested in the curve of his calf and shin bone.) Christians do commonly think of God, in fact, as their Heavenly Father, for so did Jesus Christ address Him.

On the other hand, because people simply cannot bridge the gap between what must obviously be the impersonal Creator of such a vast universe and an anthropomorphic (human-shaped) being, they come up with concepts that seem to be, according to their understanding, more logically satisfying. I mentioned one of these brave attempts earlier: "The Cosmic Ground of Being." People, in suggesting concepts like these, no doubt congratulate themselves on their philosophical nicety. They don't stop to consider that they've provided no clear image at all. If God is love—as everyone with direct experience describes Him—then such intellectual definitions deprive the Almighty of the only clarity we can have about Him.

God is no mere abstraction: no force, merely, like the wind, lightning, or even energy. What has one understood, after sticking such a label onto the Infinite as "The Cosmic Ground of Being"? A bottle of strawberry jam may have a label calling it that, but unless one knows what strawberries are and what jam is, the label won't have any meaning for him. Can anyone say what is meant by a "ground of being"? Does it help anyone to call it, moreover, cosmic?

All right then (one may ask), does the word "love" suggest a clearer meaning? Not unless we tie it down to something we have ourselves experienced. Otherwise, the objection of abstraction, here too, is valid. "Love" is nothing more than a word. To a Frenchman who knows no English, it is a sound without meaning. Were he, on the other hand, to speak of "*amour*," a Scotsman might think he was talking about a moor with gorse on it. I hope I don't sound too facetious. What I'm trying to say is that the only way to get some "handle of understanding" on *any* concept at all is to relate it to something we know already.

That is why even the description of God as Love needs to be tied down to something comprehensible in human terms. In Spanish the expression, "I love you," translates as *"Te quiero,"* which is to say, "I *want* you." In Italian the expression is, *"Ti voglio bene,"* which is to say, "I want the best for you." Both cases imply the concept of *desire.* Divine love, however, is beyond all desire. How can people even conceptualize divine love as it truly is?

In Sanskrit, there are several words for love, prominent among which are *kama* (desire), *bhakti* (devotion), and *prem* (cosmic, selfless love, which beholds all beings with kindest feeling as manifestations of the one Self). This last aspect of love is the most difficult of all to understand for ordinary human beings.

The answer, then, is simply to start with whatever understanding we have already. A "cosmic ground of being," as a concept, offers no ground to stand on at all!

Let us begin with that masculine pronoun: "He." If we identify it exclusively with a male being we overlook, or even reject, the equal reality of the feminine. If, on the other hand, we try to express ourselves too exactly by referring to God as "He/She," we may perhaps satisfy some personal desire to avoid bias in the matter, but we won't really clarify anything. God is both masculine and feminine, true, but God is also *neither* masculine *nor* feminine. As a great woman saint in India, Ananda Moyi Ma, said of that Infinite Consciousness: "It is and it isn't, and neither is it nor is it not." (Try to figure that one out!)

The commonly used masculine pronoun for God poses a problem only as long as one thinks of it as *exclusively* masculine. The word, "He," is also, at least in English, the impersonal pronoun. It spares one the redundancy of repeating "one" too often: "When one listens to music, he [not "one"; and not "he/she"] likes to enjoy it." "He" works better than "it" if one is trying to describe a conscious being, to whom we can relate also personally. I myself like to think of God as my Divine Mother. If I'm trying to communicate with others, however, I speak of God as "He"; in my mind that word embraces both the masculine and the feminine aspects, whereas "She" would stand out in my mind as sounding artificial.

We are all human, and must think and communicate in limited terms for the simple reason that our human understanding is, itself, limited. "Father" is not an absolute concept when referring to God. It shows shallowness even to try to be absolute. Far simpler is it—and, because it is comprehensible, far clearer also—simply to discard all attempts at intellectual preciseness and concentrate on concepts that uplift the heart's feelings in an undefined but clearly experienced, loving aspiration toward the changeless Bliss for which all of us, consciously or unconsciously, yearn.

The West has been conditioned to the Aristotelian method of reasoning, with its "either . . . or" alternatives. In India, a different—and perhaps also more "reasonable"—concept is in common use: "both . . . and." This attempt to combine seeming opposites, though it is sometimes scoffed at as "woolly-minded" in the West, offers a way out of the dilemma Christians face when they try to visualize a reality so vast and impersonal as to be, ultimately, incomprehensible.

All saints who have experienced God describe "Him" (or Her) as Love Itself. With alternatives that are mutually *inclusive*, instead of *exclusive*, there is a greater possibility of universality. My earnest plea to the reader is, Don't get caught up in the thought that you'll ever be able to define God perfectly; try to experience His presence in your heart. As that experience grows, it will gradually encompass more and more of the cosmic reality which God really is.

The divine consciousness is simply beyond conceptualization. Jesus Christ said, **"Even the very hairs of your head are all numbered."** (Luke 12:7) His words lead inescapably to the conclusion that the Divine Consciousness is *both* vastly infinite *and* minutely infinitesimal: aware equally of the largest galaxy and of the smallest electron. Indeed, since the concept of omniscience has never been theologically challenged, this concept demands that we think of God as *both* impersonal *and* personal.

God wants nothing from us. In that sense, then, He is completely impersonal. At the same time, however, He is very intimately personal where we ourselves are concerned, for He wants for each of us, His creatures, the perfection of absolute Bliss. *Sanaatan Dharma* (I prefer this ancient name for what is commonly referred to as Hinduism, which Christians falsely accuse of idolatry) offers a blend, one which, to reason itself, is perfectly acceptable, between God as both impersonal and personal.

God, as Krishna explains in the Bhagavad Gita, and as I said earlier, *dreamed* everything into existence. He couldn't *mold* anything, outwardly, for there was nothing "out there" to mold—nothing in all existence but His own consciousness. As trees grow from seeds, and as animals develop from the union of two cells, male and female, even so the Infinite Spirit brought everything into existence *from an infinity of individual centers*—dreaming outward, so to speak, from the center of each of them.

Artificial, man-made threads are solid all the way through. Nature-made threads have a hole passing through the center of them to allow the life force to pass through.

Thus, Divine Consciousness was described by my Guru as "center everywhere, circumference nowhere." This, surely, is what Jesus meant also when he said, **"Neither shall they say, Lo here! or, lo there! for, behold, the kingdom of God is within you."** (Luke 17:21)

Many teachings in the Bible are either allegorical or metaphorical. This statement by Jesus, however, is more *suggestive* than allegorical. "Within *what*?" one asks. Kingdoms cover large expanses of territory. What could Jesus have meant by this implication that God's vast kingdom lacks any outward dimension at all? One hears of someone making a confession by "baring his breast," but even heart surgery hasn't shown that any "kingdom" resides in there!

Let us begin with the most literal explanation: God, residing at the center of everything, dwells at the heart of every atom. He knows us human beings from the "inside out," and perceives the least flicker of our thoughts and feelings. In a true sense, indeed, He *is* those thoughts and feelings.

"Kingdom," then? What can he have meant by that word? Only this, surely: Time and space, in Divine Consciousness, are illusory. So also, indeed, is creation itself.

Until recent times, mankind had to be satisfied with believing that God simply *did* it all, somehow. His "magic" was quite beyond man's power of conceptualization. One might say that, in popular fancy, He produced the universe (as I suggested earlier) like a magician producing a rabbit out of a hat. Nowadays, however, with the expansion of man's knowledge to infinity, and with the subtle

insights science has given us into the inner workings of the atom, it is possible at last to ponder a
little realistically the "hows" of Creation.

Be warned, however: The explanation will take
you farther afield than you may expect!

Science, as I stated earlier, has discovered that
matter is composed of innumerable vibrations of
energy. Indeed, Yogananda said that vibrations of
energy are only a part of the picture. On a subtler
level, energy is projected by vibrations of ideas,
which in turn are projected by will, which is itself
a vibration of pure consciousness. The stillness of
the Supreme Spirit's awareness is set in motion
to produce cosmic ideation.

Thus did Paramhansa Yogananda explain the
whole of Creation. The Spirit—ever calm, ever motionless, Absolute Bliss—set in motion a portion
of its consciousness. Since movement itself is not
absolute, and always, in any direction, moreover,
implies its own opposite, Infinite Consciousness
had to manifest the principle of duality—*dwaita*,
in Sanskrit. Movement in any direction must be
compensated for by an equal and opposite movement. Thus, the tuning fork produces sound,
when its tines are struck, as they move in opposite directions from a state of rest in the middle.

More suggestive even than the tuning fork is the
image Paramhansa Yogananda often gave of an
ocean, with its waves ever rising and falling. No
rising wave, regardless of its height, can make the
slightest change in the overall ocean level, for

every upward movement is matched by a corresponding downward one. Every crest is matched by a trough.

The Eternal Spirit remains ever untouched and unaffected by cosmic creation. The word, "vibration," signifies opposite movements from a state of rest at the center. On this principle of vibration, called *dwaita* or duality, not only the material universe but all manifested existence was brought into being.

Here we find ourselves suddenly stumbling upon a deep scriptural truth. The Christian Trinity of God the Father, Son, and Holy Ghost (or Spirit) is, Yogananda stated, a fundamental and universal truth, stated symbolically. In the traditional human household, the father goes out from home to provide sustenance for the family. Though he comes back in the evenings, he is less directly involved with the family life than the mother. God the Father, similarly, remains aloof, in a sense, from His creation, though sustaining it. The mother symbolizes the Holy Ghost, or Holy Spirit, which manages and maintains the home. The Son is the outcome of the union of these two.

The Book of Genesis states:

"In the beginning God created the heaven and the earth.

"And the earth was without form, and void; and darkness was upon the face of the deep. And the Spirit of God moved upon the face of the waters." (Gen. 1:1,2)

Here we see the inspiration for Yogananda's image of the ocean. God "moving" upon the surface of the vast ocean of consciousness, like the wind passing over it and raising waves, affords a clear image of how the Supreme Spirit vibrated its consciousness to produce the "waves" of vibratory manifestation.

God, the Spirit, *is* those waves: He didn't produce them out of nothingness. The universe is a vibration of innumerable thoughts upon the surface of the infinite ocean of consciousness. That Holy Vibration constitutes, as I have indicated, what the Bible calls the "Holy Ghost," or "Holy Spirit." The word, *Ghost*, suggests an invisible, self-conscious reality. In essence, the Supreme Spirit is beyond movement and therefore beyond all duality. Movement is not a *created* reality. Rather, it is a *manifestation* of the Supreme Being, Existence Itself. Because creation depends on consciousness—indeed, *is* a manifestation of consciousness itself—that Supreme Spirit, untouched by all movement, is also present throughout creation. The cosmic Stillness is *reflected* in every atom.

The still, unmoving consciousness is not only aloof, but is also present in all things as a reflection, just as reflections of the sunlight appear in countless slivers of glass. That reflected presence is omnipresent in creation. This omnipresent reflection of the Supreme Spirit in all creation is a cosmic reality. It is the one and only true Christ, for which "the only begotten Son" is but a metaphor.

Jesus had attained that state. Therefore he was called the Christ. All souls who merge consciously into the Infinite attain that all-pervading state of consciousness.

I once asked my Guru, "To what state must one have attained to be called a master?" He replied, "One must have reached Christ consciousness."

The Christ has no form, for it is omnipresent. As the ocean is present in each of its drops, but no drop can be identified with the whole ocean, so the universal Spirit of Christ was manifested in Jesus, but could not be even remotely defined in terms of his human form. All souls who attain the state of oneness with the Christ consciousness lose, inwardly, their sense of fundamental individuality and become what are called masters. All of them are equals of Jesus Christ.

Does what I've written sound blasphemous? Please consider this important truth: Jesus was not born on earth to show people how great *he* was. *He came to show us how great is our own divine potential.*

When the Jews accused him of blasphemy for his statement, "I and my Father are one," he answered them, **"Is it not written in your law, I said, Ye are gods?**

"If he called them gods, unto whom the word of God came, and the scripture cannot be broken [gainsaid];

"Say ye of him, whom the Father hath sanctified, and sent into the world, Thou blasphemest; because I said, I am the Son of God?"
(John 10:34–36)

From what I have stated so far it should be obvious that countless layers of misconception need to be removed from popular understanding before these truths can be widely understood. Consider this point, however: How could God, the Infinite Spirit, have produced one unique human offspring, a tiny human being who lived a mere thirty-three years on this little mud ball, our Earth—a single, tiny being in the vast universe with its hundred billion galaxies. How could one such being be, in some unaccountable way, unique?

Imagine yourself living on a vast continent, educated into the universal realities that modern science has revealed, but knowing nothing of the teaching that Jesus Christ was the only son of the Almighty Spirit, Creator of the whole universe. Then imagine a missionary arriving on that continent from a little island in the Pacific and trying to persuade you that the founder of his religion taught that he alone was identical with God. What would you think? Wouldn't you say, "Your view is unbelievably insular"? And if he announced, further, that you could be saved only by accepting that one human being as the Son of God, wouldn't your first question be, "Saved from *what?*"

Imagine all this, I say, and then ask yourself,

Would that missionary succeed in his efforts to convert you? Surely not, if you were blessed with the slightest measure of common sense. To be converted *from* ignorance is desirable; to be converted *to* it seems, however, absurd. And how else could that missionary's efforts be described?

There is no reasonable justification for insisting that spiritual and scientific truths be kept in separate, airtight compartments. Yet that is what they simply must be if one persists, in the name of religious truth, in making claims that fly in the face of what everybody knows to be reality.

These apparent contradictions can be resolved, however. Paramhansa Yogananda was sent to America to explain to Christians the truth that unites science and religion. Indeed, what he taught soars high above the relatively pedestrian claims of material science, for he showed that life everywhere is divine. He showed, further, that the mission of mankind (and, eventually, of all creatures) is to transcend the cosmic illusion and rediscover one's own, eternal nature as ever-existent, ever-conscious, ever-new Bliss.

A certain amount of spadework may be necessary for the layers of misconception to be removed, but let us see whether I can explain these things more clearly, next.

Our question now must relate to who we, ourselves, really are.

CHAPTER TEN

WHO ARE WE?

"And one of the scribes came, and having heard them [Jesus Christ and the more-or-less atheistic Sadducees] reasoning together, and perceiving that he had answered them well, asked him, Which is the first commandment of all?

"And Jesus answered him, The first of all the commandments is Hear, O Israel; the Lord our God is one Lord: And thou shalt love the Lord thy God with all thy heart, and with all thy soul, and with all thy mind, and with all thy strength: this is the first commandment.

"And the second is like [unto it], namely this, Thou shalt love thy neighbor as thyself. There is none other commandment greater than these.

"And the scribe said unto him, Well, Master,

thou hast said the truth: for there is one God; and there is none other but he:

"And to love him with all the heart, and with all the understanding, and with all the soul, and with all the strength, and to love his neighbor as himself, is more than all whole burnt offerings and sacrifices.

"And when Jesus saw that he answered discreetly, he said unto him, Thou art not far from the kingdom of God." (Mark 12:28–34)

IN MY FIRST FULL-LENGTH BOOK (WHICH IS STILL, TO me, a major work of mine), *Out of the Labyrinth* (subtitled, "For those who want to believe, but can't"), I quoted two contrasting statements: the first, by the French nihilist Jean-Paul Sartre, and the second, from the sacred works of India: "Jean-Paul Sartre [I stated] said it for the lower elements in human evolution when he wrote, 'To be conscious of another means to be conscious of what one is not.' And the *Taittiriya Upanishad* of India said it for the highest with this ringing cry: 'The Spirit Who is here in a man, and the Spirit Who is there in the sun, it is one Spirit and there is no other!'"

Let us, from a point of view of simple reason, based on modern scientific knowledge, consider the question, "Who are we?" I say "based on," because science of course, being fundamentally materialistic, thinks of consciousness itself as a mere product of brain activity. Still, science has discovered that matter is only a vibration of energy.

Several scientists have come, individually, to *suspect* that energy is only a vibration of thought. And from there it requires no great mental leap to see that thought can only be a vibration of consciousness. The French philosopher René Descartes was mistaken with his famous declaration, "I think; therefore I am." His mistake lay in the fact that consciousness cannot but precede thinking; it cannot, therefore, be a *product* of anything. Deep awareness actually demands a suspension of mentation. It would be truer to restate Descartes in these words: "I am aware that I exist: therefore, I am able to think."

St. Teresa of Avila described the fourth stage of prayer as coming when the one who prays, while intensely aware, is yet *incapable* of thinking at all. Thought, to repeat, is a lower level of conscious activity, and belongs only to the conscious mind, not to the Superconscious.

Let us, then, address again a subject we touched on more lightly earlier. Of present concern are two essential questions: first, How did God create the universe? and second, How did He create us human beings? Nothing existed, in the beginning, except His consciousness. It was only out of that consciousness that he could create anything at all. Consciousness itself is the fundamental reality of all creation. Whence, then, our own, human awareness? It could only be a manifestation of God's Infinite Consciousness. (As that scribe we quoted said, "There is none other but he.") And whence, finally, comes our *self*-awareness? This, too, had to manifest itself out of God's consciousness. God alone is—and indeed, has to be—our Infinite Self.

Consciousness that is completely lacking in Self-awareness is possible only, if at all, at very dim levels of awareness; the lack is impossible at higher levels in more evolved creatures, what to speak of in Absolute Superconsciousness? For even though the sense of separate individuality must, at that highest level, be transcended in absolute oneness, there can only be, in that state, the consciousness that one is still aware!

Material scientists are shallow in believing that consciousness is a product of brain activity. They even postulate the possibility that computers will someday become sophisticated enough to be conscious. Literary fiction in the early twentieth century was fairly littered with science fiction accounts of man-made machines that rose up in revolt against their human creators. The earthworm, however, which displays a minimum of physical complexity, is sufficiently aware, even so, to squirm away from a threat if it perceives one. Earthworms have even been successfully trained to select one channel through which to move in preference to another, when a tempting reward was placed at the end of one channel, and an electric shock awaited them at the end of the other.

Self-evidently, consciousness *precedes* brain activity. It is, indeed, present in everything. It is the "bedrock reality" even of granite. All things are, in the last analysis, emanations of Infinite Consciousness.

Orthodox science tells us (strange, that we should be speaking already of scientific orthodoxy!) that matter is composed only of vibrations of energy. Why, then, do rocks seem so hard and solid? Why do our bodies seem so substantial? And why is it that the air itself, though seemingly insubstantial, shows an awesome power to destroy during a hurricane?

Consider once again the tines of a tuning fork. As they vibrate, they create the illusion that a certain mass exists between the outer limits of their movement. An airplane propeller in rapid rotation appears as a solid disk. An infinite number of vibrations can be understood, similarly, as producing the vast array of appearances in the world around us. All things are simply manifestations of energy at different rates of vibration.

Energy, again, is only a product of the vibration of will, projected out of an infinity of formative ideas. The inner flow also of energy to the body depends, Yogananda said, on the strength of the will.

All, then, is consciousness. All is God. There is no other reality possible in the entire universe.

You and I may seem very different from each other, separated as we are by our bodies as well as by our personalities. But what if we hadn't bodies and personalities at all to define us? We should still be self-aware, if consciousness is the cause of our bodies, brains, and personalities. We'd have to be aware of having some individuality as long as there remained even the slightest degree of self-limiting definition: the thought, for instance, "I am happy," or, "I am sad," or indeed any other self-defining concept that we've added to our accumulating burden of outward, human existence.

What, then, if even the most nebulous self-definition were to disappear? What would remain? What if there were nothing left but consciousness itself?

This had to be the dilemma people faced who came after the Buddha and who never fully understood him. Once all human qualities have disappeared in the final extinction of karma and, with that, of all individuality, which is the meaning of *nirvana*, what can possibly remain? Well, for one thing, what remains is consciousness itself.

The ocean still exists, even when all of its waves subside. Consciousness is not a product of anything: It is self-existent. Consciousness is the One Reality out of which everything manifests.

Many people ask the question, Who made God? The answer is quite simple: No one! No one possibly could have. Causation is possible only in this realm of relativity. God, the Supreme Cause, is beyond relativity itself. He is absolute because nothing really exists but God; nothing, therefore, can be in any relation to Him.

One may ask, then, Is it possible to define consciousness beyond merely stating that it exists?

Do you see where I'm heading? My problem is how
to explain myself logically. Every human state of
consciousness identifies itself with some outward
appearance—with something we identify with this
realm of relativity. Peace suggests something to
which it can be contrasted: conflict, or turmoil, or
the simple absence of peace. Light suggests its opposite: darkness. A sense of power suggests the
existence of something over which power can be
exerted. The concept of energy suggests some
kind of kinetic activity. Even potential energy suggests the possibility of eventual kinesis. Happiness, too, suggests contrast with its opposite: unhappiness. Even love suggests an object of some
kind. Bliss, indeed, may be defined as the fulfillment of love, but in itself Bliss alone is absolute,
implying as it does the perfection of calm joy. Otherwise, joy too is an emotion, and may be compared to a rising wave. Just as every rising wave
sinks in time to become a contrasting trough, so
every emotion alternates, wavelike, between itself
and its opposite. Joy, too, sinks in time, to become
its opposite, sorrow.

At this point, logic itself becomes so finely drawn
that one would need to view it with suspicion until
one had actual supporting evidence. For logic, too,
must be based on something substantial. Of feeling one can say that it, too, must arise from *something*: It cannot manifest itself from nothing. As
consciousness cannot arise out of unconsciousness, and as *something* cannot manifest itself out

of *nothing*, so feeling, too, must be included in this syllogism. The fact that feelings exist means they must arise out of some actual "reservoir" of feeling, and not out of a total absence of any feeling at all! If absolute consciousness exists, then feeling too must be an aspect of that consciousness.

When the waves of feeling—which man experiences as ego-motivated emotion—become completely stilled, they cannot but sink into a calm "reservoir" of *feeling*. They cannot be a product of unfeeling awareness.

One question remains: What must be the nature of this vast feeling? Could it, even possibly, be misery? Absurd! Misery springs from an awareness of lack, and simply could not exist were there no such awareness. Only absolute fulfillment could provide the sense of completeness that is absolutely satisfying. The simple fact that consciousness itself has to be self-existent and complete in itself can only mean that conscious feeling, too, is absolute, self-existent, and complete in itself. Emotional joy, on the other hand, is not absolute, for it is inevitably accompanied by its opposite, sorrow. Bliss is what *remains* after every qualification of emotional ups and downs has been removed.

So far logic can take us, and point the way ineluctably to our conclusion. Logic alone, however, cannot ever satisfy completely, for at best it can only point to the doorway, beyond which lies Bliss. Bliss, then, must ever remain the one sublime truth which can never be proved, but can only be experienced. It can be inferred by the process of logic, but that is all logic can accomplish. Therefore the *Shankhya* philosophy states, *"Ishwar ashidha"*—"God is not proved [or provable]."

Here again, therefore, we find ourselves thrust back upon the need for *superconscious experience.* The universal *experience* of all Self-realized saints is the same: God, yes, but *God as Bliss!*

What of *self*-awareness? As human beings we are accustomed to thinking of "self" in terms of our bodies, personalities, and our "little bundles of self-definitions"—terms which admit the existence of selfhood also, but separately, in others. Our underlying consciousness, too, is of an inner center in ourselves, separate from other people's centers. Where there is separateness of any kind, there has to be a self-isolating circumference. In our case, that circumference consists of our self-definitions.

What, now, if that circumference were completely removed?

Paramhansa Yogananda described divine vision as "center everywhere, circumference nowhere." If our delusive circumference of self-definitions were wholly removed, then either what remained, Conscious Bliss, would be aware of itself or it would be aware of nothing at all.

The term, Self-realization, means the discovery that we are, in our deepest reality, that eternal, absolute, infinite, ever-blissful Self.

Swami Shankara, many centuries ago in India,

confronted the Buddhist dogma of atheism with the realization—common to every enlightened master, including Buddha himself—of the supreme truth: God is *Satchidananda*—Ever-existing, Ever-conscious, Ever-new Bliss.

All of us are individual *reflections* of Absolute Bliss. Therefore we all seek to avoid (or to escape) pain, and to find happiness. We are circumscribed by our self-definitions, as I've said, but there must be something within us that does the defining. Those self-definitions comprise our "circumference." And when all self-definitions are removed, the circumference itself disappears.

Think of an onion. When it is peeled, nothing is left; the onion consists of its peels. With us, however, there *is* something left, something real. That "real something" is conscious bliss. Everyone who has gone this route has discovered *from experience* that this is, eternally, what remains: Bliss. Cosmic Bliss is also, of course, *self*-aware.

Your ego and mine, stripped to their essence, have no individuality. We are manifestations, both of us, of the Eternal Self: the Supreme Spirit. That is why the goal of all spiritual endeavor is well described by that combined word: Self-realization.

Everything in existence—including, as a logical necessity, every creature and every ego-motivated human being—has its reality only as a manifestation of Blissful Self-Awareness. The goal of all striving *cannot* be anything but reabsorption into that Infinite Self.

Yogananda used the illustration of the flames on a gas burner. Every flame appears to be individual, but we know that it is a manifestation of the one reservoir of gas underneath. We can even imagine each flame as different *in appearance*—if, for example, a different chemical powder is sprinkled onto each of them. All of them, nevertheless, manifest the same *underlying* gas.

Each of us, similarly, is unique. "Every atom," as Yogananda put it in *Autobiography of a Yogi,* "is dowered with individuality." The Supreme Spirit is the true Self of everything and everyone in existence. Being "center everywhere," moreover, the Eternal Reality exists *individually*, at the center of each appearance.

What this deep truth signifies is that you, I, all beings, and everything in the universe are expressions of that one Reality. All of us, tiny bundles of self-definition, must gradually strip away our separate identity and realize ourselves as the infinite, eternally blissful Self.

To know everything about even one atom would be to know the secret of existence itself. We can never know anything, however, outside ourselves—except as an extension of our own understanding. A turtle cannot appreciate the beauty of a great painting. A sex addict cannot appreciate the inner freedom that comes from living a pure life. The only point in creation that can ever be probed to its ultimate reality is one's own self, one's ego.

To understand all that there is to know about a single drop of ocean water is, in a sense, to understand the whole ocean. Granted, one might not, with this knowledge, know anything about the ocean's vastness, or about the awesome power of ocean water during a typhoon. Still, vastness and power exist only in the realm of relativity, and have no separate reality of their own. Where perfect understanding concerns consciousness, to be one with the ocean means to achieve Absolute Consciousness.

The apotheosis of all seeking can be achieved only by offering our little self up to God in deep, prolonged meditation. When the soul succeeds at last, by deep spiritual effort, in merging into God, it becomes omniscient.

There remains one further, important truth: In omniscience, one never forgets that he also manifested for a time as a particular, egoic reality. Thus we see resolved the dilemma of how the deepest instinct in all life, self-preservation, can achieve that goal permanently by losing itself, and as it were "dissolving" itself, in God.

Therefore did Jesus Christ say, **"He that findeth his life shall lose it: and he that loseth his life for my sake shall find it."** (Matt. 10:39) His reference in the verse just prior to this one, to "taking up one's cross," must be understood in the deepest sense of offering up more than physical life—which seldom brings more than temporary, and never completely satisfying, relief. It means, rather, offering up to God one's limited self-awareness itself.

In God, nothing is lost. God is our deepest reality—"Nearest of the near," Paramhansa Yogananda used to call Him; "Dearest of the dear." In the attainment of divine omniscience, the soul never loses the memory of having once lived as a separate, individual identity.

Thus, when Jesus Christ was born it was he himself who came: not an abstract manifestation of Infinite God, but a fully self-aware, individual expression of God's Infinite Consciousness. Jesus could rightly say (as he is quoted as saying in the Book of Revelation) **"even as I overcame."** He was, as I've said, a living expression of that never-lost individuality, and was by no means a mere manifestation of the Abstract Absolute. Even though he had, in the deepest sense, transcended that individuality, he was that same being, returned to earth for the salvation of mankind, who had lived on earth before. If he didn't, in fact, come "for the salvation of all mankind," he came at least for the salvation of **"as many as received him."** (John 1:12)

CHAPTER ELEVEN

SALVATION FROM WHAT?

WHAT DOES IT MEAN, TO "BE SAVED"? SOMEONE once demanded of me, "Do you believe Christ died for your sins?"

"How could God die?" was my reply.

Of course, we all know what that man meant, and we all know what others mean when they ask, "Are you saved?" Their meaning is, "Do you accept Jesus Christ?" and, "Do you believe he died on the cross to atone for your sins?"

The alternative to "being saved" is to be damned eternally in hell. Implied in that damnation, moreover, is the concept that, without the Crucifixion, our "natural gravity," owing to the weight of our sins, is so great that it can only sink us down, down, ever farther down among the damned.

What, then, if we haven't really been all that bad? What, in fact, if someone dies while he is still a baby, and hasn't had time, therefore, to sin at all: what then? Or what if, as Yogananda put it, our good and bad deeds are so evenly balanced when we die that we can neither rise nor fall: What then? The whole thing seems like a puzzle wrapped in an enigma. How can intelligent people believe something so barbarous as the tenet that a loving God would damn *anyone* to eternity in hell, even the greatest of sinners? But then, intelligent people used to believe that a round Earth would mean that if anyone were to try to go to the other side he would fall off into space. Intelligent people do sometimes succeed in having many untenable beliefs!

Paramhansa Yogananda once attended a revivalist meeting led by the famous evangelist, Amie Semple Macpherson. Thousands were present. At one point in her harangue she shouted, "You are all sinners! Get down on your knees."

Yogananda later commented, "I was the only one who remained standing, because I wouldn't accept that I am a sinner!"

He was always fair, however; he saw things all-sidedly. When that same evangelist became a focus of scandal, years later, he wrote an article urging people to remember all the good she had done.

He used to say to us, "The worst sin is to call yourself a sinner! Why identify yourself with your mistakes? Say, rather, 'Naughty or good, I am a child of God.'" He also said, "A saint is a sinner who never gave up!" By emphasizing our sinfulness we only give ourselves all the excuse our egos want to go right on sinning! By emphasizing our potential for perfection, however, as Jesus did, we stiffen our spines to go on bravely until we reach perfection.

To accept one's sinfulness is to *affirm* it. True, many do so from a wish to show humility. Humility, however, is not self-abasement. If one bows continually to the ground, casting dust onto his own head, his mind is focused on the ground, on dust, and on his head. If, on the other hand, a person stands under the heavens at night, gazes up at the stars, and sees in them a reminder of his own littleness, particularly if then he thinks of the stars and not of his own lack of significance, he does well, for he passes beyond the thought of his insignificance to the thought of infinity. The secret of humility is *self-forgetfulness*. People who make a big issue of their humility make themselves the big issue!

I remember when I was new as a disciple, and was working hard to overcome a tendency toward intellectual pride. I awoke one morning to the dismaying awareness that I was becoming proud of my humility!

"Humility," Yogananda used to say, "is not a put-up job!" It comes with simply not thinking about one's self. It isn't what you *say* that matters. When great saints like Francis of Assisi have referred to themselves—as they have sometimes done—as sinners, they've done so to deflect praise from themselves. In that spirit Yogananda, too, never hesitated to refer to himself self-deprecatingly. In fact, however, his humility meant that his attention was always directed *away from* himself, as a human being. As I mentioned earlier, I heard him say one time, of himself, "How can there be humility, when there is no consciousness of ego?"

Surely it is clear from everything I've written so far that salvation means to be saved from the delusion of being a little, ego-centered dot in the universe, a human being separate from God for long aeons and condemned to live (for how much longer?) in a succession of little bodies. Christians imagine that salvation means living in heaven in a body for eternity. If that definition of salvation, however, means that we remain trapped through eternity in these little bodies and personalities, one wonders: Can hell itself be much worse?

In truth, what it means to be saved is to be freed from ego-consciousness, in the realization that God is the one, only, and eternal Truth: the sole reality behind every deed, every thought, every feeling of every being, and of every inanimate-seeming object in the universe. Our little, egoic selves will be with us until at last we break out of our enclosing walls of limited self-definition, and expand our consciousness to become one with the eternal, true Source of all being which is God, the Supreme Spirit: Ever-existing, Ever-conscious, Ever-new Bliss.

In eternal freedom, our self-awareness, as I have said, is never lost: It is only expanded to infinity, to oneness with the Cosmic Spirit. In God, nothing is lost. For although the ego is dissolved in Infinity, yet there remains always, in omniscience, the memory of that one, unique individual who lived for many lifetimes as your own, or as someone else's, limited ego. When an enlightened soul comes back to earth, as Jesus did, with the pure purpose of uplifting others spiritually, it is indeed that person, *himself*, who comes back, and not some cosmic abstraction.

Yogananda put it this way: God would never send to earth for man's upliftment a special, eternally perfect manifestation of Himself, labeled God. What message of hope, indeed, would that give us? It would be tantamount to saying, "I want you all to try, but it will of course be eternally impossible for you ever to be really perfect like Me." Doesn't it make supreme sense that He would descend through souls who are already eternally enlightened, who have themselves labored and achieved salvation in the past, and have *attained* perfection?

This is what Jesus meant by the commandment, **"Be ye therefore perfect, even as your Father which is in heaven is perfect."** (Matt. 5:48)

Salvation, then, does not mean salvation from that otherwise certain fate: eternal damnation in hell. Our true "fate" ought, rather, to be called our divine destiny. All of us must eventually be saved. How long it takes to reach perfection depends entirely on us. Saved we must be, in the end. The divinity inherent within each one of us will not leave us tranquil until we accept true freedom at last, and surrender to it our very egos.

Think of the commonly accepted alternative destiny: hell. Then imagine a boy born and raised in a city slum, exposed to nothing better, and knowing no other way of living. For him, life itself is a city jungle, a struggle to take advantage or be taken advantage of: to down others or be downed by them, to kill or be killed. To him, it must seem perfectly natural to join a gang, if only for his personal protection and security.

Then let us say that at the age of eighteen he becomes involved in a gang war, shoots someone to death, and then is himself killed.

Now, imagine the fate, according to orthodox Christian dogma, awaiting him. He is condemned to hell for all eternity. That is a *long* time! Christian tradition speaks glowingly of "the millennium" as if that meant something. A millennium is a mere thousand years! In eternity, a billion years pass in the blinking of an eye.

Now, then: Supposing, after a couple of billion years or so, someone says to this ex gang member, "What are you down here for?" How would he respond?

"Why," one imagines him saying, "now that you mention it, I don't really remember! I just figure it

must be what happens to everyone. In fact, by
now I've grown kinda used to it."

A finite cause cannot have an infinite effect.

One day Paramhansa Yogananda, dressed in
the orange robe of a swami, was traveling by train
in America. A fundamentalist Christian preacher,
traveling in the same carriage, saw this "heathen"
as he considered him, strode up to him, and demanded loudly, "Do you believe in Jesus Christ?"

"Yes, of course," Yogananda replied.

Well, this wasn't what the preacher had hoped
to hear.

"Do you accept Jesus Christ," he persisted, "as
your only savior?"

"I accept God as my Savior," calmly replied the
swami, "and I believe He has effected His salvation through many of His awakened sons, not only
through Jesus Christ."

This was more like it! "Unless you accept Jesus
Christ as your only savior," the preacher thun-
dered angrily, "you will go to *hell!*" (Everyone in
the railroad car was, by this time, listening in-
tently.)

"I may get there by and by," the Christian missionary to a Christian country replied, "but my
friend, you are there *already!*" From the wrath
that contorted the man's face it was evident that
he was indeed far, at that moment, from "the
peace of God, which passeth all understanding."
Everyone in that car burst into laughter.

As long as we live in ego-consciousness, and

therefore define ourselves by our likes and dis-
likes, attractions and aversions, fulfillments and
disappointments, we cannot but live in a hell we
ourselves have created. Ego-centeredness extends
an open invitation to an endless succession of disappointments, heart-breaks, losses, and failures.

Yogananda used often (quoting Krishna) to cry
out to his audiences, "Get away from My ocean of
suffering and misery!"

Jesus lamented, **"O Jerusalem, Jerusalem,
thou that killest the prophets, and stonest
them which are sent unto thee, how often
would I have gathered thy children together,
even as a hen gathereth her chickens under
her wings, and ye would not!"** (Matt. 23:37)

Those who think themselves wise or knowledge-
able, but who know nothing of their own spiritual
nature, are condemned to an existence of repeated suffering until they learn their divine lesson at last: The ego is only a mask for the eternal,
indwelling Self.

It is foolish to insist that the whole of truth be
contained in only one scripture. A Moslem caliph
in the nineteenth century, firmly convinced that
all truth lies in the Koran, attempted to demolish
the great pyramid at Giza, Egypt, with canon fire.
That ancient monument was an offense, in his
eyes, against the supposedly "complete revelation"
of Mohammed. The great pyramid is, however, so
massive that the caliph's attempt to destroy it had
to be abandoned at last. The disfigurements

wrought by his canons were so slight as to be almost unnoticeable.

The purpose of religion is to bring people closer to God. If any revered ancient text offers a new slant on teachings that are familiar to us in another context, then, instead of denouncing it, why not simply accept what it teaches with gratitude? Why denounce it? No civilization could, by any remotely possible contingency, be ever in a position to claim a monopoly on Truth itself! The important thing is that Truth always be supportive of differently worded statements of the same truth.

Again, if we accept that India's scriptures, written (as is claimed in Indian tradition) in a higher age than our own, may have announced facts relating to the universe that have only recently been corroborated by science, why not respond, simply, "We're happy to learn the truth *wherever* it exists, and by *whomsoever* it is stated!"

The geologist J.H.F. Umbgrove, in his learned treatise, *Symphony of the Earth*, wrote, "Nobody can foresee whether these modern speculations (on the problems of life and matter) will ever be susceptible to condensation into a social or religious system. Remarkably enough, however, they remind one of certain aspects of the Brahmanese Upanishads."*

*Quoted in my book, *Out of the Labyrinth*, p. 221, Crystal Clarity Publishers.

The purpose of the present book is to introduce
a new slant on the teachings of Jesus Christ, a
slant based on divine realization and not on
dogma, nor on any new, scholarly "revelation."
God does intervene, sometimes, in human history.
He did so with the descent of Jesus Christ, whose
teachings were founded on the highest revelation
of truth. For Jesus Christ was a great master,
worthy of the deepest reverence from all sincere
seekers of Truth. It has been the tragedy of Christian history, however—one that, if not a part of
God's plan, must certainly have been foreseen by
Him—that his teachings have become distorted by
human ignorance.

Christianity was introduced into the world in an
age when mankind was passing through a period
of relative mental, material, and spiritual darkness: a materialistic age which lasted for centuries, and brought with it the conviction that
matter itself is the only reality.

Christians too, in consequence, have identified
their religion with a strictly materialistic world
view. When an increase in human knowledge
began to reveal once more how vast and how very
subtle the universe really is, people were shaken,
in their religious beliefs, to discover how far from
reality their understanding of it had been. Even
at that, however, human ingenuity managed to
cope with the challenge. Truth, many Christians
decided, is of two types: the spiritual, and the
scientific.

In recent times, however, as declarations by scholars, novelists, and others have undermined people's belief even in the divinity of Jesus Christ, more and more people have been asking, "How valid is this, our Christian faith?" Sincere Christians naturally *want* to believe, and cling to their belief, even without reason, out of love for God and Jesus Christ. There has entered into that belief, however, with a certain quiet desperation the thought: What, exactly, shall we believe? In their hearts they *know* that God, the Bible, and the life and teachings of Jesus Christ are true. What their hearts know determines the core of their religious faith. Yet they've been shaken in their intellects by the double onslaught from science and the so-called "new revelations" regarding Christian history that are being proposed by an increasing number of people. What really *are* the facts? What *is* the truth?

God has intervened many times in human history. If ever there was a time when His intervention was needed, that time is now. My purpose in writing this book is, therefore, to offer Christians spiritual support based on revelation. It is badly needed.

CHAPTER TWELVE

STILL, WASN'T JESUS ALSO UNIQUE?

A FASCINATING ASPECT OF TRUTH IS THAT IT IS, LIKE Paramhansa Yogananda's improvement on Shankara's definition of bliss, *ever new*. The message of Jesus Christ was, therefore, not only *Sanaatan Dharma* as it has been taught elsewhere in the world, but a restatement of *Sanaatan Dharma*, and was therefore also *new*: both fresh and refreshing, both timely and timeless, and, though different in some ways, in complete agreement (as it would have had to be) with timeless Truth itself.

I once asked my Guru, "Is the teaching you've brought a new religion?"

"It is a new *expression*." His answer held a careful correction.

Much that Jesus Christ brought was new also— though at the same time wholly compatible with the eternal truth taught by great masters through the ages. God's truth can never become stale: it is ever fresh, ever thrilling, and ever both thrillingly fresh and freshly thrilling, ceaselessly rich with inspiration.

Thus it must be added that, although much of what Jesus taught was contained in the ancient tradition—and he himself referred back constantly to that tradition in Judaism—much even of the teaching he brought was arrayed in new clothing. He offered ancient but ever-new truths as, indeed, they must often be taught: from a new angle.

One reason for the special new aspects of his mission, and also of the character he displayed, was that Jesus, unlike the ancient *rishis* in India (many of whom saw it as their duty simply to perpetuate their lofty tradition), had also to create and establish a new tradition: not one in any way different from *Sanaatan Dharma*, but at the same time a particular expression that took into consideration the specific needs of the people of his country—a message, moreover, which they'd be capable of accepting.

There is a further, and forever fascinating, aspect of Spirit's ever-newness. It is that when the seeker achieves Self-realization and has dissolved his ego in the Infinite, he doesn't leave behind him his particular (and, as people like to think them, unique) qualities as a human being. Quite the opposite, he *discovers* at last the actual, eternal uniqueness of his own soul expression of God!

It is said that no two snowflakes are exactly alike. God is not only centered in every atom, which thereby (in Yogananda's statement) is "dowered with individuality": He has also his own special (in a way of speaking) melody to sing through each individual. No spiritual master ever expresses the Divine in quite the same way as any other. All of them do, of course, express the essential characteristics of divine perfection—divine love, for example, always universally and impersonally. At the same time, however, the particular way every enlightened master expresses the divine qualities is unique.

Does this mean that all saints and masters agree with one another on every issue? Not at all! They cannot but agree on the deeper issues, which relate to *Sanaatan Dharma* itself, but I myself have noted human differences both of personality and of opinion. I remember one saint, whose nature was withdrawn to the point of being almost taciturn, who disparaged another saint's tendency to laugh a lot. My own Guru was once speaking of land as the best investment, when Rajarsi Janakananda (his chief disciple, "Saint Lynn" as the Guru had previously called him) frankly, though without emphasis, disagreed.

Ordinary human beings, on the other hand, being spiritually unawakened and completely centered in their egos, borrow from others almost all their values, opinions, personality traits, mannerisms, and reactions. (I've often thought of a man coming out of a theater after seeing a cowboy movie, walking with a slightly rolling gait as though having just alighted from his horse!)

A child brought up in a completely different culture from that of his parents will reflect the values of his new environment, not those of his own flesh and blood. Heredity does play a role too, of course, in people's outlook on the world, in their behavior, and in their personalities. So also—even more so of course—do their karmic tendencies (*samskaras*), which they've brought over from past lives. Still, much of people's nature is influenced also by their present surroundings and by the prevailing attitudes there.

Shakespeare's plays portrayed the general understanding of his times. He fairly consistently described children of aristocratic parents, therefore, who, although perhaps raised in peasant homes, nevertheless showed innate nobility. There is indeed some truth to this concept—and also to its opposite: that children of peasants who are raised in noble homes may well retain certain peasant-like characteristics. A child of aristocrats raised among louts will probably acquire also some of their loutish characteristics, unless his own nature, brought over from the past, is exceptionally refined. A "fishwife" by nature will behave like a fishwife, or at least will tend to be shrewish, even if she is raised in a palace. It is common enough, moreover, to see very ordinary human beings born and raised to positions higher than their innate qualities merited.

I remember seeing once, outside the Howrah railway station in West Bengal, India, a group of beggars standing together. They had their hands outheld, and were pleading for alms. Among them stood a young girl with her hand held out also, who was obviously inwardly remote from the rest, as if thinking, "What am I doing *here*? This isn't where I belong!" She looked like a queen who had found herself, owing perhaps to selfishness in her personal karma, thrust into that low station in life.

In America one sometimes hears the expression, "I gotta be *ME!*" Who is this "me" that people feel they "gotta" be? It is nothing but a bundle of self-definitions, often selected from similar "bundles" which other people have themselves lumped together! Would the fiercely independent type of "far-West cowboy" be just the same fellow if he'd been raised in a marble palace? It is more likely that he'd display in new ways the arrogance and the affirmation of independence he'd developed already in the past.

One can be determinedly cheerful. (I'm reminded here of a cartoon I saw years ago of a man in hell, pushing what might be called an eternal wheelbarrow, but whistling cheerfully. A devil standing nearby turns to another one with the lament, "He just isn't getting the idea!")

Or, if one prefers, one can also be determinedly

angry, or sad. Here I'm reminded of a story about a man who ordered a meal in a restaurant. He was outraged, upon tasting it, at the way it had been prepared. "I know the owner. I know many important people in this town: the mayor, the council members. And yet you dare to present me with this slop!"

The chef, anxious for approval, prepared a new meal especially for this customer. It was served obsequiously. The man, still disgruntled, merely glanced at it, then shouted angrily, "Take it away! I'd rather be mad!"

One can be happy, or one can be dour. No one, however, manifests his actual, God-given nature until he has rid himself of those ego-limitations, which he has developed by constantly revising his self-definitions, until he learns to allow the Divine Light to shine through him clearly. Otherwise, every human being is like a cloudy pane in a stained glass window, through which the sunlight shines only dimly. The pane must be cleansed before it will permit clear passage to the light shining upon it. Only then, in the case of human beings, will the light of God's consciousness shine through us clearly and beautifully.

The saints may be said to be the only human beings on earth who are entirely themselves. Otherwise, the common expression, "I'm only human," deserves to be answered with a rebuttal: "No, you are not yet human, for you have yet to realize, to the fullest degree, your own human potential."

Therefore did a great woman saint, Lala Yogish-
wari, centuries ago in Kashmir refuse to wear any
clothing. When the scandalized residents in her
village demanded, "Why don't you wear at least
something?" she replied, "Why should I? I don't
see any men around!" To her rather drastic view,
no one deserved to be considered a man so long as
he was still living in delusion. One day, it is said,
another saint (a man) came to see her. Hastily,
then, she donned some apparel in preparation for
his visit.

Have the saints personalities? Of course. They'd
have to have them, to function as human beings.
My Guru once said to a small group of us, "When
I incarnate again and see the personality I'm going
to have to assume, it feels a little uncomfortable—
like a heavy overcoat on a hot day. Once I actually
have it, however, I get used to it."

The difference between a saint's personality and
the personalities of unenlightened people is that a
saint is not motivated by any consciousness of
ego. When people are told they must learn to offer
up their egos to God, they find it difficult to understand how to do it. It isn't, however, that in ego-
free action there is no sense of acting at all.
Rather, the ego-liberated saint enjoys the stream
of divinity he feels flowing through him. He merely
"pushes action along" with egoic will as its driv-
ing force. He sets action into motion, but sees the
entire flow as coming *through* him, rather than
being impeded by the usual egoic sense of impor-

tance, responsibility, and "doership." The saint may be described—in our analogy of the stained glass window—as allowing his own color to shine, like a finally cleansed pane in that window, and no longer obstructing the flow with impurities of ego-identity.

Many years ago I did office work in my bedroom. Above my desk was a large window through which I would feast my gaze on a beautiful garden out of doors. One day there was a big rainstorm. It splattered mud on my "picture" window so badly that I could no longer enjoy the outdoor scene, and had to endure those splatters of mud for several weeks. Finally, one Saturday, I had the free time to go outside and clean my window. I remember, when the job was finished, going inside, stepping back from the window, and exclaiming, "Ah, what a *beautiful* window!"

Then I smiled, for I realized that what made the window beautiful was that I could see *through* it clearly once again. It wasn't the window I was seeing, but the garden beyond it.

Similarly with mankind, and with the saints: When one becomes a clear channel for God's grace he becomes beautiful, but that is only because his personality is transparent now, and permits a clear view of the divine wonders beyond!

Saints might be called the true eccentrics of the world—not in the sense that their personalities shout, "Look at *me!*" but because they seem quietly to say, "Look *beyond* me to the truth, which

lies at the heart of every man." The saints are by
no means self-centered in the usual sense of the
expression. They are completely centered, however, in the divine Self within, and are often (perhaps always) not greatly interested in the mere
opinions of others, nor even in their own opinions.

In Matthew 9:14 the disciples of John compared
John to Jesus, emphasizing the differences in
their two ways:

**"Then came to him the disciples of John,
saying, Why do we and the Pharisees fast oft,
but thy disciples fast not?"**

Jesus answered, **"Can the children of the
bridechamber mourn, as long as the bridegroom is with them? but the days will come,
when the bridegroom shall be taken from
them, and then shall they fast."** (Matt. 9:14,15)

This story points up two interesting truths. One
is that which I've already stated, that each Master
is forever and completely himself, and not necessarily like any other except in perfect virtue and
utter dedication to God and Truth.

The other truth is the *special* uniqueness of
Jesus Christ. Grammarians might quibble over
that qualifying adjective, "special," but it fits the
case perfectly. Seldom has a great master come in
such an outwardly commanding and heroic role.
Jesus *was*, very specially, himself. His mission
was not only to deliver new statements of Eternal
Truth around which he had to create a new tradition: it was also his role virtually to *wrench* old

traditions (both practices and attitudes) in a completely new direction. As he went on to say after that last passage:

"No man putteth a piece of new cloth unto an old garment, for that which is put in to fill it up taketh from the garment, and the rent is made worse.

"Neither do men put new wine into old bottles [commentators have pointed out that the word he used must really have been, "wine skins"]: else the bottles break ["crack" would, again, have been the correct translation], and the wine runneth out, and the bottles perish: but they put new wine into new bottles, and both are preserved." (Matt. 9:16,17) (I'll present a whole chapter, later on, called "New Wine.")

Thus, Jesus brought truth as a "new wine" to the people of his times. Most of those people were like "old wine skins"; they could not accept his teaching and would have "cracked" had they even tried to accept it. Jesus, as a human being, was loving, joy-filled, magnetic, and utterly wonderful. He'd have had to be, to attract multitudes of simple, ordinary people. He was also, to an amazing degree, courageous. Small wonder that those old "wine skins," the orthodox Pharisees, rejected him as fiercely as they did. One might almost say that Jesus, by his outspokenness, virtually *invited* their rage, causing it to erupt, finally, in the Crucifixion!

Jesus said, **"Think not that I am come to send peace on earth: I came not to send peace, but a sword. For I am come to set a man at variance against his father, and the daughter against her mother, and the daughter-in-law against her mother-in-law.**

"And a man's foes shall be those of his own household.

"He that loveth father or mother more than me is not worthy of me: and he that loveth son or daughter more than me is not worthy of me.

"And he that taketh not his cross, and followeth after me, is not worthy of me." (Matt. 10:34–38)

And then Jesus spoke those immortal words, quoted already before this: **"He that findeth his life [who clings to it, in other words, and finds comfort in it] shall lose it: and he that loseth his life for my sake shall find it."** (Matt. 10:39)

Jesus was summoning his listeners to offer up their egos entirely to God.

What can these statements have seemed to non-believers, but incendiary? Yet Jesus told Peter in the Garden of Gethsemane, **"Put up again thy sword . . . , for all they that take the sword shall perish with the sword."** (Matt. 26:52)

The conflagration Jesus sought to ignite was a fire of pure love for God, underscored by renunciation of every lesser attraction and attachment. He didn't comport himself like a rabble-rousing firebrand—a suggestion that a few modern commentators have made. He did speak, however, with magnetic courage, joy, and unshakable faith. Masters are often viewed as "social inconveniences" by self-satisfied worldly people. It is very evident from the Gospels, however (Yogananda, too, corroborated this statement), that Jesus never spoke with personal anger. It is true he did sometimes reflect the divine wrath of God, as (for instance) when he drove the moneychangers out of the temple! Yes, he could speak, when the occasion demanded it, with fiery power and conviction, and he always expressed firmly his refusal to compromise in matters touching on high, spiritual truths.

To those who like their saints "soft and cuddly," Jesus would have been—shall we say?—an embarrassment. Indeed, to some people he must have seemed glaringly offensive! But then, so also are, to some extent, many true men and women of God. One wonders how the expression ever got started: "Gentle Jesus, meek and mild"! Meek he could be in the true sense, meaning harmonious. That is to say, he never demanded or wanted anything for himself, but always acted in harmony with the divine will. Mild he could be also, for under the greatest stress he remained always inwardly kind and loving. In fact, he fitted perfectly the Vedic description of the man of God, as Paramhansa Yogananda quoted it in *Autobiography of a Yogi*: "Softer than the flower, where kindness is concerned; stronger than the thunder, where principles are at stake."

The age Jesus lived in was a hard one. He had
to survive a public mission in a rough, dogmatic,
and intolerant society. Never did he hesitate to
"thunder" when the occasion called for a divine
rumble.

It is amusing how often his later followers have
tried to imitate that "thunder"! Usually their
shouts and posturings are more like pop guns and
firecrackers! They ought to look, rather, to their
own inner dedication to Christ and God than to
others' lack of it. *Personal* sincerity is what Jesus
demanded. What others think and demand of us
is really "none of their business"!

Jesus, completely—one might even say, "gloriously"—himself, wanted to inspire all to seek God
with the same ardor he showed, the ardor of dedication to the divine search. Sooner or later, everyone will have to disappoint his mother, his father,
his family members, his neighbors and worldly
friends, and, in his search for the eternal verities,
"go on alone!" This world will always fight against
anyone's efforts to escape its net. One may con-
sole oneself with the reflection of this one eternal
truth: Once one finds liberation in God, seven
generations of his human family in both directions (this truth my Guru averred to me personally) will be saved, or at any rate will be greatly
furthered in their own spiritual evolution.

Some people take the thought of individual independence to the point of saying that, because they
prize their own personal freedom, they will never

follow anyone as a guru. They don't realize how bound they are already by the shackles of misunderstanding! Even mental attunement with one who has achieved freedom in himself, and whose will is to do only God's will, will enable one to find in himself that essence, which is, indeed, divine but is also eternally unique.

A mistake constantly made by unenlightened people is, like those disciples of John the Baptist, to say of every new saint, "But he isn't like that other one, whose sainthood is well established." Saint Francis of Assisi, for example, set a radiant example of sanctity for all mankind. My Guru used to describe him as his "patron saint." When one of Yogananda's disciples, however, asked him why his path was in so many ways different from that of St. Francis, the Master replied, "This is how God wants to play through you and me."

God has a different song to sing through every soul that has achieved wakefulness in Him. That song is not different in quality, for it always manifests God's perfect love and bliss. It is ever itself, however, and every melody, being divine, is in some very special way the perfection of divine beauty.

CHAPTER THIRTEEN

SON OF MAN VS. SON OF GOD

"I and my Father are one," Jesus said.

"Then the Jews took up stones again to stone him.

"Jesus answered them, Many good works have I shewed you from my Father; for which of these works do ye stone me?

"The Jews answered him, saying, For a good work we stone thee not; but for a blasphemy; and because that thou, being a man, makest thyself God.

"Jesus answered them, Is it not written in your law, I said, Ye are gods? If he called them gods, unto whom the word of God came, and the scripture cannot be broken [that is to say, gainsaid]; Say ye of him, whom the Father hath sanctified, and sent into the world, Thou blasphemest; because I said, I am the Son of God?

"If I do not the works of my Father, believe me not. But if I do, though ye believe not me, believe the works: that ye may know, and be- lieve, that the Father is in me, and I in him." (John 10:30–38)

THE FIRST PART OF THIS PASSAGE WAS QUOTED IN an earlier chapter. What I emphasized there was man's own innate and eternal divinity. I quote the passage here again to call the reader's attention to two other fascinating aspects of what Jesus said here.

I'd like first to point once again to his delightful, and at the same time notably courageous, sense of humor. Put yourself in his place on that occa- sion. The Jews had just accused him of blas- phemy; they were about to stone him. What, then, was his answer? He replied (I paraphrase): "I've done all these good works among you. For which of them do you intend to stone me?" There could be no other explanation than courageous open- ness to anything, based on perfect non-attach- ment, in the way he replied. Only such supreme detachment could have made possible his good humor. Think of it: There he was, threatened with disaster by a hostile mob. Could what he said have been due to self-pity? ("Just look at all the favors I've done you. Is *this* your way—sniff!—of showing gratitude?") Absurd! He *challenged* them, almost laughingly!

The other thing about that saying is that his

words and attitude would not have "flown" in high society. For instead of deprecating himself, as people in that milieu soon learn to do, mixing as they do with others who, like themselves, have "arrived" and want to demonstrate "good form" to their peers, Jesus virtually dared the mob to swallow its words and listen *only to him*!

Repeatedly through the New Testament we find Jesus referring, without the slightest hesitation or reticence, to himself. Sometimes he spoke of himself as the son of man; sometimes, as the Son of God. "Scarcely good form," one can hear the members, for example, of the British aristocracy saying. "Not the straight bat." To those at the top of any social ladder, Jesus might well have seemed "pushy" and "a bit over the top." Let's face it, he *was* "pushy." It wasn't himself he was pushing, of course, but divine Truth and God. His listeners, however, were obviously incapable of understanding what it was, exactly, that he was pushing. He had come as a way-shower, a road builder, a carver-out and conqueror of unknown territories. The more restrained and socially approved way of expressing oneself, always with tactful care, was not at all what was needed in his times.

Jesus used two expressions: **"Son of man,"** and, **"Son of God."** Paramhansa Yogananda pointed out something I myself had neither noticed nor thought of before. I wonder, therefore, how many others have ever noticed it. When Jesus spoke of the "son of man" he was referring,

Yogananda said, to his own human self: to his body, his personality, his egoic "I-ness." When he spoke of "the Son of God," he meant the Christ, the "anointed of God," the "Only Reflection of the Supreme Spirit in creation": the Christ consciousness. I suspect that the scribes who wrote, copied, or translated the New Testament never understood this subtle distinction either, and often got it wrong. When reading those chapters, however, readers should (according to their best understanding and discrimination) mentally insert this distinction, for it is important, and will help them to gain a much deeper insight into the true meaning of what Jesus said and taught.

When he asked his disciples, "Whom do men say that I the Son of man am?" that word, "son," should have been (but isn't) written with a lowercase "s," for he was speaking of his separate, human expression of Divine Consciousness, and not of the Infinite Christ.

We read, again: **"And when the tempter came to him, he said, If thou be the Son of God, command that these stones be made bread."** (Matt. 4:3)

Again: **"And, behold, they [the devils who had possessed two persons] cried out, saying, What have we to do with thee, Jesus, thou Son of God?"** (Matt. 8:29)

And again, after the miracle of Jesus walking on the water: **"Then they that were in the ship came and worshipped him, saying, Of a truth** thou art the Son of God." (Matt. 14:33)

Again: **"And the high priest answered and said unto [Jesus], I adjure thee by the living God, that thou tell us whether thou be the Christ, and Son of God."** (Matt. 26:63) The next sentence reads: **"Jesus saith unto him, Thou hast said."**

And Matthew states, **"Now when the centurion, and they that were with him, watching Jesus, saw the earthquake, and those things that were done, they feared greatly, saying, Truly this was the Son of God."** (27:54)

The Gospel of Mark begins with the words: **"The beginning of the gospel of Jesus Christ, the Son of God."**

Later we read: **"And unclean spirits, when they saw him, fell down before him, and cried, saying, Thou art the Son of God."** (Mark 3:11)

In Luke 1:35: **"And the angel answered and said unto her (the mother of Jesus, Mary), The Holy Ghost shall come upon thee, and the power of the Highest shall overshadow thee: therefore also that holy thing which shall be born of thee shall be called the Son of God."** (And what difficulty could there be in God impregnating the Virgin Mary? He himself resides within the seed of every male!)

"Now when the sun was setting, all they that had any sick with diverse diseases brought them unto him; and he laid his hands on every one of them, and healed them.

"And devils also came out of many, crying

out, and saying, Thou art Christ the Son of God. And he rebuking them suffered them not to speak: for they knew that he was Christ." (Luke 4:40,41)

In John we read John the Baptist saying: ". . . but he that sent me to baptize with water, the same said unto me, Upon whom thou shalt see the Spirit descending, and remaining on him, the same is he which baptizeth with the Holy Ghost. And I saw, and bare record that this is the Son of God." (John 1:33,34)

St. John wrote: "For God so loved the world, that he gave his only begotten Son, that whosoever believeth on him [we have seen already that to *believe* means far more than mere intellectual acceptance] should not perish, but have everlasting life.

"For God sent not his Son into the world to condemn the world; but that the world through him might be saved.

"He that believeth on him is not condemned: but he that believeth not is condemned already, because he hath not believed in the name of the only begotten Son of God." (John 3:16–18)

Clearly, this means that one is not condemned for not believing in Jesus, but for not believing in the Divinity which resided in him, and therefore not believing in one's own true higher Self. The condemnation comes, in other words, because one rejects one's own high, spiritual potential: the divine presence within us all, with which all are blessed.

John also states: **"And many other signs truly did Jesus in the presence of his disciples, which are not written in this book: But these are written, that ye might believe that Jesus is the Christ, the Son of God; and that believing ye might have life through his name."** (20:30,31)

CHAPTER FOURTEEN

DOES SATAN EXIST?

S ATAN IS AN EXAMPLE OF A TEACHING THAT BELONGS side by side with the *Sanaatan Dharma* teachings of India, but that is touched upon in them only lightly. Satan, a Hebrew word, signifies the adversary, enemy, or accuser. Spiritually speaking, Satan indicates the conscious power of evil, which influences mankind by making sin attractive to him, or by blocking his attempts to grow spiritually. Satan also obstructs man's sincere efforts to increase the influence of goodness in this world.

In India, the satanic influence is implied in teachings that concern *maya*, or cosmic delusion. Most people's impression of *maya*, however, is that it is simply there: a state of mind in which people entrap themselves, but not something with its own conscious power to entrap, which reaches out to the unwary in a deliberate effort to snare them in delusion. The Hebrew Satan is an entity—cosmic, as well as individual—which tries consciously to draw men into the ways of evil.

St. Matthew's description of him as the "tempter" who appeared to Jesus after his forty days in the wilderness implies that there was a deliberate outside influence, one beyond the conscious, personal will of Jesus. The "tempter" urged Jesus, first, to eat. Here's how the passage reads:

"And when he had fasted forty days and forty nights, he was afterward an hungered. And when the tempter came to him, he said, If thou be the Son of God, command that these stones be made bread.

"But he answered and said, It is written, Man shall not live by bread alone, but by every word that proceedeth out of the mouth of God." (Matt. 4:2–4)

That expression, "mouth of God," deserves (and will receive) treatment later on. It is important, but deeply esoteric, and requires a certain preparation on the reader's part. For the present, therefore, let us concern ourselves with that word, "tempter." Anyone with even the slightest understanding of human psychology might easily object, "Well, after fasting so many days, Jesus would certainly have needed no external 'tempter' to suggest to him the thought of food! The thought would have been, by that time, already somewhat more than pressing!" Are we to toss off the Bible's mention here of "the tempter" as evidence of a perfectly natural human desire, one that could only have been subjective? Many commentators would be, and probably have been, glad to explain away the phenomenon as a very understandable and perfectly natural urge.

I quote here, however, a fascinating statement Paramhansa Yogananda once made. "I used to think," he said, "that Satan was only a mental concept. Now that I have found God, however, I join my testimony to that of all who have gone before me: Satan does exist, and works *constantly and consciously* to encompass mankind's spiritual destruction."

I myself, when I first studied my Guru's teachings in depth, was inclined to explain away as allegorical some of his statements: for example, that for every beautiful thing in the world, Satan has created something ugly and unclean to offset it. For the lovely flowers, he has created noxious weeds; for medicinal herbs, he has created poisonous plants; for every upward inspiration, he has created something degrading to exert a downward-pulling influence on man's consciousness, such as drugs, pornography (and other inducements toward sex-intoxication), and alcohol, all of which influence man to lose himself in the senses and in his constrictive ego-identity. I see now, however, not only the inherent logic of this teaching, but also how it fits into the larger picture of *Sanaatan Dharma* as it has been taught in India.

Satan is not, in other words, a new teaching: rather, it is a *new expression* of the ancient, timeless, ever-changeless Truth that is true *Sanaatan Dharma*.

Those ancient teachings explain that the ocean of Supreme Spirit created movement at its surface. That movement might be described as the storm of *maya*, which raised the waves of duality, or cosmic vibration—*AUM*, the Holy Ghost or Holy Spirit— and made possible the appearance of everything in outward existence. God's grace calls to man unceasingly from within the soul to return to the state of oneness with the Infinite Ocean. (Much has been written about the silent, hidden, ever-active Divine Presence in men's hearts.)

Satan, however, has seemed to many thinking people an anomaly, presupposing, as the concept does, a *counter-force* to the inward pull of Divine Love. Can there actually be a force in cosmic creation that works *against* the divine will? Whence could such a force have come? Could there be *two* cosmic forces, each one in eternal opposition to the other: God, and Satan? Is Satan something quite different from God? It seems utterly bewildering!

We considered before now those words of Jesus, quoted from the Hebrew scriptures: **"And Jesus answered him, The first of all the commandments is Hear, O Israel; the Lord our God is one Lord."** (Mark 12:29) God is the Sole Reality. That reality, therefore, is but one. How, then, can the

one Lord have created a force in opposition to itself?

On the other hand, if God created everything,
must He not also have created Satan? The answer, no matter how inconvenient or unpalatable,
can only be: Yes, of course He did! Satan is a
part—necessarily so—of the divine scheme: a part
of the one reality which is God Himself. Without
Satan, there could have been no creation; no outward manifestation of anything; no universe; no
cosmic drama! As Yogananda said, "The villain is
needed in the play, to personify evil. Without him,
we might not feel the necessary incentive to love
the hero, who represents the good."

Philosophically speaking, Satan, or conscious
evil, represents the outward-flowing, creative force,
which brings Invisible Spirit into manifestation.
AUM has two aspects: the inner, cosmic Sound
heard in deep meditation, this aspect of *AUM* being
known in Sanskrit as *"Paraprakriti,"* the pure vibration. Inward-calling Mother Nature draws back
to Herself those souls who love God and are uplifted by the inspiring, increasingly magnetic power
of divine grace.

AUM in its outward, creative manifestation is
called in Sanskrit, *"Aparaprakriti"*: that influence
which draws man outward through the senses,
and induces him to participate in worldly pleasures and to seek their delusive fulfillments.

This outward manifestation is not passive. It
does not merely offer to man an attractive

alternative to the inner, "supremely relishable" bliss of the Divine. *Every influence in creation, both good and bad, is consciously active.*

Satan, then, tries actively to keep everything in a state of outward manifestation, and man himself in a state of mental responsiveness to that manifestation.

We may say that God, having once set a portion of the divine consciousness into motion, needed to create, along with that cosmic manifestation, a *conscious impetus, or will, toward ever-further, outward movement.*

Christian tradition speaks of Satan as a "fallen angel." People think of him as an angel who once lived in heaven with the other angels, where they were all gathered about the throne of God. Satan, as a result of foolish pride in his own power, rebelled against God and was cast out from heaven into "outer darkness." These may be termed excellent metaphors, and perfectly in keeping with a basic Truth, as well as with traditional ways of explaining it. They *are*, however, only metaphors. In our more literal-minded age, a more exact explanation of allegorical truths is needed also.

Yogananda compared creation to the ocean's waves. The high waves are those which become most agitated and affected by the great storm of delusion. The low waves represent the consciousness of saints, who prefer, in their humility, to live close to God, and who recognize His power alone as the source of their very existence. Tall waves, however, pull as far away as possible from the ocean bosom, and are more responsive to their own inner, egoic power, which rises, with the storm, in prideful competition against others.

Another allegory, closer to literal reality, is that the conscious power of delusion (Satan) is the storm itself, deliberately whipping up waves on the ocean surface. That force is needed to keep the "show" going; otherwise, everything would sink back again into the oneness of Spirit.

Did God create Satan? Yes!

Did God *want* to create Satan? Again, insofar as He may be described as wanting anything at all, he *had* to "want" that aspect of His cosmic reality!

Is God, then, as much evil as He is good? Most certainly not! Both good and evil exist only in the realm of *maya*, of duality. God is *beyond* them both.

Again, however, God may be described as the "Supreme Good," for goodness, in this realm of *maya*, at least *points in the direction* of the Supreme Good, which is God. Evil, on the other hand, points in the opposite direction: away from God and bliss, and toward ever-greater suffering and pain.

God is beyond merely relative goodness. Relative good, however, points, one might say, *in the direction of God*. God is beyond good and evil, but evil enshrouds the divine reality in an increasingly dense veil, whereas good holds up an ever-thinning veil over the Supreme Good, which is God.

Philosophically minded people, who love to

ponder abstractions, may end up hopelessly confused on this issue—even to the point of pooh-
poohing the very existence of evil. Christian Science, a relatively recent but well-known sect of
Christianity in America, teaches: "God does not
know evil." Paramhansa Yogananda, commenting
on that statement, remarked, "In that case, God
must be very stupid!"

What is evil, really? That which looks evil to us
may not be evil at all in the greater scheme of
things. A tiger has to kill in order to eat; that is its
nature. The tiger cannot legitimately be called evil,
therefore. To the human being strolling through
an Indian jungle, however, the animal is a men-
ace, and may therefore appear evil. Good and evil
depend to a great extent on the effect they have
on man himself.

We may take that thought farther and put it this
way: That is evil which takes man *away from* his
divine source within; and that is good which
draws him back in the direction of that source.
Moreover, a level of goodness may lie above whatever level of spirituality one person has attained,
who is himself steeped in evil. In another person,
however, that same level of goodness may lie far
below his own actual level of spiritual attainment,
if he is already soaring toward God, and may
therefore not be good at all.

To be more specific, it may be a mistake for a
saint to take personal credit for a good act, but
that same act, for a convinced materialist, may be

something for which he has every right to take personal credit. For in his case, the affirmation of personal goodness will encourage him to be better. To give even a penny to a beggar may be accounted, in him, a good deed, and one in which he may take justifiable pride. For a saint to preen himself for giving even a hundred dollars to that beggar would be absurd.

Alcohol is not, in itself, an evil. The sensory numbness it produces can even, in its proper place, be a good thing: for example, when used medically in an operation. Drunkenness itself, however, is evil because it dulls a person's awareness, and decreases his ability to function with mental clarity.

Thieving, again, is bad not merely because it breaks the law. Even more important, it is bad because it offends against man's own higher nature, causing his sympathies to shrink inward upon himself.

Anything that causes the ego to shrink inward upon itself produces inner suffering. I don't say that thieving might otherwise be good, objectively speaking—assuming, for example, that the thief believes himself capable of rising above "that shrinking feeling." The withdrawal I've described is, in fact, inevitable, the only reason for not feeling it being that the ego has already shrunk so far into itself that the effect of mere thievery no longer works upon him like a winepress. The clearest incentive not to steal is that its harmful effect is greatest on the perpetrator himself. In one, however, who is already inured to that effect, the ego-shell that surrounds him only becomes more hardened. Spiritual sensitivity may be a vanishing index in his psychology, but there is always the Law. In his case, the police are there for a good reason.

Assuming the presence of any sensitivity at all in a person, it must be said, of all moral errors, that what makes them wrong is that they go against man's innate nature. Some cultures may—indeed, some actually do—endorse thieving, lying, cheating, committing murder, and even cannibalism. People who err morally by habit are not usually over-concerned, anyway, about the effect their crimes may have on other people. *Any* contractive energy in itself, however, must inevitably inflict more suffering on the perpetrator himself than on anyone else. The harm inflicted on one's self is less instantly apparent, and is usually laughed off as something easily borne. "I may pay in the end for robbing that bank, but meanwhile—just look at all that lovely moolah!"

What people don't see is that heaven and hell lie, equally, *within* man. They are not places, but *directional flows* of energy and consciousness in one's self. The spine itself is the highway both toward and away from the "kingdom of God" which, Jesus said, lies *within.*

In every tradition, heaven is described as somewhere "up there," and hell as "down there." Objectively, there is no justification for this belief. No telescope has ever shown angels flitting about on clouds or in outer space. No devils, moreover, have ever been spewed up protestingly with oil gushers. The direction *up*, in North America is *down* in Australia. Up or down, in other words, have no cosmic significance: they relate entirely to directions in the human body itself. Anything that will raise our consciousness, or expand it and help it to embrace a larger reality than the ego, is good in the sense that it gives one a greater sense of happiness and fulfillment. And anything that lowers our consciousness, or that contracts it and our inner feelings inward upon the ego, thereby intensifying our sense of ego-separateness from others and from the world around us, increases in us a sense of restriction, pain, and suffering.

Outer influences that raise or lower our consciousness begin by acting upon our own thoughts and feelings. Kindness, generosity, aspiration, and, indeed, all uplifting feelings affect us by raising our consciousness. Selfishness, anger, greed, and other unkind or self-boosting sentiments, on the other hand, depress us, and cause within us a downward movement of energy, feeling, and awareness.

There is also, however, a much deeper aspect to all this. It is hinted at in a single sentence in *Autobiography of a Yogi*. "Thoughts," Paramhansa Yogananda wrote, "are universally and not individually rooted." Thoughts and impulses do not originate in man's own mind: They have their roots in infinity.

God and Satan, both, are active influences in this world. Their presence is active within man, also, according to whatever invitation man himself first extends to them. We might describe those cosmic influences as "sounding boards," which augment whatever note is first struck in man himself. Whatever positive or negative thoughts and feelings man emits (and none of us lives in a mental vacuum) are reinforced by divine or by demonic currents of consciousness flowing through the universe.

Both angels and demons are realities. Good forces abound wherever uplifting influences and vibrations are set into motion: in churches and temples, for example, and in the vibrations felt in clean, pure, and uplifting environments. Evil forces gather where low vibrations are prevalent: in bars, nightclubs, and similar places where the prevailing consciousness is base.

I remember Yogananda once exclaiming during a Kriya Yoga initiation (in 1949): "Thousands of angels passed through the room today!" By contrast, the evil forces that surround low "dives" (in itself, a suggestive word!) are actually demonic. Demons and devils are by no the means products of mere imagination. They are living, conscious entities that, having steeped themselves in evil, reflect in their consciousness, and even in their bodies, the evil thoughts and feelings that permeate them.

I once read a fascinating account of an American in Tibet who, during the 1930s, managed to get a native to smuggle him incognito into a seance of black magicians. Hooded, so that none of them would be recognizable, the whole group chanted together in a circle, "*Yaman taka, Yaman taka,*" with the purpose of summoning up the Great Spirit of Evil, from which they hoped to draw more energy for their dark practices. First what appeared in that circle was a succession of demons with grotesque, human-like shapes. It was easy, the American later reported, to see which demonic quality was represented in those lurid forms, for each of them was a horrible caricature of some human failing: anger, lust, passion, greed, avarice, vengefulness, and other base qualities.

At last the Supreme Spirit of Evil began to manifest itself. Slowly it materialized before their eyes, emanating a great, magnetic power which threatened completely to possess their consciousness. The whole group then put out a united mental force to drive him away before they themselves lost control of the situation. As the Spirit of Evil slowly vanished, something of his evil remained in their consciousness. No doubt they came indeed, to some extent, under the sway of his power.

A terrible story, but illustrative also of a terrible reality: Satan does exist. If you open yourself to him, he will come, and will infect you with the disease of evil itself. He comes more readily, moreover, than the divine forces, for Satan is eager to possess human beings, whereas angelic forces, before they'll reveal themselves, want to feel that we really *are*, in our love for goodness and truth, quite pure and selfless.

Do not play with those dark forces! They are real. They exist. And they can determine whether you rise toward happiness or fall into wretched misery and despair. Man is little more than a pawn in the cosmic game. Wars are waged first in heaven, between forces demonic and divine. Mankind on earth is capable in that struggle of serving as an instrument for one side or the other. Most people don't take sides, but wander distractedly between the two, neither particularly good nor particularly bad. Essentially, all that such people do is mark time for yet another incarnation, after death comes to claim them and give them another chance to "make good." Of such people Jesus said, **"Let the dead bury their dead."** (Matt. 8:22)

Above all, therefore, invite goodness into your consciousness. The battle will be half won, once you realize that you yourself are not the *source* of any virtue that you manifest, nor of any delusion, but that you can, if you choose, become an instrument for divine love and bliss in the world.

Jesus, in his parable of the sower and the seed, spoke of seeds falling by the wayside, **"And these are they by the way side, where the word is sown; but when they have heard, Satan cometh immediately, and taken away the word that was sown in their hearts."** (Mark 4:15) One might interpret this as the simple negligence of worldly people, who cannot inwardly absorb a truth even when they hear it, for the power of delusion is too much of a conscious presence within them, seeking ever to draw them deeper into worldly consciousness.

Yogananda used to say: "Here is a line. On one side of it is God; on the other side, Satan. Neither can influence you until you yourself turn toward the one or the other. Once you allow yourself to turn either way, however, the divine or the satanic influence will begin to act upon you consciously." You yourself, in other words, first extend the invitation. God or Satan then comes to you, and influences you further in the direction you've already indicated.

"Then entered Satan into Judas surnamed Iscariot, being of the number of the twelve.

"And he went his way, and communed with the chief priests and captains, how he might betray him unto them." (Luke 22:3,4)

A recent book, called *The Gospel of Judas*, pretends to be a faithful account by Judas of his closeness to Jesus. It claims that Jesus conspired with him to bring about his own betrayal. Intriguing? It is utter nonsense! I myself tried to read it, and soon gave up. The last straw was finding that Jesus was supposed to have taught Judas—contrary to Hebraic tradition, which of course Jesus himself taught and fully accepted—that there are nineteen Gods. (**"And Jesus answered him, The**

**first commandment is Hear, O Israel, the Lord
our God is one Lord."**) Jesus himself said there is
only one God—not that there are nineteen of
them.

I once had an interesting talk with my Guru on
the subject of Judas. He told me, "Of course,
Judas was a prophet."

"*Was* he!" I exclaimed in astonishment.

"Oh yes," he replied. "He would have had to be,
to be one of the twelve." He paused a moment,
then added, "I knew him in this lifetime. After two
thousand years of suffering, Jesus appeared on
his behalf to a great master in India, and asked
him to give Judas, in this incarnation, final liberation."

"What was Judas like?" I inquired, naturally
eager for more information.

"Always very quiet and by himself," my Guru responded. "He still had some attachment to money.
The other disciples began to make fun of him for
it one day, but the guru said to them, 'Don't.
Leave him alone.'"

Judas's money attachment showed up in this
incarnation in a giving way, not as the delusion of
avarice, for that disciple took it upon himself to
raise money to support the guru's wife after his
death.

So, although Judas acted under the influence of
Satan (in John 13:27 Jesus is quoted as saying to
him, "That thou doest, do quickly"), the story of
Judas must be strictly understood as not indicat-

ing a permanent state of alienation from God. As great as was Judas's betrayal—owing, my Guru said, to "a little bad karma"—its fruits were only temporary. Judas *was*, inherently, a great and true disciple. His problem was merely that there were in him still a few deep-seated faults that remained to be worked out.

For ourselves, we must understand that no matter how many times, or how far, we fall, God will ever wait for us with outstretched arms until we return to Him. Even those, moreover, who fail spiritually are leagues ahead of the most successful materialists of this world.

Never fear, therefore, but give to God as much of yourself as you are capable of giving. He will ever do the rest.

Chapter Fifteen

A New Revelation

W HEN JESUS CHRIST APPEARED IN THE NINE-
teenth century to Babaji, the great
"Yogi-Christ" high in the Himalaya, he addressed these words to him: "What has happened
to my religion? My followers are doing good works,
but most of them have forgotten the essence of my
message, which concerned direct, inner communion with God. Let us send again to the West the
secrets by which they can achieve that communion."

Thus, paraphrasing those words, what Jesus
said was, "Let us send to the West a teaching
which will enable my followers to understand and
appreciate once again the deeper message I
brought them." This is another example—several
others were listed earlier—of the truth that God
does intervene, sometimes, in human history.

Jesus Christ asked Babaji to send to the West a true master, fully qualified to fulfill the mission they envisioned together.

India has given birth, through the ages, to many great saints and masters. Its ancient religion gives people the freedom to teach according to their own understanding, rather than forcing them to adhere to some carefully pre-formulated dogma. That freedom is theirs because Hinduism has never been organized—enclosed, that is to say, in the straitjacket of administrative control. Those teachers whose instruction is deluded soon find their words swept aside by the power acquired over time by the strong currents that flow through a well-established tradition.

Swami Sri Yukteswar, Yogananda's guru, quoting what Babaji had told him during their first meeting—it had been at a *Kumbha Mela*, or religious fair, in Allahabad—told his young disciple Yogananda (I am quoting from *Autobiography of a Yogi*), "[Babaji said] You, Swamiji [Sri Yukteswar], have a part to play in the coming harmonious exchange between Orient and Occident. Some years hence I shall send you a disciple whom you can train for yoga dissemination in the West. The vibrations there of many spiritually seeking souls come floodlike to me. I perceive potential saints in America and Europe, waiting to be awakened. [To his young disciple, Sri Yukteswar then said] My son, you are the disciple that, years ago, Babaji promised to send me."

As I stated earlier in this book, part of Yogananda's mission to the West was to bring back to universal awareness "the original teachings of Jesus Christ." He always added after that, "and the original yoga teachings of Krishna in the Bhagavad Gita."

What about the findings of modern science, which seem, in the evidence they provide that life is without meaning, almost hostile to spiritual truth? Science claims that evolution is completely accidental, and that there is no observable purpose in anything. I have addressed these issues, basing my arguments on the Vedanta teachings and on those of my own Guru, in two books (to me, they are important): *Out of the Labyrinth*, and, *Hope for a Better World!* In those books I examine some of the spiritually damaging claims made by materialistic science, and the excessive rationalism of recent scholars and philosophers who base their findings on science. I've shown in those two books that, *in terms of those people's own reasoning*, their arguments admit of other, very different, and far more hope-inspiring interpretations.

Paramhansa Yogananda's commentaries on the words of Jesus Christ were profound, convincing, and of inestimable inspiration to Christians everywhere who want answers to the doubts that are being forced upon them nowadays—indeed, forced upon every thinking person: the apparent conflict between old religious concepts and the ever-expanding horizons of modern knowledge;

the mounting influx of discoveries of supposedly ancient scriptural texts in Near Eastern countries; the never-ending flood of scholarly opinions, the main attempt of which seems to be to humanize Jesus, and almost to make him out as a fairly ordinary human being. People need, now more than ever before, to understand the relevance of Christ's teachings to their daily lives and to present-day understanding of the universe. Indeed, spiritual truths ought to be far more relevant and far-reaching in our lives than materialistic science can ever hope to be.

Alas, Christians who believe in Christ's teachings, and (for that matter) religiously inclined people everywhere, find themselves on the defensive, instead of "standing tall" in their claim to a rightfully prominent position in this world, declaring their faith openly and with confidence. The tendency is widespread today to apologize for one's religious beliefs, as if saying, "Well, I happen to be someone who"—here they smile self-deprecatingly—"actually believes in God." Religious tradition as they know it has left them with antiquated ideas about how the universe was made, about its inconceivable vastness, and about man's true place in the grand scheme of things. Nor does their tradition give them any clear concept of man's chances of redemption, and of the possibility of eventually attaining divine perfection.

Christians go to church, sing hymns, offer formal prayers to God, and come together on other occasions for congregational functions. They perform their Christian duties, however, as if not daring to approach God intimately. They see themselves as petitioners standing (or kneeling, or crouching) before the throne of God, arms upstretched metaphorically in supplication. How beautiful it would be if they could sing, pray, and speak to Him lovingly, with deep, personal fervor! Indeed, some of them surely experience tender feelings toward Him. Nevertheless, even the hymns they sing are seldom addressed directly *to* God: They are paeans *about* Him. Some Christian hymns are thrillingly beautiful—such as, for instance, that glorious anthem, "A mighty fortress is our God." They are hymns only of praise, however, and lack the informal, confiding intimacy and trusting adoration of a child. Many of those hymns are, indeed, far from beautiful, either melodically or lyrically. Most of them fall short, moreover, of being devotionally inspiring.

One gloomy hymn (sad in its melody, sadder in its words) that we used to sing at our Anglican church in Ploeşti, Romania, began with these words:

> There is a green hill far, far away,
> Without a city wall,
> Where our dear Lord was crucified,
> Who died to save us all.
>
> We may not know, we cannot tell
> The pains he had to bear,

> But we believe it was for us
> He hung and suffered there.

More stanzas follow. Some of them are rich with genuine feeling; I needn't repeat them all. The idea behind this hymn, of course, was that Jesus, as he hung, crucified, on that hilltop, suffered unimaginably for our redemption. The theology implicit in these lines is appalling. From what was it that he saved us? I've addressed that question elsewhere already, but still the thought floats to the surface: What is the destiny awaiting us as an alternative? Eternity in hell? What does that say for God's love? True spiritual mastery means transcendence. It *absolutely must* render a person personally immune to all ordinary suffering. Christ's suffering *could not possibly* have been for himself. He had expressed its true nature already as being by no means personal, but for all mankind.

Recall his lament as he gazed down upon the Holy City:

"O Jerusalem, Jerusalem, thou that killest the prophets, and stonest them which are sent unto thee, how often would I have gathered thy children together, even as a hen gathereth her chickens under her wings, and ye would not!" (Matt. 23:37) His suffering, though intense, was by no means personal, either in or for himself. What he felt was *compassion*—indeed, *anguish*— for the suffering people inflict on themselves by ignoring God, while clinging obtusely to the misery they bring on themselves by ego-drenched desires and attachments.

Contrast the words of that hymn with this simple chant by Yogananda. Both the words and the melody are soul-stirring:

> Cloud-colored Christ, come!
> O my cloud-colored Christ, come!
> O my Christ! O my Christ!
> Jesus Christ, come!

People who want to believe, but find they cannot do so sincerely, will find in Paramhansa Yogananda's writings, and in those books of mine which I have listed above, a solid basis for the conviction that spiritual truth is as far above materialistic science as direct spiritual insight is above the merely intellectual deductions of philosophy.

More than fifty years have passed since Yogananda left his body. What he taught during his lifetime is even more relevant today, half a century later. Science is veering ever more in the direction of an understanding that consciousness, far from being the mere product of cerebral activity, is the underlying *essence* of everything. This basic truth is the key to all right understanding of Christ's teachings.

I have had to build gradually, through these pages, to the point where I can finally make this statement firmly and clearly: *Everything manifests God's consciousness.* As Krishna stated in the Bhagavad Gita, even the atheist manifests God.

Speaking of God's manifestation in all, he adds: "In the atheist, I am his atheism"!

Important also to a right understanding of Christ's teachings is the fact that truth, albeit universal, must also be understood by each person individually. Outward religion must ever remain, to a great extent, a social phenomenon: necessary, but at the same time watered down to be acceptable to the majority of people, who prefer that a teaching give them relative upliftment, and let them aspire to high truths without really trying too hard to attain those truths personally. For if religion is to be widely embraced—a better alternative, certainly, than having it widely rejected—it must respect the general consciousness of mankind by offering truths that people can accept comfortably.

Those truths, on the other hand, which challenge men to become saints must still be, for all that, at least hinted at—even if, at the same time, the truths are kept somewhat in abeyance. For didn't Jesus himself announce repeatedly, **"Those with ears to hear, let them hear!"**? Popular religion cannot afford to offer too generally those uncompromising teachings which comprise the highest truths.

Thus, many Hindus, too, will assure you that their scriptures sanction *kama* and *artha*: desires for pleasure (sexual, especially) and for wealth. Granted, these "fulfillments" do, if attained legitimately, have scriptural sanction. Desires are of course an obstacle in the search for God, but since people will have desires anyway, the important thing is to offer those desires up to God, and to fulfill them in ways that are sanctioned. No one can afford to teach too widely the universal and loftiest principles of *Sanaatan Dharma.* Unfortunately, but also realistically, most people are simply, in their present condition, not ready to be lifted up too high!

Christianity is not essentially, however, a religion for congregational worship alone. Churches, where congregations gather, are of course a good and necessary part of Christianity. God-believing (let us eschew that unfortunate term, "God-fearing"!) men and women want at least to be faithful to divine principles. Dilution of the higher truth comes, however, when people insist on what they define as the fullness of Christ's message as being a watered-down, "God-fearing" attitude. Christianity is also, and above all, an expression of the highest, universal, and most sublime truths. It is more than anything else for those few who desire—the more earnestly they desire, the better—to commune directly with God.

As for the rest, the churches, too, give people worthwhile truths to live up to, and are light years ahead of the plodding quest for facts that is the chosen domain of the material sciences and of intellectual scholarship.

Yogananda made an important prediction: "A great change is coming in the churches. Real *souls*, someday, will go there." Congregational worship is a wonderful thing, especially if it encourages the individual to seek inner communion with God rather than believing that all God wants of him is to "make a glad sound unto the Lord." Congregational worship can serve also to put a brake on individual delusions, like some of those which arose during the time of the Gnostics. (For, as I wrote earlier, there were Gnostics and Gnostics.) There is, therefore, a *need* for people also to worship God together in company with others.

Yogananda was once invited to hear a famous Christian choir who sang especially for him. After they'd finished, they asked him how he'd enjoyed it.

"It was all right," he said, his tone of voice a little non-committal. Naturally, they'd expected praise, even enthusiastic applause. Their fame, after all, had been well earned.

"You mean you didn't like it?" they pressed him. He then saw that he had no alternative but to give them a completely truthful answer.

"As far as technique was concerned," he said, "you sang beautifully. But whom were you trying to please? For whom was the music written? It was written for God. You should have been thinking only of Him when you sang. In future, please don't sing for your audiences. Sing to God."

The direction he foresaw for the future of Christianity was a move toward deeper love for God, and for other people *in God*.

He wrote commentaries on all the four Gospels. A very interesting fact is that the month he left his body—March, 1952—was when the last issue appeared containing his Bible commentaries. It had been appearing regularly in Self-Realization Magazine for more than twenty years. What a marvelous example of cosmic timing!

His commentaries will not all appear in this book. My purpose is to offer highlights from them. The commentaries themselves have already been published in their entirety in a large (two-volume) tome titled *The Second Coming of Christ.* My hope, here, is (so to speak) to skim the cream off the top.

To be honest, I must confess to a certain disappointment in that work. It was done by certain of my fellow disciples, and took many years to publish. Their version is, in my opinion, over-edited and difficult to read. Paramhansa Yogananda himself told me to edit his writings, and I have felt it my duty to offer, here, at least the essence of his commentaries. I do not think I will be given the time, however, at my age (I am eighty) to undertake the far more voluminous labor of editing all his commentaries. Meanwhile, however, I do recommend that the reader at least work his way through the rather complex structure of that book. If, in other words, you succeed in managing the potholes in that road, you will find yourself traveling through wonderful terrain. I do therefore recommend that book—with qualifications, admittedly, but sincerely.

I have also written a shorter work, *The Promise of Immortality*, in which—ever basing my thoughts on Yogananda's commentaries—I compare passages from the Bible with passages in the Bhagavad Gita. At present, that work is contained in one volume. I hope, in time, to complete a second volume.

The question must arise: Why was I not able to influence the editorial work of my fellow disciples? Those who know something of the story of my life will understand. Destiny has obliged us to plow in different fields.

Meanwhile, what I hope to accomplish in these pages is to give you the *essence* of the teachings of Jesus Christ that Yogananda brought to the West. Those teachings have, I truly believe, the power to change people's lives and to bring them closer to God.

What I have written so far constitutes only a kind of introduction to Yogananda's deep commentaries on the teachings of that great master of Galilee, Jesus Christ. What follows hereafter will be an overview of highlights in those great teachings.

Part Two

GEMSTONES IN
CHRIST'S TEACHINGS

CHAPTER SIXTEEN

HOW IT ALL BEGAN

"In the beginning God created the heaven and the earth. And the earth was without form, and void; and darkness was upon the face of the deep. And the Spirit of God moved upon the face of the waters. And God said, Let there be light: and there was light. And God saw the light, that it was good: and God divided the light from the darkness. And God called the light Day, and the darkness he called Night. And the evening and the morning were the first day." (Gen. 1:1–5)

IT IS A PITY THAT RELIGION AND SCIENCE HAVE BEEN treated, by their own "votaries," as separate realities. It is surely natural, especially in the matter of teaching truth, to begin discussions—especially of religious truth—with the question,

How did it all begin? What is the nature of objective reality? What is man's place in the universe?

Thus begins the first book in the Bible: the Book of Genesis. That passage continues:

"And God said, Let there be a firmament in the midst of the waters, and let it divide the waters from the waters. And God made the firmament, and divided the waters which were under the firmament from the waters which were above the firmament: and it was so. And God called the firmament Heaven. And the evening and the morning were the second day." (Gen. 1:6–8)

What is meant by that word, "firmament"? Paramhansa Yogananda explained that it means space, which he said is an actual vibration, separating the material from the astral realms: the waters above (heaven) and those below (Earth).

The most mystical of the four Gospels, the "Gospel According to St. John," also begins with the cosmic beginnings, setting in its proper context the deeper meaning of Jesus Christ's mission.

"In the beginning was the Word, and the Word was with God, and the Word was God." (John 1:1)

Both Jews and Christians identify the Word of God with the Holy Bible itself. Could any written scripture, however, have come into being even before the universe was created? Absurd!

Was God's word, then, something uttered with ordinary lips? How could it have been? To imagine the Creator of the vast universe, with its hundred billion galaxies, as possessing a human form and speaking human words is too fantastic to be taken seriously.

Words, as we know them, are the outward vibrations of their animating thoughts. Thus far reason can take us without making us stub our toes, metaphorically, on the incomprehensible. Before even mankind existed, however, and before there were tongues to utter human speech, the expression, "word," can only have had a very different meaning. In John, "the Word" refers to Cosmic Vibration itself, which is part of the Eternal Trinity and is therefore an aspect of God Himself.

God's "Word" is the vibration of His thought. That thought, through the medium of the Holy Vibration, produced the vast universe. The Infinite Spirit dreamed creation into existence by setting in motion, at the surface of its consciousness, that Cosmic Vibration. Wherever there is vibration there is movement. Vibration is movement in opposite directions from a state of rest at the center. Thus, the Cosmic Vibration produced duality (*dwaita*). As the ocean waves rise and fall without even slightly affecting the overall ocean level, so the waves of the Cosmic Vibration may be described, figuratively, as rising and falling above and below the state of absolute rest between them, in the Supreme Spirit. Their true, inner reality, however, is not that dual movement itself, but the state of rest at the center.

Vibration manifests outwardly in two ways especially: as sound, and as light. The first chapter of Genesis tells us, **"And God said, Let there be light."** St. John describes the holy vibration as the "Word"—as sound, in other words. Both these phenomena, Light and Sound, are experienced in deep meditation. Indeed, it may be said that listening to the Cosmic Sound, inwardly, is even more deeply thrilling than gazing into the inner light, even as music can affect us more instantly and deeply than painting.

John goes on to say, **"All things were made by him; and without him was not any thing made that was made."** From *AUM*, the Holy Ghost, were all things manifested. **"In him was life; and the life was the light of men."** Human life and consciousness, too, emanate from the Cosmic Vibration: the Word, or Holy Ghost (or Spirit). We owe our individual existence to that vibration. Our perception of having a separate existence is only an illusion created by the conscious, Holy Vibration.

"And the light shineth in darkness; and the darkness comprehended it not." Behind the darkness of closed eyes there ever scintillates the inner, spiritual light.

Jesus said, **"The light of the body is the eye: if therefore thine eye be single, thy whole body shall be full of light."** (Matt. 6:22) How many translations put those words differently: "If thine eye be whole"; "If thine eyes be healthy," "If your eyes see goodness,"* and so on. No one should be blamed, for people can only transmit to others what they have themselves understood. The light that "shines in darkness" is not beheld by those who are spiritually asleep, their consciousness darkened by spiritual ignorance.

A fascinating passage in the Old Testament of the Bible follows: **"Afterward he brought me to the gate, even the gate that looketh toward the east: And, behold, the glory of the God of Israel came from the way of the east: and his voice was like a noise of many waters: and the earth shined with his glory."** (Ezekiel 43:1,2)

The Hebrew word for "east" is *kedem*: "that which lies before." The same word applies also to the body, and refers to the forehead. (North, in mystical terminology, signifies the top of the head; south, the base of the spine; and west, the back of the head in the region of the medulla oblongata, the seat also of ego-consciousness.)

The "spiritual eye" is described in the Bhagavad Gita as located in the forehead midway between the eyebrows. It is not a physical organ, but a light which is actually visible there, "behind the darkness." Through that light (the "spiritual eye"), the deep meditator can gaze into subtler-than-material realms. As Ezekiel states, **"The glory of the god of Israel came from the way of the east . . .**

---

*This one is, I confess, only my invention.

and the earth shined with his glory."

Some years ago, Ananda Sangha, near Assisi, Italy, wanted to place a replica of the spiritual eye above the altar of its new temple. Ananda representatives went to Murano, a city famous for its works in glass. Approaching a well-known artisan, they described to him what they wanted. The man replied, astounded: "Why, that is something I have seen all my life!" He was deeply excited. "Tell me: What is this light?" He was a devout Christian, but knew nothing of the teachings of yoga. When that inner light had been explained to him, he was thrilled with devotional fervor.

Many yoga students have indeed told us over the years that they'd seen this light long before they first heard what it was. This light, in other words, is no hallucination created by subjective expectation. The spiritual eye exists already in everybody. All can see it, when their minds are deeply focused and calm.

What does the spiritual eye look like? When seen perfectly, it is a halo of golden light surrounding a field of deep blue, in the center of which is a silvery-white, five-pointed star.

The spiritual eye is, in fact, a reflection of the cosmic energy entering the body and sustaining it. Its portal of entry is the medulla oblongata at the base of the brain. I find myself suddenly in a position, here, of having to explain a number of deep, esoteric, but fundamental and important spiritual truths that are well known in the yoga teachings, but that are completely foreign to most orthodox Christians.

For now comes the question: What's all this about energy entering the body? We quoted earlier the words that Jesus addressed to the "tempter" (Satan), after his forty-day fast in the wilderness. Satan had urged Jesus to ask God to appease his hunger by converting the surrounding stones into bread. It is against highest spiritual usage to pray for oneself, since man's ultimate duty is to rise out of ego-consciousness altogether. I don't mean to suggest that it is always wrong to pray for oneself. Still, in the case of someone fully enlightened, like Jesus, a higher dimension of spiritual truth is manifested.

A story comes to mind which was told me by my Guru. A saint in India once became ill; his disciples said to him, "Sir, you've prayed for many of us so often in our illnesses. Why don't you now pray to the Divine Mother that She heal you, also?" Thinking it over, the guru decided they might be right. He prayed to God, therefore, as the Divine Mother of the Universe, and asked Her to heal him. She appeared to him with a stern visage and said, "Of all things! You have realized your oneness with Me. How is it that now you want to descend from that height and pray for your little self? Shame on you!" The saint, of course, hastily retracted his prayer.

Therefore also Saint Bernadette refused to seek healing from the miraculous waters of Lourdes, which she herself had brought into existence through her ecstatic visions. (On her deathbed she cried, "The spring flows not for me!")

And so we can understand the reply that Jesus gave to Satan: **"But he answered and said, It is written, Man shall not live by bread alone, but by every word that proceedeth out of the mouth of God."** (Matt. 4:4)

I didn't discuss, the first time I quoted this passage, what Jesus meant by that reference to "the mouth of God." Paramhansa Yogananda explained it this way: All of us have two points of entry through which we draw energy into the body: our physical mouths, which enable us to eat material food; and the medulla oblongata at the base of the brain, through which the life force and cosmic energy enter directly into the body from the surrounding universe.

The Bible is, in fact, full of esoteric teachings that might be described as "pure yoga." How could it be otherwise? For truth is simply a fact. As I have stated many times before, Truth is universal. There is no such thing as a "true, Christian vision," from which anyone belonging to some other religion is, by his "wrong structure of beliefs," automatically debarred. We become worthy to experience a divine truth not by what we believe, but by the purity of our hearts, and by our calmness of mind and feeling.

"Not every one that saith unto me, Lord, Lord, shall enter into the kingdom of heaven;

but he that doeth the will of my Father, which is in heaven." (Matt. 7:21)

As Christians can address God in their own language, whatever that may be, using, therefore, different words and different appellations for the Lord (calling Him, variously, *Dieu, Gott, Dio*, Jehovah, etc.), so also it must be clearly understood that God is pleased with man according to his purity of heart, which he offers up to Him with love. God cares *not at all* whether we love Him in Christ's name or in the name of some other great savior, or even if we visualize Him in some other way, so long as we love Him. Everyone who has loved God finds, in his ensuing clarity and expansion of consciousness, a window opening onto the Infinite, Divine Consciousness.

So then, you may ask, "What's all this about energy entering the body through the mouth of God"? Modern man is still deluded in his belief that our consciousness is produced by brain activity ("I think, therefore I am"); that the body is what gives us life; that any energy acquired by the body has to come to it in the form of material food, or from air. *It is consciousness alone, in the first place, which makes it possible for the brain to think.* Similarly, without energy coming to us from an inner, subtler source—the *true* source of all life in the body—we would not be able even to eat or digest our food!

Sufficient proof of this truth has been offered mankind through certain of the great saints, such as Therese Neumann in Germany, who lived for many years without eating any food at all.

We live always by that energy, drawing from it more than we consciously realize. Yogananda explained that will power is the secret by which we draw energy consciously into the body.

Here's an example of how we draw on it at will. Imagine yourself living alone. One day you return home from work utterly exhausted. This, you tell yourself, is one evening that you want only to flop down on your bed and sleep for long, long hours. You may even wonder whether you have the energy to get undressed and slip under the covers.

And then, suddenly, the telephone rings. An old friend you haven't seen for years is in town, and must leave again the following morning. Can the two of you, he asks, spend a little time together this evening?

Imagine your response. *Of course* you want to see him! *Of course* you're thrilled he's in town! *Of course* you have all the energy to go "out on the town" with him! You may even return home late that evening. Even so, you rise the next morning full of energy in the recollection of the happy evening you spent together.

"The greater the will," Paramhansa Yogananda often said, "the greater the flow of energy." He taught a set of what he called "energization exercises" by which one can learn how to live, ever-increasingly, by cosmic energy, drawing on that energy with the power of will. Regular practice of those exercises enables one also to be less dependent on outer, physical sustenance.

The medulla oblongata is the one part of the body that cannot be operated upon directly. It is the seat of life in the body. Energy enters into the body through this point. The medulla is reflected, as I said, in the forehead, where it is seen as the spiritual eye. The reason for the concentric rings in the spiritual eye, which I described earlier, with its five-pointed star in the center, has to do with our subtler astral and causal bodies, and with the channels of awakening in the spine of each of those bodies.

Well, then, shall I say, "In for a penny, in for a pound"? How can I suddenly plunge you into these deep waters, when I haven't been able even to ask you whether you know how to swim? Well, let's give it a try, anyway.

There is another consideration. The Bible (in the Book of Genesis) says, **"And God said, Let us make man in our image, after our likeness."** (Gen. 1:26) This passage has been taken to mean that God has a man-like appearance. This is, however (as we've seen already), quite impossible. Study that sentence more closely, however. You'll see that it isn't God who has the form of a man, but man who was made, somehow, in the image of God. There is, indeed, something about the way our bodies were made that clearly reflects the divine image.

The five-pointed star at the center of the spiritual

eye is the doorway through which our minds can penetrate into the inner kingdom of God. The five points correspond, interestingly, to the shape of the human body. Stand with your arms stretched out to the side, and your legs wide apart. That shape, with your head at the top: Do you see its general resemblance to a five-pointed star? The original design of our bodies was based on that star in the spiritual eye. We were literally made "in the image of God." This wasn't a merely poetic image meant to indicate somehow a higher *potential* in ourselves. And it didn't mean, as orthodox dogma would have it, that only human beings possess souls. In fact, we *are* souls: we possess bodies.

I mentioned the Star of Bethlehem, earlier. It was the star in the spiritual eye, which the wise men of the East followed eastward (they were, in literal fact, traveling westward) to the Christ Child. Any star in the heavens, as I pointed out, if it's seen over a stable would appear over something else if one went behind that stable. The star, here, has a deeply esoteric meaning.

The story of the wise men means, for "those with eyes to see (or ears to hear)," that they'd perceived a wondrous truth: The Lord Himself had incarnated on earth in human form, through Jesus Christ! The divine light had descended from the Supreme Spirit itself. The Biblical account was written to imply, to those who could understand, that Jesus Christ was no common baby, but the Lord Himself descended to earth in a human body. The wise men had been appointed by God to make this sublime fact known.

And so (to return to Ezekiel) when one is deeply focused in prayer and meditation on the spiritual eye, he beholds the light of God, and sees that all things have their being in that light. **"And the earth shined with his glory."** (Ezekiel 43:2)

Ezekiel described another phenomenon. **"His voice,"** we read earlier in that passage, **"was like a noise of many waters."** These words speak of the mighty sound of *AUM*, the Holy Ghost (or Holy Spirit). The Book of Revelation, also, states: **"and his voice [was] as the sound of many waters."** (Rev. 1:15)

That sound has been described variously in the Bible, as well as in many other scriptures. In the Acts of the Apostles we read that on the day of Pentecost the disciples (to whom Jesus had promised to send the Holy Ghost) were gathered together, and heard **"a rushing mighty wind."** (Acts 2:2) Indeed, one sometimes feels in meditation a sensation as though an actual breeze were blowing (usually, however, rather gently) on the body when one is sitting perfectly still. It can happen in a closed room, and bears no relationship, in other words, to any outer movement in nature. This breeze, too, is a manifestation of *AUM*.

You may have gone occasionally to some place where deep silence reigned. Haven't you sometimes been aware, in such places, of a quiet, rushing sound in your ears? It occurs usually in the right ear, and may suggest the gentle sound of the wind through pine trees. This, too, is a manifestation of the *AUM* sound, the Holy Ghost, or Holy Spirit.

Don't think that it is only a soothing sound, however. The Book of Job tells us, **"God thundereth marvellously with his voice; great things doeth he, which we cannot comprehend."** (Job 37:5)

And again the Bible says: **"Thou calledst in trouble, and I delivered thee; I answered thee in the secret place of thunder."** (Psalms 81:7)

AUM is a sound with which all can commune, and into which also, in time, all can merge. It will help greatly to learn the method for deepening this communion. It was for this reason that Jesus told Peter, **"And I will give unto thee the keys of the kingdom of heaven."** (Matt. 16:19) That marvelous passage will be treated again at some length later on. My intention, here, is to share with you an important statement Yogananda made. He said the "keys" Jesus referred to are the spiritual techniques by which true seekers of God can achieve the high aim of union with God.

Yoga is a very ancient science. It is based on simple realities of human nature that are, indeed, universally recognized. The techniques and teachings of yoga are a highly spiritual science. We'll devote more space, in the next chapter, to correlating the exotic-sounding yoga science with everyday, human realities. Here let me state only that what is involved is simple *recognition* of those realities, and not any strained, "far out" *invention*. For now, I offer two universally recognized facts, in the hope of convincing you that I am not, myself, being merely "far out."

1. Yogis say the seat of the will, of the intellect, and of concentration is a point in the forehead midway between the two eyebrows. It is a commonly known fact that, when we exert our will or try to puzzle out some complex thought, or when we make a special effort to concentrate deeply, we tend quite naturally to knit our eyebrows. This slight frown is a clear indication that we are attempting to focus our mind's energy at that point.

Is there—we may then ask—something special about that point in the forehead itself? No, not there exactly, but *just behind* that point, in the brain.

The frontal lobe of the brain is associated with intellectual effort, and with the higher aspects of mentation. It is no great mental stretch to consider that there may exist, just behind that point in the forehead, the exact area (as yogis claim) on which to concentrate if one wants to develop the higher aspects of his consciousness.

In focusing at that point, the eyes are drawn upward naturally. It is, indeed, no accident that saints in a deep state of ecstasy have been seen, and have been so depicted in works of art, with their eyes gazing upward.

2. Yogis say that emotional feeling, deep love,

and intuition are all centered in the heart. It is again a simple fact that our deep feelings are centered there. The area of the heart is also the location of a woman's breasts—owing, again, to woman's enhanced capacity for sensitive feeling. A "love-sick swain" may lament, "My heart is broken!" but he'll never say, for example, "My knee hurts!"

The heart has, I've been told, been found to contain an even greater complex of nerves than the brain. The heart is, in any case, much more than a mere physical pump to send blood throughout the body.

Actually, yogis say that the spiritual center of feeling lies at a point in the spine just *behind* the physical heart. (We'll go into this subject more deeply during a discussion of the spine, in the next chapter.) Yoga teaches the importance of concentrating energy in the heart—or, more specifically, in the spinal center behind the heart. That is where the feeling quality must be awakened. From there it must be directed upward to the point between the eyebrows. The heart's feeling should be kept reined in, and not allowed to spill outward and waste itself in emotion, nor to flow downward in the spine. If the energy flows to the lower centers in the spine, one's consciousness becomes drawn downward also, to lower states of consciousness.

The experiences I've described are universal to all humanity, and may help to explain that, when one develops sensitivity to them, he can deepen his insight also into the Bible and into the teachings of Jesus Christ.

Jesus said, **"Say not ye, There are yet four months, and then cometh harvest? behold, I say unto you, Lift up your eyes, and look on the fields; for they are white already to harvest."** (John 4:35)

Again, Psalm 121:1,2 states, **"I will lift up mine eyes unto the hills, from whence cometh my help. My help cometh from the Lord."**

And, regarding the heart, Jesus said: **"Blessed are the pure in heart: for they shall see God."** (Matt. 5:8) Only when one is free from any ulterior, ego-generated motives, and is able to be wholly absorbed in God's love, can he know God.

Again, Jesus said, **"A good man out of the good treasure of the heart bringeth forth good things: and an evil man out of the evil treasure bringeth forth evil things."** (Matt. 12:35) Yoga emphasizes the importance of keeping the heart filled with "good treasure": kindly thoughts, devotion, love, calm feeling, non-attachment to everything material.

"Evil treasure," on the other hand, lies heavily on the heart, and pulls one's energy downward. Therefore we read, of Judas Iscariot when he betrayed Jesus, **"And supper being ended, the devil having now put into the heart of Judas Iscariot, Simon's son, to betray him. . . ."** (John 13:2) The impulse toward treachery is one of the heart's "evil treasures." Evil is called such when it is more than a mere suggestion in the mind, but is entertained and "treasured" by people who harbor dark motives in their hearts. Those dark "treasures" are manifestations of satanic influence on those people whose hearts have turned "desirefully" toward delusion. Evil motives plunge one's consciousness downward into ever-increasing mental darkness.

It is interesting that the Biblical account describes "the devil" putting the thought of betrayal "into the heart of Judas." Indeed it so happens because, as Yogananda said, "Thoughts are universally and not individually rooted." We first tap the source of negative consciousness in the universe by ourselves thinking wrong thoughts, and by mentally toying with any desire we harbor even lightly in our hearts. Those thoughts and desires send rays of magnetic energy into the infinite, attracting a compatible energy. It depends on whether our "invitation" is positive or negative. In either case it can uplift us, in turn, heavenward, or cast us down into ever-deeper darkness and suffering.

If a person wants to cleanse himself of impure motives, or to strengthen his inner purity, the best place to start is by spurning every impure imagination, which people tend too easily to "play with" in an effort (they may tell themselves) to "understand" and reason their way out of that thought. Instead, one should concentrate on raising his feelings from the heart to the higher centers in the throat and the head. If he can harmonize those feelings, uplift them, and then channel them to the spiritual eye (the "Christ center") in the forehead, he will find that his tendency to objectify impure feelings onto the world around him will change completely. Almost automatically, they will be purified.

Without subtle techniques such as these, which Jesus called "keys to the kingdom," it is difficult for people to develop spiritually. They may try, for example, to direct love toward God but, despite their best efforts, find their feelings being dispersed in a thousand different directions of restless emotion. They may try to concentrate on God, but, having no idea how to do so, find their thoughts running riot.

A cousin of mine gave birth to a baby with a defective heart. The mother prayed desperately.

"It was so discouraging," she later admitted to me. "Even though I desperately longed to pray with all my heart, my thoughts kept straying off toward useless distractions. I found myself wondering whether the milkman had delivered the milk that day; asking myself what to prepare for lunch; hoping my husband would return from work in time for dinner. Intense though the pain was that I felt for my baby, I simply *couldn't* concentrate. It made me weep with frustration to realize that I was simply unable to help myself!"

I told her she should take up yoga.

Yoga is not some unnatural, pagan ritual. It is
no more foreign-seeming than you are, yourself!
It puts to practical use, rather, certain realities
with which everyone is completely familiar. Is
yoga, then, unchristian, simply because it is a foreign word? Preposterous!

Let me quote for you one more passage in that
first chapter of St. John. **"No man hath seen God
at any time; the only begotten Son, which is in
the bosom of the Father, he hath declared
him."** (John 1:18) It is heart-rending to read this
passage through the eyes of someone who believes
himself *essentially* different from God, and
doomed by original sin to eternity in hell unless
he accepts Jesus Christ and believes that Christ
died for our sins.

I still remember my mother's tears of anguish
when, at the age of sixteen, I told her I would not
go to church with her anymore. She came to my
room later that day, and cried, "Oh, how it pains
me to think that my own child is condemning
himself to eternal hell!" (And she had given me
with heartfelt love to God, as her first child, while
still she carried me in her womb.) I next remember her coming to me a few days later, with profound relief in her eyes. She told me with deep
hope that she had just read somewhere that rejection is often the first step toward deeper acceptance.

I replied, "You've understood." Sadly, I was
never able to share with anyone, not even with my

mother, my own deeply spiritual search.

Yogananda's most important message on the teachings of Christ was that man is, and *cannot but be*, a child of God. There is nothing, anywhere in all creation, but God's consciousness. As my Guru often told us, "To call yourself a sinner is, it-self, the greatest sin!"

Truly, human sight cannot behold God. Only the eyes of the soul are clear enough to perceive Him. The above passage is deeply true, but the way it ends: **"the only begotten Son, which is in the bosom of the Father, he hath declared him,"** is open to so many misinterpretations that I cannot but suspect those words were somehow "refined" to fit in with dogmatic understanding.

Well, they're all that we have of that passage, and in essence they are true; they simply need to be understood deeply enough to correspond to *Sanaatan Dharma*—the eternally true religion, which embraces the whole universe. Yes, it is only in Christ consciousness that God becomes fully revealed. But yes, also, we all can—indeed, we *must*, eventually—attain Christ consciousness ourselves.

What happens during deep meditation? First, the sacred *AUM* vibration is heard in the right ear; then, later, in the whole body. As meditation deepens, one finds his consciousness merging in the Cosmic Vibratory sound. One then realizes it as the one, true Self. After hearing and feeling its vibration pervading the body, one's consciousness expands to embrace all creation.

One then feels, subtly underlying the vibrations in the body, the still reflection in the body of the Christ consciousness—"only begotten," because, in all creation, no other reflection exists of the still, ever-unmoving, vibrationless Spirit *beyond* creation.

With continuously deepening meditation, one's consciousness expands, ultimately to embrace the Christ consciousness everywhere. It is omnipresent in all creation. That is the Christ, the only begotten Son, who, the Bible says, "declares" God, by revealing Him in the soul.

Really, it may all appear as though one had to learn a new language! So many false concepts abound in "Churchianity"! The chief incentive for learning this "language" is that, if we reject it, we turn our backs on what we most deeply want in our own hearts.

Too many challenges have been hurled at Christianity: hurled by science; hurled by those who comprise so much of modern scholarship; hurled by an evolving world view, in our modern times, that is ever-increasingly at variance with almost all one hears when he goes to church. The supreme justification for learning this new language—the ancient language of spiritual awareness—is that, literally, nothing else works.

If any other alternatives worked, I'd say with Shakespeare in Hamlet, "grapple them to thy soul with hoops of steel." But the fact is, they simply don't! They are, all of them, only snares and delusions. Show me a truly happy scientist and I'll say to you, "And why is he happy? Simply because, in addition to being a scientist, he is also a saint." Outside of God, so long as one roams in the thick woods of ego-consciousness, nothing ever works!

People for countless incarnations do their best to "make it" on their own "out there" in the world. Always they fail. There is, literally, only one way "out": to seek God. His is the language Yogananda came to teach us. This was the language that Jesus, too, spoke. It is the language of the soul.

CHAPTER SEVENTEEN

THE SPINAL HIGHWAY

"The sabbath was made for man," Jesus said, **"and not man for the sabbath."** (Mark 2:27)

EVERYONE KNOWS THE STORY: HOW THE DISCIPLES were picking corn on the sabbath, and the Pharisees criticized them for "working" on the Bible-ordained day of rest. The answer Jesus gave them has been applied, no doubt, to many different situations, for it means also that all rules are for man's sake, primarily, and aren't there to satisfy a more abstract demand. Probably, however, that story has seldom, if ever, been taken to its ultimate conclusion. For in truth, the whole of Christ's teaching refers not to external, but to internal realities: not to some blessed eventual existence amid "heavenly surroundings," but to the inner man. Above all, every rule of religion, also, is there to uplift us spiritually, and not to satisfy any demand God makes of us.

I've quoted the following passage before: **"The kingdom of God cometh not with observation: Neither shall they say, Lo here! or, lo there! for, behold, the kingdom of God is within you."** (Luke 17:20,21) As I've also said, every religious tradition on earth (as far as I know) thinks of heaven as situated somewhere "up above," and of hell as being "down below." In cosmic terms, these concepts obviously don't work, for wherever we happen to be on earth, what seems *down* to us is *up* for people on the other side, and what seems *up* to us is, again, *down* for them—who, of course, aren't walking about upside down, as people once imagined. The realities of heaven and hell refer universally, as in the case of the Sabbath, to realities within man himself—in fact, to the directional flow of energy in his own body.

Whatever uplifts our consciousness brings us more inner happiness. And whatever lowers our consciousness diminishes our happiness and even makes us unhappy. It is a common description of happiness to say, quite literally, "I feel uplifted," or, "I'm flying high today." By contrast, when we are unhappy we use expressions that describe a downward flow of energy and consciousness. People say, "I feel low," or, "I'm feeling downcast," or, "depressed."

Christian truths must be understood above all, then, in relation to universal, even if still human, realities. Every true scripture is concerned much less with abstractions than with the truth as it affects man himself.

There is a book, which claims to be a scripture, that enjoyed a certain popularity when I was young, and is still read (though perhaps less widely so). Its name is *The Urantia Book*. The book deals with all sorts of supposed phenomena such as the various categories of angels, and gives detailed descriptions of the astral worlds. I haven't read much of it, and perhaps am not being wholly fair. It does seem to contain fascinating stuff, perhaps especially for the sort of people who are interested in science fiction. Its subject matter is not at all the domain of genuine scripture, however. The whole message of true scripture, and certainly of Jesus Christ, was directed, by contrast, toward uplifting man's consciousness, and concentrates on what will lift him toward God. Christ's message concerns, also, necessary warnings against what might alienate man from his own potential for Divine Bliss.

When the "mother of Zebedee's children" came to Jesus with her sons and said to him, **"Grant that these my two sons may sit, the one on thy right hand, and the other on the left, in thy kingdom,"** (Matt. 20:20–22) the account goes on to say, **"But Jesus answered and said, Ye know not what ye ask."** Indeed, the question was a foolish one.

People have too long imagined Jesus and his

Father seated in heaven on exalted thrones, as if holding court. The divine consciousness, however, is omnipresent. It exists already, albeit unrecognized, within everyone, be he king, courtier, or commoner. The Divine is subtly present within every creeping snail and crawling beetle—indeed, in every rock. Certainly it is not ensconced forever, in stasis, on a throne!

Jesus once compared the kingdom of heaven to a tiny mustard seed (Matthew 13:31). Has anyone ever made the leap from that thought of a sprouting, and then upward-growing mustard seed to the shining astral heavens? If so, it is a leap my own little brain is incapable of making. What Jesus referred to in that parable was, again, man's own latent potential to *raise* and *expand* his consciousness, spiritually, into oneness with Omnipresent God. That expansion is accomplished by removing, one by one, all the self-enclosing veils which constitute our egoic limitations.

Jesus said he had come to fulfill the law and the prophets (Matt. 5:17). From those words we may understand that what the ancient prophets taught were truths implicit also in Christ's teachings.

Isaiah declares: **"The voice of him that crieth in the wilderness, Prepare ye the way of the Lord, make straight in the desert a highway for our God.**

"Every valley shall be exalted, and every mountain and hill shall be made low: and the

crooked shall be made straight, and the rough places plain:
"And the glory of the Lord shall be revealed."
(Isaiah 40:3–5)

The "highway for our God," which Isaiah said must be "made straight," is the spine. The "rough places" are the ups and downs of duality (*dwaita*), which are smoothed out when human consciousness finally comes to rest at its true center in the Self within.

Here again, common understanding soars above common belief. Everyone, that is to say, knows that a straight spine indicates someone who is upright, honest, and who possesses noble and lofty ideals. Someone lacking in will power, on the other hand, is commonly described as "spineless." In English, at least, a dishonest person is described also as "crooked"—an image suggestive of someone whose spine is far from straight. Few people, unfortunately, are aware of how important a straight spine is to their own *spiritual* development.

Physically speaking, one thing is obvious. A bent spine makes it more difficult to fill the lungs with air and, therefore, to breathe properly. Mentally or attitudinally, a straight spine indicates courage. Discouragement, on the other hand, or a lack of strong will power, reveal themselves instantly in a bent spine. Spiritually speaking, therefore, it can easily be understood that a straight spine is important for lifting the body's energy upward. A bent spine indicates a downward flow of both energy and awareness.

When energy is centered particularly in the heart—that is to say, usually, in that region of the spine which is located *behind* the heart—it means that the feelings, or emotions, are deeply affected. Feeling may be evoked either spontaneously from within, or by inner reaction to some outside occurrence. All emotions are indicative of at least somewhat excited feelings. Calm feeling alone brings true, intuitive perception.

When the feeling quality is directed upward, particularly to the "Christ center" between the eyebrows, one develops aspiring love for God.

Again, when energy becomes centered (especially by deliberate effort) in the area of the spine behind the throat, calmness is induced, and an inner feeling of expansion.

Energy centered in the medulla oblongata must be allowed to flow on toward the positive pole of the medulla, which lies in the front of the brain at a point between the eyebrows, in the "Christ center." If, on the other hand, that upward energy flow is blocked in the medulla, it increases one's focus on the importance of his ego. (Therefore it is that egotists are said to "look down their noses" at others. The concentration of energy in the medulla creates tension in that region, and draws the head backward.)

Energy centered in the lower centers of the spine draws the mind down toward matter-attachment.

Even the gestures of dance suggest varying mental states. Sinuous movements, for example, especially of the hips, suggest sexual desire, or an effort to tempt others sexually. Strong movements of the legs and feet suggest strong involvement in earthy attachments. Gracious, upward movements of the arms suggest a more uplifted spiritual consciousness. Movements of the head indicate a variety of attitudes, whether gentle, uplifted, or arrogant. Arrogance is displayed by movements in which people toss their heads backward, or energetically from side to side. Such movements are often displayed, for instance, by singers of "pop" (meaning popular) music. Movements that toss the head backward are also, of course, indicative of contempt. Inclining the head forward in a position suggestive of the humble bow indicates a release of tension at the back and top of the neck, which can mean offering one's consciousness forward toward the Christ center, or upward to God, or generously offering deference to others.

"I was in the Spirit on the Lord's day," says the Book of Revelation, **"and heard behind me a great voice, as of a trumpet, Saying, I am Alpha and Omega, the first and the last: and, What thou seest, write in a book, and send it unto the seven churches which are in Asia."** (Rev. 1:10,11) Paramhansa Yogananda explained, first, that that "great voice" is the mighty sound of *AUM*. Second, he said, "the seven churches" indicate "for them that have ears to hear" an inner, not an outer reality: the centers in the spine. The entire Apocalypse (as this book is often called also) is not a book of prophecies concerning the future—unless that future be understood as a reference to man's own future inner enlightenment. The above passage continues:

"And I turned to see the voice that spake with me. And being turned, I saw seven golden candlesticks [candle holders]." (Rev. 1:12) What did St. John the Divine mean by, "I turned"? One explanation of this expression would be that John turned his head to see what was behind him. Another—indeed, the intended—meaning is that John "turned within." Normally, man's energy flows outward to the body and onward, through the five senses, to the surrounding world. To turn one's energy backward, then, means to redirect it inward: to withdraw the energy from the outer body in deep meditation.

A voice isn't something one "sees." Probably the original statement was that John *perceived*, rather than *saw*, the voice, which was the great inner sound of *AUM*. One can both hear and see ("perceive" in both cases) the subtle spinal centers. The topmost of them is higher than the spine, at the crown of the head. The spiritual centers, then, are seven in number. The passage continues:

"And in the midst of the seven candlesticks one like unto the Son of man, clothed with a garment down to the foot, and girt about the paps with a golden girdle.

"**His head and his hairs were white like wool, as white as snow; and his eyes were as a flame of fire;**

"**And his feet like unto fine brass, as if they burned in a furnace; and his voice as the sound of many waters.**

"**And he had in his right hand seven stars: and out of his mouth went a sharp twoedged sword: and his countenance was as the sun shineth in his strength.**

"**And when I saw him, I fell at his feet as dead.**" (Rev. 1:13–17) The scripture goes on to speak of the blessings that accrued from this experience.

"**I fell at his feet as dead.**" Those words, Yogananda explained, have a subtle meaning. They indicate the state of deep inner ecstasy, when one's energy is completely withdrawn from the senses and the body, freeing the soul to soar in the Infinite. In this context, Yogananda often quoted the words of St. Paul, "**I protest by your rejoicing which I have in Christ Jesus our Lord, I die daily.**" (I Cor. 15:31) Many Christian saints have been observed in a state of such deep inwardness, in meditation, that their bodies have actually appeared "as dead."

The "son of man" refers here, not to Jesus the Son of God, but to John's own human form (the son of man) in his astral body, which is in fact very much like the physical body, though in fact the human body is only a replica of the astral body and not the reverse.

"His head and his hairs were white like wool, as white as snow; and his eyes were as a flame of fire; and his feet like unto fine brass, as if they burned in a furnace." (See above) These are descriptions, again, of the astral body. The highest center, at the top of the head, is called in the yoga teachings the *Sahasrara*, or "thousand-rayed lotus." It is so described because rays of light radiate outward from that point in all directions. The Book of Revelation describes that "crown chakra" as **"white like wool, as white as snow,"** for the purest light of the astral body emanates from this highest center.

His eyes were **"as a flame of fire."** This was because great energy flows out through the eyes. The quality of that energy depends on the thoughts and feelings that animate it.

The feet are described as being **"like unto fine brass, as if they burned in a furnace,"** because the lowest, and therefore (relatively speaking) the dimmest, energy in the astral body emanates from the feet.

The **"golden candlesticks"** and **"seven stars"** indicate the spinal centers (including the spiritual eye, or reflection of the medulla, which in Sanskrit is called the *agya chakra*. The spiritual eye does double duty as the positive pole of the medulla oblongata). The real seventh center in the body is situated at the top of the head in the *Sahasrara*. This center, however, can be reached only by opening and passing through the spiritual eye. Therefore I've described the seventh center as the spiritual eye: the positive pole, provisionally, of the sixth center.

"And out of his mouth went a sharp two-edged sword." (See above) From each *chakra*, rays of energy flow out to bring sustenance to corresponding parts of the body. **"Out of his mouth"** is a reference, not to the physical mouth, but to the medulla oblongata, or *agya chakra*. In the physical body, the mouth takes in physical food. The astral body, however, lives mostly by energy, which it draws in through the medullary center. The two rays that "go out" from the medulla oblongata move outward from that center *into* the body, not outward *from* the body. These two rays represent the *ida* and *pingala nadis*, as they are known in Sanskrit: nerve channels, in other words, which travel along the length of the astral spine. (In fish, these two nerves may be seen running alongside the whole spine.) These nerve channels represent central bodily realities, producing the *impulse* to inhale, without which one would feel no inclination to breathe. The subtle cause of inhalation is an upward flow of energy through *ida* in the astral spine. The subtle cause of exhalation, similarly, is a downward flow through *pingala*.

Energy flowing upward and downward through the *ida* and *pingala* nerve channels accompanies our emotional reactions to the world around us:

upward, when the reactions are positive; downward, when they are negative. (This is a common human experience, as I've indicated before. When a person feels good about something he tends to inhale, and also to sit up straighter. When he feels badly, on the other hand, he usually sighs, and also slumps forward as if unwilling to take another deep breath.)

When a baby is born, it utters its first cry (in disappointment, Yogananda said, at having to cope once again with matter!). Before it can emit that first cry, however, it must inhale. At death, one's final act is a prolonged exhalation.

The highest technique of yoga, known as *Kriya Yoga*, requires that one magnetize the energy in the spine, first by deliberately controlling the energy-flow in the two superficial nerve channels (*iḍa* and *pingala*), and then by neutralizing that superficial flow in breathlessness. Complete inner, bodily stillness then causes a withdrawal of one's energy into the central, or deep spine.

The deep spine contains three concentric channels of energy, each of which must be entered and passed through in turn. They correspond to the ring of golden light, the circular blue field inside it, and the silvery white, five-pointed star in the center, all of which together form the spiritual eye.

"Blessed is the man that heareth me, watching daily at my gates, waiting at the posts of my doors." (Proverbs 8:34) The **"posts of my doors"**

are the spiritual centers of the spine through which the energy must be directed upward for enlightenment. **"Heareth me"** (above) signifies listening to *AUM*, and also to the sounds that emanate from each of the *chakras*. (These are all subsidiaries of *AUM.*)

Even in outward, physical imitations, these sounds can be thrilling. A drum sound (or, alternately, a humming, beelike, droning sound) emanates, when stimulated, from the lowest (coccyx) center.

A flute sound (or, alternately, a sound resembling crickets, or a rippling brook) emanates when the second (or sacral) center is stimulated.

The sound of plucked harp strings, or of any plucked string instrument, indicates that the third, or lumbar center has been stimulated.

A deep gong bell sound is a sign that the inner heart, or dorsal, center has been stimulated.

A rushing sound, like the wind through tall pine trees, indicates that the energy is centered in the cervical center, opposite the throat.

And a symphony of all the sounds (the mighty *AUM*) comes when the energy is deeply centered in the *agya*, or medulla oblongata, or at the positive pole of that *chakra* in the spiritual eye.

"Watching daily at my gates" (above) signifies meditating on the chakras. In meditation, try chanting *AUM* mentally at each *chakra* (three times each is a good number), and endeavor to see the light emanating from each of them. Chanting

AUM at the chakras stimulates the upward flow of energy through them, toward the brain.

The **"garment down to the foot"** (above) indicates what is known as the *aura*, a light which surrounds the astral body.

The girdle, mentioned in the words, **"and girt about the paps with a golden girdle,"** is that extra energy of love which surrounds the heart region.

"When the enemy [Satan] shall come in like a flood, the Spirit of the Lord shall lift up a standard against him." (Isaiah 59:19) The standard, here, is the spine, which must be raised "against him" by straightening the spine, thereby allowing the energy to flow upward to the brain.

"Thou hast been in Eden the garden of God. . . . Thou wast upon the holy mountain of God . . . ; thou hast walked up and down in the midst of the stones of fire." (Ezekiel 28:13,14) The "holy mountain of God" is what Christian mystics have called "Mount Carmel," symbolic, for them, of the pinnacle of spiritual attainment. The **"stones of fire"** are the spinal *chakras*, each blazing with its own particular light.

And what, finally, do those words mean, **"Thou hast been in Eden the garden of God"**? Much effort has been expended by Christian scholars of various types to determine where on earth the Garden of Eden might have been located. That location is, in fact, *within every one of us!* Eden is discovered when a person's consciousness becomes fully centered in the spiritual eye.

Adam and Eve experienced a spiritual fall because they had succumbed to the wiles of the
"serpent." They were "cast out," therefore, from
the Garden of Eden. The serpent, here, signifies
especially (as we shall explain later) the temptation to indulge in the instinctive creative desire for
sexual procreation and enjoyment. (Interesting,
isn't it, that all sinuous dances, suggestive as they
are of a serpentine movement, are particularly associated with sexual temptation?)

More of this, however, in the next chapter.

Let me return now (at the end of this chapter)
to Christ's admonition, which I mentioned early
on in this book: **"It is more blessed to give than
to receive."** (Quoted by St. Paul in Acts 20:35)

When we give from our hearts to others, the
very gestures that often accompany that giving,
and also our energy-flow, are outward and self-
expansive. Giving to others is blessed, because it
brings us more "bliss." That is to say, it makes us
happier, for it expands our self-identity to include, in our own well-being, the well-being of
others.

The contrary is true also: When we clutch our
feelings to ourselves, as if holding them to our
chests, we become more *un*happy, for thereby we
narrow our own self-identity.

There is another aspect to giving also, however.
When we give of ourselves outwardly to others, we
expand our self-identity, but that act can't alto-

gether *release* us from identity with the little ego. *Sattwic,* self-ennobling qualities enlarge the sympathies, but are not enough *in themselves* to bring soul-liberation.

To free ourselves completely from ego-involvement, we must "give" also (and primarily) upward, to God, rather than only outward, to others.

When the heart's energy is offered up through the spine, and is allowed to flow freely through the medulla oblongata (instead of being blocked there) to the spiritual eye in the forehead, the ego-sense (which is centered in the medulla) is released, and spiritualized, to become soul-consciousness.

Medically speaking also, there is a connection between the heart and the medulla. The medulla controls the rate of the heartbeat. Spiritually speaking, when one's feelings (centered in the heart region) grow light and "airy," their energy rises naturally upward. The medulla oblongata also, in this case, becomes "light," for, receiving that upward flow of energy, it passes the energy onward to the spiritual eye.

When, by contrast, the feelings in the heart grow heavy, they exert a downward pull on the ego in the medulla also, and as a result bring one's conscious self-identity down into the lower spinal centers. Thus, heavy feelings lower the consciousness.

Our duty, if we love God and the teachings of His son Jesus Christ, or merely if we want our own true happiness, is to raise our hearts' feelings and energy *upward*, toward that kingdom of God which, Jesus declared, lies "within."

CHAPTER EIGHTEEN

THE SERPENT POWER

"And as Moses lifted up the serpent in the wilderness, even so must the Son of man be lifted up: That whosoever believeth in him should not perish, but have eternal life." (John 3:14,15)

IT MUST BE NOTED SPECIFICALLY, HERE, THAT IT IS Jesus who speaks these words. Their very context, especially as the passage continues, clearly suggests his future crucifixion. This passage occurs quite early, however, in the Gospel of John, even before the story of his encounter with the woman of Samaria. There *simply has* to have been some other interpolation here—a reshuffling of certain statements and events. I don't mean to suggest that those who later wrote Christ's story might have resorted to outright invention. How else to explain, however, this clear reference to the

Crucifixion, an event about which no one listening to Christ's discourse could have had even the slightest suspicion?

What makes sense here, surely—and in many other passages as well—is that Christ's words, although recorded conscientiously (as I truly believe they were, for they ring with divine power),* were nevertheless selected from things Jesus said at *different* times, and were later compiled in a way that seemed reasonable to those who were writing later on from memory, even many years after his death, or who tried to reconstruct his sayings in such sequences as seemed to them best. Indeed, even the most conscientious amanuensis has little choice, sometimes, other than to replace a word, or an expression, that is unfamiliar to him with another that he can at least understand.

The reference to Moses lifting up a serpent in the wilderness is deeply esoteric. The reference to "the wilderness" makes it doubly so, as we'll see presently. Again, this reference to the "son of man" had to have a universal meaning, referring to all men, for the essence of its teaching here is universally true. The passage following it, which I'll quote in the next chapter, seems clearly to be a non-sequitur. Speaking of Moses raising the serpent, and relating that story to Christ's Crucifixion, seems highly inappropriate,

---

*I reject completely the claims made by certain modern scholars who say that some of the teachings attributed to Jesus were scholarly inventions.

besides—indeed, somewhat unfortunately so, since Jesus Christ, in that case, is comparing himself to a serpent! Calvary, moreover, was never described as resembling, or as being anywhere near, a wilderness.

Intellectual analysis can take one very far away from the truth. I do, however, remember once asking my Guru, "Was Moses a master?"

"Oh yes!" he replied emphatically. "He would have to have been: He lifted up the serpent in the wilderness." It was obvious to me, from the vigor of his reply, that he was speaking from revealed wisdom. Yogananda knew Moses, inwardly in his soul. He only gave that further explanation in order to underscore the truth of his reply. Still, what my Guru said Moses had accomplished in "raising the serpent" indicated that Moses was divinely awake in God. That "lifting up" in no way referred to any external event like the Crucifixion.

"Wilderness" was an expression used often in the East as a spiritual symbol. We should remember, moreover—as Yogananda sometimes reminded us—that Jesus Christ lived in what Europeans considered the East. "Wilderness," in this passage, symbolized the perfect stillness of deep meditation, in which no "wild flowers" of worldly distraction bloom.

Also, in the *Rubaiyat of Omar Khayyam*—a true Persian scripture of the eleventh century A.D., and one about which Yogananda wrote a deeply

inspiring commentary*—there is the quatrain
(*rubai*), dearly familiar to English speakers:

> Here with a Loaf of Bread beneath the
>   Bough,
> A Flask of Wine, a Book of Verse—and Thou
>   Beside me singing in the Wilderness—
> And Wilderness is Paradise enow.

Yogananda's "Paraphrase" of this passage,
taken from his book, precedes his longer explanation of it. The paraphrase reads:

"Withdraw your life-force [bread, or life-sustain-
ing energy] into the center of the tree [the bough]
of life, the spine, and bask there in the cool shade
of inner peace. As the sensory tumult dies away,
drink the wine of bliss from the flask of your
devotion. Commune inwardly with your Divine
Beloved.

"And in stillness, listen: For the Singing
Blessedness will satisfy your every heart's desire,
and entertain you forever with melodies of perfect
wisdom."

The "Book of Verse" (not mentioned in the above
paraphrase) is defined four pages later as: "The
inspirations emanating from the book of the
heart, once the restless emotions have been
soothed, transformed into calm feeling."

Let us study the original account of Moses lift-

*Available in the book, *The Rubaiyat of Omar Khayyam Explained*
by Paramhansa Yogananda (edited by me), from Crystal Clarity
Publishers, Nevada City, California 95959.

ing up the serpent in the wilderness.

"And the Lord said unto Moses, Make thee a fiery serpent, and set it upon a pole: and it shall come to pass, that every one that is bitten, when he looketh upon it, shall live.

"And Moses made a serpent of brass, and put it upon a pole, and it came to pass, that if a serpent had bitten any man, when he beheld the serpent of brass, he lived." (Num. 21:8,9)

Brass is a shiny substance. Here, it symbolizes the light of inner energy as it travels up the spine. This story is deeply esoteric. In the last chapter I referred briefly to the sinuous movement of the hips that one sees in certain dances. The clear intention behind that movement is a sexual invitation. A rotary movement—usually counter-clockwise when viewed from above—suggests energy moving downward from the second *chakra*, or sacral center. When that center is stimulated, and the energy within it flows outward, sexual desire awakens in the body. (With the first stirring of sexual desire, the spiritually aware person will also feel a slight stirring of energy in his second *chakra*. He should recognize, even in that faint stirring, a preliminary warning: sufficient, let us say, for the wise.)

Let us return this discussion to our "beginnings." At conception, the sperm and ovum cells unite, then subdivide to produce the physical body. Their creative activity begins at the medulla oblongata, which remains ever thereafter the seat of life in the body. From that point, the energy moves outward and downward to create the brain, the spine, the nervous system, and the rest of the body.

When the life-energy has completed its creation of the spine, its downward flow comes to a stop, physically speaking, at the base of the spine. The nerves emanating from the lowest center (the coccyx) flow outward to the organs of excretion and to the lower limbs. The base of the spine now becomes the negative pole of a magnet somewhat similar to a bar magnet.

Bar magnets are formed when their molecules, each with its own north-south polarity, all face in a single north-south direction. So long as those molecules face randomly, the overall magnetism of the bar is neutralized.

An ancient Hermetic teaching contains the words, "As above, so below." The truth of these words may be seen all around us. It explains the correlation between material and spiritual realities. Magnetism in a bar of metal is, as I said, in many ways comparable to magnetism in the human spine, and also to the many magnetic qualities that human beings manifest. Gravity, a universal force in the material world, is comparable, spiritually, to the attractive power of love. Physical pleasures have their spiritual counterpart in inner, soul-joy.

Again, planetary motion around the sun is reminiscent, materially speaking, of the individual

soul in its relationship to God. A planet is held—
one might even say, drawn inward—by the sun's
gravity. At the same time, however, it is kept in
outward orbit by the centrifugal force generated
by its movement around the sun. Divine Love is
thus duplicated, on the material plane, by the
gravitational pull of the sun, which holds its planets in orbit around it. And the balancing centrifugal force which pulls the planets away finds its
counterpart in our material desires, which keep
pulling us ever outward, away from God's center
within, causing us to keep our distance from Him.

The molecules in a bar magnet have their subtle counterpart in the mental tendencies, or *samskars*, that dwell in men's hearts, and that settle
at different heights along the spine. As mental
tendencies can disperse their inner store of energy
in countless different directions, seeking an ever-
imaginary outer fulfillment, so our potentially
enormous magnetism is neutralized by what Yogananda called "the conflicting cross-currents of
ego." The more those *samskars* can be directed
upward, in spiritual aspiration, toward the "Christ
center" in the spiritual eye, and from there to the
top of the head in the *sahasrara*, or "thousand-
petaled lotus" (the "seat," or "throne" of God), the
more greatly is the yogi's overall magnetism increased.

Materialistic consciousness, too, can generate
considerable magnetism when people focus their
minds on any specific material goal, and when

they direct all their energy toward achieving it. Thus, egotists and materialists are capable also, with their magnetism, of strongly influencing others, even if those others have loftier goals than their own. Thus, strongly magnetic materialists sometimes succeed even in inducing spiritually inclined people to assume their own far-less-than-noble ambitions. Even those who are devoted to doing evil can develop a strong evil magnetism if they direct their energies one-pointedly toward dark ends.

It is important, particularly for well-meaning Christians, to understand these truths, for many of them insist that one ought to love everyone equally. It is indeed important to love everyone, but I've always remembered something my Guru once told me: "You must be practical in your idealism." The love we give should, for one thing, be impersonal. In many cases, moreover, it should be restrained from outward expression, and cherished only in the heart. In one's behavior toward others, it is important studiously to avoid sending energy to people whose consciousness does not resonate sympathetically with one's own, and particularly with one's own most cherished goals in life. One should particularly avoid anyone who displays dark, evil magnetism. For you must never imagine that your own spiritual magnetism will protect you merely because you are well-meaning. In any magnetic encounter, it is always, Yogananda explained, the stronger magnet which prevails.

Those who aspire to develop spiritual awareness should avoid people who emanate either a strongly materialistic or an evil vibration. They should take care also never to reach out with sympathy to such people in the hope, perhaps, of uplifting them. Such efforts, unless one is very strong in himself, are fraught with danger.

Paramhansa Yogananda stated that this principle of magnetic exchange needs to be viewed as a definite rule of life, especially for spiritual aspirants. Always, when two persons of different, and particularly of incompatible, interests mix together, the one with the stronger magnetism will influence the other, weaker one. If the stronger magnetism is materialistic, then, no matter how idealistic the weaker one may be, that combination will produce two materialistic magnets. One who is trying to develop success magnetism of any kind may, in fact, succumb to strong failure magnetism if he mixes with failures. He should mix *consciously*, therefore, and as much as possible, with people who are successful in life, and particularly with those who have succeeded in his own field of endeavor.

Whatever skills you want to develop—be they business, artistic, athletic, culinary, or spiritual— make it a point to court, *with concentration*, the association of those who have a strong success magnetism in that field. Aspiring artists should mix with successful artists (especially with those whose tastes are compatible with their own), and should avoid those pleasant but vague bohemian types who are mere dabblers at their craft.

Aspiring devotees, then, must consider it supremely important to abide by the principle which, in India, is called *satsang*, or wholesome and uplifting spiritual company. The aspirant shows particularly clear discrimination if he seeks the company of saints, or lives together with other devotees who spend dedicated lives in a monastery or spiritual community.

Therefore also the early Christians—who must surely have received their first encouragement in this direction from Jesus Christ himself—gathered in groups for worship, and also lived together, later on, in little Christian communities.

No illustration is ever perfect, of course. Thus, a bar magnet has the drawback that its molecules are inert. Thoughts, on the other hand, are conscious and vibrant; they can be directed deliberately, by an act of will, toward any desired goal. The more one-pointed that focus, the greater will be one's magnetism. Human beings can develop an infinite variety in their magnetism. To succeed in any field, success magnetism in that field is mandatory.

Mix attentively, therefore, with people who have succeeded in your own field. If your aim is spiritual, keep the company of those who aspire to become holy. Try especially to mix with saints. This is a cardinal principle. If you, as a spiritual aspirant, are forced to mix with worldly people, then make it a point, if possible, to keep a "spiritual bodyguard": one or more friends who, like you, are sincerely following the spiritual path.

I quoted the next passage in an earlier context:

"Then came to him the disciples of John, saying, Why do we and the Pharisees fast oft, but thy disciples fast not?

"And Jesus said unto them, Can the children of the bridechamber mourn, as long as the bridegroom is with them? but the days will come, when the bridegroom shall be taken from them, and then shall they fast." (Matt. 9:14,15)

Jesus, while he was still outwardly with his disciples, served as their protector. People, on the other hand, with nothing to depend on but their own strength are wise to make it a point to mix as much as possible with others who are at least of similar mind.

Let us return now to our central point: the spine, and its resemblance to a bar magnet. The strongest magnetism is generated, as I said, when *all* one's energy is flowing unidirectionally. This it can never do, so long as the energy moves outwardly, away from one's center. It must, above all, be directed upward in the spine. For only the spine can channel one's entire flow of energy, whether upward or downward. On the other hand, though it is at least theoretically possible to channel all one's energy downward, toward a hypothet-

ically absolute evil, in fact such a goal cannot ever
be achieved for the simple reason that the inner,
divine Self alone is real and absolute. Any pull
away from that reality results in a diminution of
energy. Any outward flow, again, since it is a projection *away* from the source of energy in the
spine, becomes dissipated and necessarily, in
time, depleted.

Again I must emphasize that what we are speaking of here is *conscious energy*; we are not speaking any longer of the inert molecules in a bar magnet. Conscious energy has no physical limitations
either upward or downward. Passing up the spine,
that movement leads eventually to infinity. Moving
downward, one must, as a logical consequence,
be able to continue indefinitely toward the infinitesimal. The "south pole," at the base of the spine,
constitutes merely a physical full stop. The down-
ward-flowing *energy* is not so physically limited.

Everyone is magnetically pulled in two opposite
directions in the spine: upward, and downward.
The upward pull is that of spiritual aspiration—
the "divine call" within: God's love, which seeks
ever to draw us back to Himself. This pull is countered by the opposite, *downward* pull toward ever
lower states of consciousness, and *outward* toward increasing matter-involvement. These downward and outward pulls are the effects of *maya*,
which is also the conscious attractive power of
Satan.

In spiritually unawakened man, Satan has the

upper hand at least to this extent: Past memories and habits in the subconscious call to man silently, "Turn back! Seek comfort once again in what has been long familiar to you: your past, your old indulgences, your material comforts. All these things you *know*, understand, and have long *enjoyed*." The voice of Satan whispers to the mind: "Dwell on those thoughts! Was your life, then, really so bad? Why cut off every association with it? Why not reflect pleasantly, at least some-times, on that association?" The French have an expression for this allure. They call it: "*la nostalgie de la boue*: nostalgia for the mud.*"

The downward energy becomes locked, so to speak, at the base of the spine, and maintains there a firm grip. It will not release its hold, nor will it let the energy flow back upward again, until the "mud" has been vigorously shaken off and hosed away.

The energy at the "south pole" of the spine is called, in Sanskrit, the *kundalini*. When its thrust is downward, it is called the *sleeping kundalini*. When it begins at last to move upward, its move-ment is called *kundalini awakening*. To waken the *kundalini* is essential for spiritual aspirants. With-out such awakening there can be no true spiritual unfoldment.

If I seem to be expressing myself strongly here, it is because there has been much ignorant liter-ature published in the West, sternly warning peo-ple *not ever* to try to awaken the *kundalini*. This advice is sheer nonsense. It is important, on the other hand, to understand that *kundalini* awakening should be natural, never forced.

The *kundalini* has been known since ancient times, in religious circles of many persuasions, as "the serpent power." The reference is to the fact that the *kundalini* is said to lie coiled, serpent-like, at the base of the spine. Medical science, however, has discovered no passage of any kind in the bone structure at that base. What happens, rather, is that a spiral motion begins when the energy starts to rise up the spine.

When electricity is directed through an electric wire, its movement generates a magnetic field, which moves spirally around the wire. This fact suggests what occurs also with *kundalini* awakening: It is a spiral sensation in the spine itself. Often, this movement may cause the whole body at first to rotate in a circular fashion: clockwise, as seen from above. Progressive inner relaxation brings that outward movement under control.

"Davening" is the name for a Jewish practice during which men at prayer sway deliberately forward and backward. The reason for this practice may, once again, be explained by a movement that is sometimes caused by heightening states of consciousness. Inner *kundalini* awakening does often create a similar swaying in the body. A forward and backward motion is an early effect of that awakening. Merely to imitate that movement outwardly, however, is ineffectual; it cannot lead to any inner awakening.

The upwardly moving *kundalini*, or "serpent power," is blocked from further ascent by the outward flow of energy in each of the respective *chakras*, or spinal centers. These centers must, each in turn, be "opened." That is to say, their normally outward flow of energy must be reversed and directed upward, with *kundalini*'s passage up the spine. Only as each *chakra* "opens its door" to the upward-moving energy can the *kundalini* continue its upward journey.

When the energy that was formerly locked at the base of the spine is reunited at last with its highest point of origin at the crown of the head, full spiritual enlightenment is attained. That energy first reaches the medulla oblongata (the *agya chakra*). From that point it passes forward to the spiritual eye in the forehead. From there, finally, it rises and becomes united with the *sahasrara* at the top of the head.

Interestingly, Saint Teresa of Avila stated in her writings (I have not seen the passage, but was told about it by a Catholic priest) that the seat of the soul is situated at the top of the head.

This gradual awakening occurs in the "wilderness" of inner, meditative stillness. *Kundalini* is raised up the "pole" of the spine, as was the case with Moses. From then on, one can no longer be affected by delusion. Moses was also able, after his awakening, to free anyone else from the poison of delusion who had been "bitten" by the downward-moving "serpents" of worldly desires. Thus we read, in that above passage: **"And Moses made a serpent of brass, and put it upon a pole, and it came to pass, that if a serpent had bitten any man, when he beheld the serpent of brass, he lived."**

For the serpent of delusion—that which tempted Eve, and (through her) Adam, in the Garden of Eden—has a poisonous bite. It doesn't kill physically, but it can plunge to the "spiritual death" of delusion anyone who touches it willingly, and allows himself to be drawn by its fatal allure.

"Bah!" the unwary may scoff. "It's all in the mind. It can't hurt me. I know what I want!" The "serpent," however, is more subtle than the mind of man. Satan is adept at seeking out any chink in a person's spiritual armor. The wisest choice by far—and by all means the safest—is to keep a "body guard"—that is to say, to arm oneself with the company, at least inwardly, of a true spiritual master, or guru.

Thus also, we may see an explanation for that person, whoever it was—perhaps John the Apostle himself—who combined the first of Christ's words above (concerning Moses' lifting up the serpent in the wilderness) with the hint of Christ's later crucifixion. This passage occurs, as I said, very early in John's Gospel. Christ, moreover, had also raised his own *kundalini*, for he was a true master. It would be perfectly consistent with his deeper teachings for him to say, in reference to *kundalini* awakening (rather than to the Crucifixion), that "whosoever believes truly in him [the Christ] will not perish, but have eternal life."

It requires, however, a considerable mental stretch to tie this statement by Jesus, literally true though it is, to that completely unanticipated event: his crucifixion. It is, on the other hand, universally true that the "son of man"—every son of man—must lift his consciousness, through *kundalini* awakening, in order to know God.

A vitally important technique for this awakening is Kriya Yoga. A principle effect of Kriya Yoga is the circulation of energy around the spine, magnetizing it. It is also important, however, that Kriya Yoga be practiced with devotion, and with high spiritual aspiration. Too much has been made in the yoga teachings of the importance of raising the *kundalini* by merely mechanical methods. Many misguided students have, in consequence, turned an important spiritual teaching into a mere physical exercise. This, obviously, is wrong. Even without any such method, but with exalted devotion, many have experienced, during meditation, an awakening of their *kundalini* power. On the other hand, when *kundalini* awakening is accomplished by mechanical means alone, and without devotional aspiration, the energy may rise temporarily, but it will soon fall again. Until the heart has been completely cleansed of all worldly attachments and desires, the increased focus of energy in the spinal centers may stimulate any one of those centers in such a way as to flow outward, and to reawaken latent delusive tendencies.

In a book of mine, *Conversations with Yogananda,* I included an account of one time when our Guru said to us, "When one thinks good thoughts, the *kundalini* automatically starts moving upward. When one thinks evil thoughts, it moves downward. When one hates others, or has wrong thoughts about them, it moves down. And when one loves others, or thinks kindly about them, it moves up.

"*Kundalini* is not awakened by yoga techniques alone."

One significant aspect of that statement is that wrong thoughts move the *kundalini* downward. Isn't the *kundalini* already—one may ask—as low as it can go, since it is "locked" at the base of the spine? Unfortunately, such is not the case. *Kundalini* energy can move ever further down the ladder of consciousness, into the stygian darkness of the deepest delusions.

How far is it possible for the soul to fall? If it has the potential to rise toward infinity, it stands to reason that its potential for sinking downward must be limitless also. It is indeed possible, as I said before, for man to plunge down so far as to become identified again with the infinitesimal.

The implications here are far from comforting. They have been treated in my book, *The Essence of the Bhagavad Gita Explained by Paramhansa Yogananda* (as remembered by his disciple, me). Let me recommend, if you find this subject interesting, that you obtain that work and study it carefully. For it does not seem to me appropriate to go into it more deeply here.

These truths, then, must be clearly understood. Let me enumerate them:

1) All spiritual awakening depends on what we make of ourselves inwardly, and is minimally affected by outward material, social, or physical improvements.

2) The highway to God is the spine, and not some fancied outward "stairway to the stars."

3) True spiritual awakening depends on intense aspiration, and also on serious effort expended to keep one's consciousness uplifted toward God. The Lord has no favorites. "God," as Yogananda put it, "chooses those who choose Him."

4) You will win the Lord's favor not by superficial efforts, such as giving to charity (which is, for all that, a self-uplifting act, and will create good karma for you), but by sincere love for Him in your heart. Outward acts cannot ever, in themselves, bring inner spiritual freedom.

5) You will find God's guidance ever with you, the more you open yourself inwardly to His guidance. Accept wholeheartedly, therefore, whatever He sends you in life. His tests can sometimes be very difficult! Try always to refer everything back to Him. Hold *nothing* back for yourself.

CHAPTER NINETEEN

THE NEED FOR A PERSONAL SAVIOR

WHY IS IT THAT NOBODY LIKES THE BOASTFUL tendency? Is it because the boaster seems in some way to be slighting other people—by not giving them their own "proper due"? Not necessarily so at all. I think the general disapproval of boasters is because boasting contradicts a universal, intuitive perception: namely, that self-promotion is self-*demeaning*, not self-exalting. There is, as we all know, a whole world "out there" to learn from and enjoy. One should therefore, in his own interest, relate to it expansively, and not intrude himself on that vast scene by forever calling attention to himself.

Consider this wonderful truth, for people are wiser than they know: Everyone recognizes subconsciously that man is more than he appears. Science tries to deprecate man and make him feel that he is much less than he appears. This is because science views everything from the outside. Man, seen as a mere body, is tiny, frail, and almost pitiably weak compared to the elephant; dull in his ability to smell and hear compared to the lowly dog; by no means so agile as the monkey; and poor in his ability to see compared to the eagle. Viewed as a human ego, man, to quote Shakespeare, "struts and frets his hour upon the stage, and then is heard no more."

Yet somehow everyone feels, as Emerson wrote in his essay on "The Over-Soul," that when two human beings converse together, "Jove nods to Jove from behind each of us." Emerson then added that immortal sentence: "Men descend to meet."

The wisdom of the ages was expressed in such counsel as this one in the ancient Greek: "Man, know thyself (*Gnothi sauton*)." Again there is the dictum of Pythagoras: "Man is the measure of all things." Are these sayings uttered simply by people "tooting their own horns"? Everyone knows, by some deep instinct, that man is in some way, quite to the contrary, a veritable universe. His potential is, in a true sense, infinite. His ego clings almost pathetically to its minuscule self-awareness; defends it with a fervor approaching fanaticism; strives with grim determination to keep ever fresh and alive his sense of personal significance and importance. Deep inside each of us, however, we know that some essence in us exists that is eternal, and that possesses infinite significance. We are, indeed, *much more* than we seem.

It is only temporarily that we have this individuality. Something underlying our day-to-day consciousness is the true Self. In this "something," moreover, lies our hint of immortality.

God dreamed all things into an appearance of reality out of His vast consciousness. His creative work begins at the center of each point of manifested existence. It expands outward in every living thing from that point to its full manifestation. There is nothing in existence, ultimately speaking, except consciousness.

Consciousness, latent in all things, becomes increasingly distinct with the upward development of evolution. So also, with increasing clarity, does *self*-consciousness emerge gradually. The earthworm, though presumably not conscious enough to define itself specifically as a worm or as anything else, is yet capable of acting from its own center of consciousness. It can be trained, moreover—as I've said elsewhere—to seek pleasure (however dim), and to avoid pain (however vaguely perceived).

In higher animals, motivation is more clearly directed from within, both in seeking pleasure and in avoiding pain.

Man, at the summit of material evolution, knows very well that it is he, himself, who suffers or rejoices—not only physically, but mentally also.

Consciousness, quite independently of any outward shape it assumes, is the true criterion of evolution. Higher evolution depends on the soul's gradual emergence into clear, intelligent awareness. The summit of material evolution is reached when life finally expresses *self*-awareness.

In mankind, the ego is clear about its self-definition. The Divine Self, or soul, achieves at least some measure of infinite awareness, even though its sense of self is limited to the human ego.

Paramhansa Yogananda defined ego as "the soul identified with a body." All egos, as we saw earlier, are like little jets of flame on a gas burner, each one with the appearance of individuality, but each one being, *in fact*, only a manifestation of the unifying gas underneath. What gives people their illusion of individuality is the bundle of self-definitions they gradually amass, most of which are quite insignificant, but which become, in their aggregate, a heavy burden on their spiritual awareness.

As ego-consciousness becomes more clearly evident, so does man develop, along with self-awareness, more and more numerous attractions and aversions, friendships and enmities. The outwardly manifested soul—that germ of individuality with which, Yogananda declared, every atom is dowered—moves gradually up the ladder of evolution, becoming increasingly aware, until, in mankind, it becomes fully *self*-aware on an egoic level.

Though evolution is an undeniable fact, Charles Darwin misunderstood it in this one, fundamental respect. He considered it only in terms of creatures' changes in outer form. Thus, his view of evolution was through the wrong end of the telescope, as it were: he saw evolution as an entirely material phenomenon. His rejection of the spiritual reflected, of course, the norms of modern science. For science, as we know, decided centuries ago to eliminate God from its reckoning. It decided that God is "logically imponderable," and had better be left out of any scientific reckoning. Subsequently, science reached, therefore, the wholly unreasoned assumption that God, because He wasn't to be thought about, doesn't really exist. Since, however, that view was never reasoned, we may comfortably dismiss their stand as unreasonable.

The soul cannot change its intrinsic reality as a manifestation of God. It can, however, and constantly does, mutate its outward appearances. As the Indian scriptures put it, "God sleeps in the rocks, dreams in the plants, stirs to wakefulness in the animals, and in mankind becomes self-aware."

A doctor friend of mine, visiting America from South Africa, told me of his experiences in a clinic he'd established in the town of Durban. "I've sometimes seen it happen on Saturday nights," he said, "that a native will come in after a knife brawl at a local bar. I've actually seen people with their intestines hanging out of their abdomens, holding them in their hands.

"'Don't bother with anaesthesia, Doc,' they'll say. 'Just shove it in and sew me up.'

"I've seen women come in with their hands supporting one breast, almost severed from their bodies. 'Don't worry, Doc,' they'll tell me. 'Just sew it back on. I'll be fine.'"

One might think the explanation for this extraordinary indifference to pain must be that primitive people are less aware through their senses than those who are more civilized. In fact, however, primitive people often have keener sensory perception. They can see at greater distances than most "city folk" can; they can hear sounds to which most of us are insensitive. What differentiates them from us, their "citified" brothers and sisters who've had a more sophisticated education and training in the ability to reason logically, is that, in them, ego-consciousness is less highly developed. Like animals a step lower in evolution— from which level primitive people may have more recently come—their awareness of pain as an experience closely related to themselves is dimmer than our own. They may be aware that something is wrong, but they don't refer that feeling of wrongness nearly so intimately back to themselves, as man does once he learns to depend more on reason, and develops feelings that are allied much more specifically to ego-attachment.

Often, primitive people are also more intuitive

than those with an education, whose dependence on reason is greater. A friend of mine in Australia once told me of an aborigine employee of his who asked for two weeks off so that he might go visit an uncle. "He's unwell," he explained, "and has need of me."

"How can you possibly know?" demanded his employer. "Doesn't your uncle live out in the bush, far from any post office? How can you claim to be getting word from him?"

"I just know, Sir," was the only explanation the man would vouchsafe. When he returned two weeks later, his boss asked him, "And was your uncle really ill?"

"Oh yes," was the matter-of-fact reply. "He had need of me." For that aborigine, this extra-sensory knowledge was so normal he didn't consider it even worthwhile to discuss it.

Animals, too, have been known to demonstrate amazing extra-sensory knowledge. I remember reading years ago—to submit only one example out of many—of a family that had been compelled to move to the West Coast from a city in the American Midwest. They decided, with all the uncertainties they faced, to leave their cat behind them with some friends who said they would care for it. What was their astonishment when, two or three months later, that cat turned up on their new doorstep in Oregon. Their pet had come all that distance by foot!

Civilization develops the rational faculty, which

we need in order to cope with the multitude of challenges we face in a highly complex society. Proportionately, however, we lose our subtler, yet forever-natural, sensitivities. We may also develop tastes that are far outside the range of our natural physical instincts. Thus, we may lose the innate sense, possessed by many animals, for which foods are good for the body, and which foods it would be best to avoid. We may lose the instinctive knowledge of what, for an unspoiled human being, constitutes true beauty. (Look at the grotesque tastes in art that have developed in our day.) We may even lose the inborn human sense of what constitutes moral goodness.

Conscious spiritual evolution begins at the human level. Christians are mistaken, however, in their belief that only human beings have souls. Indeed, for every test that can be offered to prove that human beings have souls—reasoning ability, the capacity for kindness and understanding, mental clarity, latent intuitive ability—a parallel proof can be offered that animals possess at least some of these attributes also, sometimes to an even greater degree. Indeed, if animals don't have souls, then nothing, I suspect, could be offered in proof that human beings do have them.

Man prides himself on his reasoning ability. Animals, however, though perhaps not endowed with the gift of abstract reasoning, show a definite ability to "put two and two together" in a reasoned, even if rather more spontaneous, way. Human beings, on the other hand, over-addicted as many of them are to logic and to abstract reasoning, often possess less intuitive ability than their fellows, and less of it also than some animals. They may even lack common sense! The fact that man's overuse of his intellect produces, in some people, a mental unbalance is a sign that the intellect is not a soul-attribute. The soul is *central* to our nature: Deep attunement with it produces no imbalance of any kind. People can, moreover, lose their reason altogether without being considered, thereby, to have lost their souls.

No, what defines the soul is *consciousness*. The more *refined* that consciousness, the more perfectly does the hidden soul become manifest.

When I lived with my family as a boy in Bucharest, Romania, my brother Bobby, aged eight, went out one day for a walk with our Scottish terrier, Jasper. Local dog catchers happened to come onto the scene and, seeing this dog in the care of a little boy, decided to catch it and hold it for ransom. Bobby confronted them with courage, shouting that they had no right to take away our beloved pet. When his challenge proved unavailing, he grasped the long pole, at the end of which was a net, held it firmly, and cried out, "Run, Jasper! Run!"

Jasper, grasping the fact of his danger immediately, ran for his life. The two men went off in determined pursuit. At a certain point down Boulevard Buşteni, Jasper found himself temporarily outside their line of sight. Promptly, then, he hid behind a bush. The men rushed past him, puffing for breath. When they'd gone a safe distance be-

̣̣̣̣Jasper came out of hiding and trotted

we described this
ntelligence Jasper
 were speaking of
gue lolling out to
y clever he'd been.
er, in concealing
d of continuing to
evard, showed no
that he showed no
reaction when we
 he'd shown? If he
ent recognition re-
y what standards
eople have souls,

a more developed
nore specifically to
ms, every thing he
rience he has, and
as found in those
es about himself a
h become both his
n.

As man evolves spiritually, he develops an increasing ability to think abstractly. He can conceptualize God as being infinite. He can imagine

the Lord as absolute and omnipresent. No less-
evolved human being—what to speak of the lower
animals?—can achieve such rarefied levels of
awareness. The use of reason, on the other hand,
lessens the keenness of man's intuition. The intellect helps him to deal with reality as he perceives it through the senses. His intellect, however, as we've already seen, becomes a hindrance
to any quest for higher truth. It can suggest innumerable reasonable answers to questions. It can
never, however, give perfect certainty.

Thus, we see that the road to higher wisdom lies
in loosening and removing our self-created bonds,
including pride in our intellects. The process is
one of unraveling our cocoon of self-definitions.

Saints have loosed and severed those bonds of
ego-centricity. They understand that both direct
perception and indirect, rational understanding
must reach an intuitive level, which is forever beyond the power of involved reasoning. Only thus
can anyone retrieve, as the saints have, his natural soul-level of awareness: Superconsciousness.

The ascent up "the spiral stairway of [spiritual]
wakefulness" (as Yogananda put it in a poem,
"God! God! God!") brings one to the point where
self-awareness is no longer limited to the little ego
and becomes, rather, awareness of the Infinite
Self. Man perceives himself united once more with
the infinite Source of his existence: the Supreme
Spirit.

Human beings are so very close to that highest

realization! All of us have the same highly developed and sensitive nervous system, the same intelligence, and the same latent spiritual possibilities as have the saints. The only thing preventing people from realizing God as their own Reality is the simple fact that ego-motivated desires direct their energy outward, away from their own divine center. The lower animals, despite having instincts (which sometimes manifest as intuition, which is known also as instinct), have yet to develop the mental clarity to seek self-expansion to Infinity. Man alone, then, is capable of knowing God.

At the same time, as is stated in St. John's Gospel, **"No man hath seen God at any time."** (John 1:18) Human beings, self-enclosed as they are in their little ego-cocoons, and unable therefore to catch even a glimpse of the high, spiritual realities around and within them, cannot ever, in their human state, see God.

Our duty, then, as children of God—a duty assigned to us from the very beginning of time—is to realize once more that we are, and have always been, projections of God's consciousness, and must reclaim our oneness with Him.

Opposing that effort is, unfortunately, the weight of our self-definitions, crystallized by countless actions and reactions, and by innumerable unfulfilled (though self-created) desires and attachments. When we think of this burden—enough, surely, to sink us far under the waters of delusion—the task of achieving freedom from our little egos must appear so great as to make the labors of Hercules seem, by comparison, but child's play! The task, however, is not so bad as it seems.

On a large lake, the ice sheet that covers it in winter might take a power greater than the combined strength of thousands of men to be broken through, even if they pressed all together over its whole surface. To reach the water underneath the ice, however, is not so difficult if even one human being drills at a single spot on the ice.

The karmic burden most people carry is like that ice sheet upon a large lake. If, by deep love for God, and by earnest prayer and meditation, one succeeds in breaking through the ice of delusion at any spot of his "materially frozen" consciousness, he can penetrate to the water beneath that sheet and merge back into God, thereby becoming one with Him. The karmic burdens one has brought over from the past, represented by that large sheet of ice, still remain to be dealt with, but God's love will then melt it slowly away to nonexistence.

Therefore does the Bhagavad Gita declare, "Even the worst of sinners, if he steadfastly meditates [or tries sincerely in any other way to commune with the Lord] speedily comes to Me."

We cannot, in our present state, rise out of or expiate all of our sins of the past, which were committed with ego-motivation. As long as the center of our awareness remains the ego, it is very difficult to disavow ego-involvement altogether. Attempting to do so is like trying to overcome seasickness while tossing helplessly in a rowboat during a raging storm. Only from a higher level of consciousness can our understanding really prevent us from ever committing those errors again.

Only in God can all our past sins and karmas of every kind become expiated. Past delusions will be seen, then, to have belonged to a lower level of consciousness: mere residues of the "disease," now healed, of ego-consciousness. As long, however, as our consciousness is centered in the ego, it is from this point that every action, every sin (even of thought), will proceed.

Our present "job," then, is to get through the "ice" of delusion and enter the free-flowing water underneath. To do so, we must for the time being shelve any guilt we feel for wrongs that we committed in the past. We must simply love God, who has (let us remember) loved us eternally. As Yogananda said, "God does not mind your faults. He minds your indifference." In the communion of oneness with God, every wrong will be made right.

How soon will all this be accomplished? That, Paramhansa Yogananda declared, is up to you. "In that state of oneness," he once told me, "you don't really care whether or not you are perfectly free, for you see everything as simply a manifestation of God's bliss. You may take longer to reach final liberation, if you like, out of a selfless desire to help those who depend on you spiritually."

The real task facing every spiritual seeker, then, is (as I've said repeatedly) to shake off the ages-old addiction to ego-consciousness. How to do that, when the very understanding we would use to free ourselves is already hypnotized by the delusion of bondage?

Analyze yourself: When someone speaks to you slightingly, do you react in any way defensively? When you lose something expensive and beautiful, are you upset by the loss? Do you consider that loss to be *your own*? If someone you depend on betrays you, are your feelings hurt personally? do you, in consequence, wish that person ill? If you've been, occasionally, in a group where everyone ignored you, did you take personal offense?

Each of these events should be offered up in gratitude, with an affirmation of inner soul-freedom. By trying to extricate yourself, however, one by one from every blow to your ego—and consider how frequently life pummels your self-esteem in constant reminder of how vulnerable you are, as long as you cling to your sense of separate individuality—the job of banishing ego-consciousness will be so enormous as to seem endless. There must be another, and better, way out. Fortunately, as I hinted in the last chapter, such a way exists.

Instead of laboriously turning every molecule in a bar of metal in a north-south direction, there are two things one can do. One can direct a strong flow of electricity through that bar; or one can place that bar alongside another one that is already magnetized.

Similarly with man, one can direct energy lengthwise around one's own "bar magnet," the spine, by the technique known as Kriya Yoga. He can also make it a point to be close to, or at least mentally in tune with, the subtle influence of a saintly being who is already enlightened.

I myself faced this problem at the age of twenty-two. I had come to realize the sheer enormity of the task I faced in trying to raise my state of consciousness. It became clear to me that it might take virtually *forever* to spiritualize my altogether-too-human consciousness. Fortunately, the enormity of the challenge helped me to realize what, in my case at least, seemed obvious: *I needed help!*

Ego-centered human beings often imagine they'll be able to overcome their wrong habits and tendencies by the sheer force of will. Yogananda assured me at our first meeting, "That method just doesn't work." For one thing, he said, the very thought that one can free himself, and doesn't need help from anyone, is already evidence enough of bondage to the very ego one needs to overcome!

Therefore is it stated in the Gospel of St. John: **"But as many as received him, to them gave he power to become the sons of God, even to them that believe on his name."** (John 1:12)

Without help from above, it would be impossible

to extricate oneself from the fetters of ego-delusion. Is it sufficient even today, then, to "believe on" Christ's name? We have quoted the following passage elsewhere, giving it a different emphasis:

"Then came to him the disciples of John, saying, Why do we and the Pharisees fast oft, but thy disciples fast not?

"And Jesus said unto them, Can the children of the bridechamber mourn, as long as the bridegroom is with them? but the days will come, when the bridegroom shall be taken from them, and then shall they fast." (Matt. 9:14,15)

Jesus spoke of the importance, to his disciples, of his physical presence among them. His death and resurrection would demonstrate his divinity to the world, but he also stressed the special importance, to true disciples, of their having him with them in the flesh:

"Yet a little while is the light with you. Walk while ye have the light, lest darkness come upon you: for he that walketh in darkness knoweth not whither he goeth.

"While ye have light, believe in the light, that ye may be the children of light." (John 12:35,36)

Jesus was declaring the importance of having a personal guide and savior. This is one of the principles of *Sanaatan Dharma*, which was also the essence of Christ's teachings.

St. John's Gospel declares:

"God so loved the world, that he gave his

only begotten Son, that whosoever believeth in him should not perish, but have eternal life.

"For God sent not his Son into the world to condemn the world; but that the world through him might be saved.

"He that believeth on him is not condemned: but he that believeth not is condemned already, because he hath not believed in the name of the only begotten Son of God.

"And this is the condemnation, that light is come into the world, and men loved darkness rather than light, because their deeds were evil.

"For every one that doeth evil hateth the light, neither cometh to the light, lest his deeds should be reproved.

"But he that doeth truth cometh to the light, that his deeds may be made manifest, that they are wrought in God." (John 3:16–21)

The essence of that expression, "Son of God," is, as I explained earlier, *impersonality*. The "Son of God," as Yogananda declared, is not Jesus the man, but the infinite Christ consciousness, which dwelt consciously within him: the reflection not only in his own body, but in every atom of creation of the omnipresent, eternally motionless Spirit beyond all vibration.

The following passages may be taken as references to the *kundalini*, which we described in the last chapter. The more obvious meaning, however, works well here also:

"Then said Jesus unto them, When ye have lifted up the Son of man, then shall ye know that I am *he*, and that I do nothing of myself; but as my Father hath taught me, I speak these things." (John 8:28)

"And I, if I be lifted up from the earth, will draw all men unto me.

"This he said, signifying what death he should die." (John 12:32,33)

All of us, when we have lifted ourselves above body-consciousness in deep inner communion, will recognize the Christ consciousness that manifested in Jesus, and that has been manifested in every great master.

At the same time it would also be true to take this passage as signifying that people everywhere will see, in Jesus Christ's death and resurrection, that he did indeed have the divine power of God. Who else, indeed, could have risen triumphant over that tyrant Death himself? Nevertheless, Jesus, in telling his disciples (in effect) to "draw as much from me as you can while you still have me with you," was saying that a living guide is, for the true seeker, a necessity.

Christian tradition is not totally lacking in the concept of what the Indian teachings call the *guru.* The Eastern Orthodox Church, which is as ancient as the Roman Catholic, stressed the importance of the *staretz,* or personal teacher and spiritual guide: a concept not essentially different from that of the guru. Yogananda stressed the importance of having a guru. He also said to me that there must be at least one physical contact with one's guru. And he told me emphatically, "If you question scripture, or challenge it, it can't answer you, but a guru *can* answer you, and can set you straight on any errors in your understanding."

To attune one's consciousness with that of a true guru—one, that is to say, who is himself free from ego-consciousness and fully aware of God as the sole Reality—is the only way to break out of self-incarceration in the prison of the ego. Most people, alas, feel little or no incentive to make such a "prison break." Desires, habits, attachments, and the energy (that is to say, the karmas) they have directed outward constantly in the past—actions for which they themselves, of their own nature, feel the inner need in some way to complete—keep their attention riveted on outer fulfillment. Hence is it that the Bhagavad Gita says, "Out of a thousand, [only] one seeks Me."

It is said also, in the scriptural tradition of which the Bhagavad Gita is a foremost example, "One moment in the company of a saint can be your raft over the ocean of delusion." A saint's company carries that great blessing because, as I stated in the last chapter, his (or her) magnetism can help to redirect people's "molecules" of mental tendencies, and to reawaken in them the desire to reach up toward more truly spiritual goals in life.

In the beginning of this awakening process, people seek spiritual fulfillment by listening to spiritual discourses and reading spiritual literature. As their consciousness becomes more refined spiritually, they begin to seek out the company of saints, or of others who possess spiritual wisdom: persons who can teach them personally also.

Finally—for God is ever actively present in the souls of men—those who are deeply sincere are drawn by divine grace to someone who has been empowered to assume the duty of guiding them out of the fixations born of ego-consciousness to perfect Self-realization. This person is their divinely destined guru—or, in the ancient Christian tradition, their *staretz*, or personal link to Christ, their Supreme Savior.

The link with the guru, once forged, is eternal. Even after one achieves spiritual freedom himself, and becomes in his turn a true master, that sacred bond remains as one of eternal friendship. With final liberation in God, all souls are, of course, one in Divine Perfection; no distinction of individuality remains. Their *memory*, however, of individuality, and therefore also of their special relationship with one another in God, exists in Omniscience for eternity. Thus, if ever again master and disciple appear together in this dream-play of God's, their soul-link will remain—not necessarily as teacher and student, but always as one of eternal, divine friends.

"But doesn't aspiration to embrace something so vast as infinity"—one may ask—"create a comparably vast tension in oneself?" Most people, I imagine, at one time or another have feared, at least subconsciously, the stress that, imagination tells them, must be involved in seeking God. The answer is contained in an earlier quote from Saint Augustine: "Lord, Thou hast made us for Thyself, and our hearts are restless until they find their rest in Thee."

The popular Christian saying expresses a valid, important, and eternal truth: "If you raise one hand to God, He will lower two hands to uplift you." God Himself it is who inspires you to reach toward Him with ever-increasing love. God's love it is, again, in your heart which inspires you to cast off all sense of body and ego, like a serpent shedding its skin.

"The spiritual path." Yogananda used to tell us, "is twenty-five percent your own effort, twenty-five percent the guru's effort on your behalf, and fifty percent the grace of God." Don't let delusion-inspired thoughts whip up needless worries, like waves upon your mental lake, about tension and hardship. No one who has reached the Divine Shores has ever described that attainment as anything but a supreme fulfillment. Remember: As long as your desire for God is sincere, it will be He Himself who gives you the strength you need, which is to say, the dynamic energy to find Him.

Jesus Christ sometimes spoke in terms that, from anyone who had attained a union with God less perfect than his, must surely have seemed almost embarrassingly boastful and arrogant.

"I am the way, the truth, and the life: no man cometh unto the Father, but by me." (John 14:6)

Jesus went on to say: **"If ye had known me, ye should have known my Father also: and from henceforth ye know him, and have seen him."** (the same chapter, verse 7)

He also said, **"Where two or three are gathered together in my name, there am I in the midst of them."** (Matt. 18:20) These words were not stated in reference to himself, the man. Indeed, it would be absurd to think of him, in that little body, rushing from church to church on Sunday mornings so as to be, each in turn, "in the midst" of all his congregation of worshipers! Besides, his statement was, "There *am* I, . . .": present, not future, tense. He was not promising to get to each of them "by and by," as time permitted. His use of the present tense suggests, rather, an eternal reality, and an infinite awareness.

Saint Simeon the New Theologian, a great Hesychast master of the Eastern Orthodox Church (the "New" in that title dates back to the tenth century!) interpreted this saying also in an inward, mystical way. "Where two or three *thoughts*," he said, "are gathered together" *inwardly* in the worship of Christ, thereby focusing the mind more wholly on him, there will he be, already.

To the Jewish priests and rabbis, these and similar words which Jesus expressed were so offensive that, in the end, they crucified him. Reading his words in the Bible, one is surprised at how powerfully he affirmed the importance of his own mission on earth. That affirmation did not indicate, however, any lack of humility. He had no ego of which to be either proud or humble. It was simply necessary for him to speak in that way, because there remained so little valid spiritual tradition among the Jews of his time. It was necessary that he emphasize a truth which few would have accepted, had he declared it self-effacingly.

In truth, a God-realized master is far above any need to protect himself from personal pride by affirming humility. Usually, so as to set others a good example of humility, he affirms his own unimportance. Ananda Moyi Ma, a great woman saint whom I often visited in India, went so far as never even to refer to herself in the first person. When speaking of herself she would say, "This body." In her this was no pose. She was (as my Guru told me) a *jivan mukta*: one who has attained final oneness with God, and complete freedom from ego-consciousness. She did still have, my Guru told me, a little past karma to work out. Such a fully perfected being needs no longer to affirm his soul's freedom in God, for he has attained that freedom already. Still, it is a common practice among great saints, if only to set others a good example, to speak very little about themselves. All their energy goes, rather, toward the upliftment of others.

It is, indeed, perfectly understandable that the self-assertiveness with which Jesus so often spoke would have seemed offensive to the unenlightened rabbis of his day. They were, in their own opinion, the supreme authorities in Judaism. If Jesus were to appear and teach in the same way on earth today in any country in Christendom—not as himself, but as someone unknown—I venture to say that almost every priest, pastor, minister of religion, and every other sort of prelate would probably consider his bold self-assertion quite as outrageous as did the Pharisees. Unenlightened priests usually try at least, themselves, to make a display of humility—if only because boastfulness in them would alienate their congregations! Their humility, however, is a mask. Even their self-deprecation is only to impress everyone with how *good* they themselves are. How could things be otherwise? The ego cannot be shrugged off so lightly. It is the central reality of most people's existence.

In the next chapter we shall discuss further the reason why Jesus Christ, even among great masters, was exceptional in his mission, and in his need to affirm his own importance to that mission. For now, it is necessary first to understand that his Self-affirmation was never personal. He never emphasized his self-importance as a human being. All his utterances were divinely impersonal.

"Verily, verily," he said also, **"I say unto you, The hour is coming, and now is, when the dead**

shall hear the voice of the Son of God: and they that hear shall live." (John 5:25)

What, again, did Jesus mean by using the present tense here? He added the words, **"and now is."** Obviously, he was not referring to any particular time. He was describing a truth that is eternal. "Son of God" was, again, a reference (as Yogananda stated) to the eternal, omnipresent Christ consciousness with which Jesus was himself identified. In speaking of "the voice of the Son of God," he was referring to the Holy Ghost or Holy Spirit, the mighty Cosmic Vibration. Indeed, an insightful explanation of his subsequent statement, **"and the dead shall hear the voice of the Son of God,"** could not be that the dead, asleep in their graves (for who knows how long—*millennia?*), would hear his voice and come once more to life.

In fact, Jesus here was saying two things: First, those who are spiritually dead will someday hear, in deep meditation, "the voice of the Son of God," which is to say, the sound of *AUM.* Second, Yogananda explained also that at physical death the departing soul does in fact hear that mighty sound, manifested as a vibration which corresponds to its own consciousness. That special aspect of the Cosmic Vibration determines the nature of one's state after death during the interim period between his incarnations on earth, or on some other planet.

What Jesus is saying clearly here, however, is a

reference to people's present reality (". . . **and now is**"). Those who love God and meditate on Him can hear within them *even now* the great Cosmic Sound, which comes to waken them from their sleep of ignorance, and to raise them toward final oneness with God.

This communion first with *AUM*, before communion with Christ, explains, too, the Roman Catholic dogma which states that one must go *through* the Virgin Mary to reach Christ. The Virgin Mary symbolizes the feminine aspect of God, which is the Holy Ghost, or Holy Spirit. To unite one's soul with God, one must first pass through *AUM*. Next, one must unite himself with the Son (the Christ consciousness). Finally, passing through Christ consciousness, the soul reaches the highest possible (because absolute) state: union with the "Father," the Supreme Spirit.

Jesus specifically described persons who are as yet spiritually asleep as being dead. Consider in this context the following passage:

"Another of his disciples said unto him, Lord, suffer me first to go and bury my father.

"But Jesus said unto him, Follow me; and let the dead bury their dead." (Matt. 8:21,22)

His teachings, as we have emphasized repeatedly, were concerned above all with raising people from their *present* state of ignorance: from their material to a spiritual identity. As Jesus Christ said, **"God is not the God of the dead, but of the living."** (Matt. 22:32) He was concerned only minimally with outward cosmic abstractions. His real issue was not the end of the world; it was not Judgment Day, nor Gabriel's horn (which of course symbolizes the *AUM* Vibration in its all-dissolving aspect). His mission was to help those refined souls whose egos were still trapped in limitation, but who desired earnestly to get out of their egos and to know God.

What was his meaning, in the earlier quotation above, ". . . **the dead shall hear the voice of the Son of God**"?

Popular fancy has depicted people moldering in their graves until "Judgment day," at which time "Gabriel's trumpet" will raise them to be judged for their actions, and sent to wherever they are to spend eternity: in heaven, or in hell. This concept—barbaric, surely—might be excusable in people with over-literal minds, such as most men had back when Christians expected the Second Coming to occur almost any day. Indeed, Jesus himself was quoted as saying, **"There be some standing here, which shall not taste of death, till they see the Son of man coming in his kingdom."** (Matt. 16:28) And again he announced, **"Verily I say unto you, This generation shall not pass, till all these things be fulfilled."** (Matt. 24:34)

He was speaking of people's *present* potential for communing with God. Today, more than two thousand years have passed. It must be accepted that everyone who heard him speak those words did indeed "taste of" physical death. Thus, it must be obvious that Jesus, if he spoke the truth, was speaking of people's inner state of consciousness, and of their soul-potential for God-realization.

Jesus said also, **"And then shall appear the sign of the Son of man in heaven: and then shall all the tribes of the earth see the son of man coming in the clouds of heaven with power and great glory."** (Matt. 24:30) Even granting the possibility that Jesus literally meant he would appear in the sky, let us visualize him standing on a cloud over New York City. That cloud would be invisible over nearby Boston. How, then, could "all the tribes of the earth" behold him? The curvature of the earth—about which people two thousand years ago knew nothing—would make it necessary for millions of Christs to appear on an equal number of clouds—simultaneously, one supposes. Is it merely facetious to ask, further, What about broad deserts, which often have no clouds at all?

Jesus *has* appeared *already*, however, in clouds of light to true devotees in all countries who loved him deeply.

Actually to understand what it means to be a divine Savior is to realize that Jesus was not identified with his human body, but was identified inwardly with the Christ consciousness.

Jesus' mission was indeed special, even when compared with the missions of other masters. This, however, is a separate subject, and will be discussed in the next chapter. Meanwhile, let us keep in mind that Jesus Christ himself stated (as we have seen above) that his physical presence provided his disciples with special spiritual protection. That physical protection was taken away from them—as he himself averred it would be—by his crucifixion. And his removal occurred, relative to our own times, nearly two thousand years ago.

It is written in St. John's Gospel: **"Jesus himself [while he still lived] baptized not, but his disciples."** (John 4:2)

Though only a relatively few true masters live on earth at any one time, there has yet been no dearth of them over the centuries. Wise is that spiritual seeker who understands how desperate his own need is for a personal guru.

I was once challenged by a skeptic, "Why do you say I need a guru?"

"You don't!" I replied firmly. "You don't need one at all! Why even think about it? Just be sincere in your own search for truth."

I then added, "When you realize, however, that it is God you want, and nothing else, then you will understand also that you need help in finding Him. *That* is the time, and not before, when you'll understand that you do indeed need a guru!"

CHAPTER TWENTY

NEW WINE

S*ANAATAN DHARMA*, THE "E<small>TERNAL</small> R<small>ELIGION</small>," has to be the same everywhere in the universe. It concerns the path which all manifested beings must take who desire eventual reunion with their Divine Source, the Supreme Spirit. There is nothing but the Spirit in existence. Everything in creation is a mere appearance, manifested by the Divine Consciousness.

Sri Ramakrishna, a great master in nineteenth century India, used the image of sweetness to explain how the Eternal Truth could have assumed so many different forms. Sweetness, he said, can be enjoyed as honey, as sugar, as chocolate, as Indian "sweetmeats," and (in the West) as candies. All of them have in common that one quality, sweetness. The truth of *Sanaatan Dharma*, similarly, is expressed in different ways according to the different "tastes" and levels of spiritual refinement manifested in the different cultures at various times in history.

Christ, who taught that Eternal Religion, gave it particular emphases that were suited to the understanding of the Judaic people of his day. He referred, for example, to the cosmic power of *maya* (delusion) as Satan, and emphasized (as great masters in India have not, to my knowledge, done) that Satan is a conscious force dedicated to man's spiritual downfall. The emphasis of Jesus Christ on this subject differs from the teachings of India on *maya*, but the *truth* of it isn't different. Both *maya* and Satan refer to a conscious force—not to a specific being, but to a universal reality, for nothing in creation is unconscious. In Hinduism—which is, as I've explained heretofore, only one expression of *Sanaatan Dharma*—the emphasis, in discussions of *maya*, has been on subjective delusion rather than on *maya's* cosmic, all-pervasive power consciously to influence all men to submerge themselves in ever-deeper delusion. In fact, however—as Hinduism teaches also, even though less explicitly—the satanic influence is not only individual, but universal.

In *Autobiography of a Yogi* Paramhansa Yogananda wrote, "Thoughts are universally and not individually rooted." Jesus Christ's allusions to Satan as a conscious force, therefore, while they may sound strange to Hindu ears, belong nevertheless intrinsically with the truths of *Sanaatan Dharma*.

The Bhagavad Gita states, "O Bharata [Arjuna], whenever virtue [*dharma*, right thought and action] declines, and vice [*adharma*] is in the ascendant, I incarnate Myself on earth [as an *avatar*, or divine incarnation]. Appearing from age to age in visible form, I come to destroy evil and to reestablish virtue." (4:7,8)

God Himself, in other words, the Infinite Lord, incarnates on earth through a fully liberated master whenever a special need appears among men. When He does so, the essence of what that master declares, though it is always the same eternal truth, often appears dressed differently. Thus, although the Jews often challenged Jesus with the claim that his teaching was alien to their own religious tradition, the error was in fact theirs, not his.

His mission was to break down a growing tendency in Judaism to depend excessively on rules. He was sent to promote, instead, an appreciation for the supreme importance of divine love. Thus, when he and his disciples picked corn on the sabbath, and were accused therefore of breaking the commandments, he replied, **"The sabbath was made for man, and not man for the sabbath."** (Mark 2:27) In the next verse he went on to say, **"Therefore the Son of man is Lord also of the sabbath."** (How those concluding words must have set the Pharisees' teeth grinding! In their eyes, Jesus, in his apparent unorthodoxy, was anyway a mere upstart.) And when the Pharisees tried to "tempt" him on the subject of divorce by asking him, **"Why did Moses then command to give a writing of divorcement [to one's wife], and to put her away?"** Jesus replied, **"Moses because of the hardness of your hearts suffered you to put away your wives: but from the beginning [that is to say, in the pristine state] it was not so."** (Matt. 19:7,8) His subsequent words have secondary importance in the present context, where we are emphasizing the freshness, and at the same time the fidelity, of Christ's teachings to true *Sanaatan Dharma*.

God's message to the Jews of his times, which Jesus Christ had been sent to declare, had universal significance, but it was also specific and special, being intended for the Jews of his times primarily. As he said to the woman of Samaria, **"Ye worship ye know not what: we know what we worship: for salvation is of the Jews."** (John 4:22)

Again he said elsewhere, **"I am not sent but unto the lost sheep of the house of Israel."** (Matt. 15:24)

The essence of his teaching was divine love. He wanted to show the supreme importance of that love even over the commandments. For salvation cannot come by following the law alone. Krishna too, in the Bhagavad Gita, states that by good karma alone (that is to say, by doing all the right things) one cannot achieve liberation from ego-consciousness. Divine love, in *Sanaatan Dharma*, is the supreme secret.

Following the theme we were beginning to develop in the last chapter, I am also concerned particularly with another apparently novel teaching: the "saviorship" of Jesus Christ through all future ages. In the last chapter we saw the need for a personal guru. In Christianity, Jesus Christ has always held the position of the supreme personal Savior. Is this, in light of the points we've discussed before, a valid belief?

I must reiterate that a personal guru is most certainly a necessity for everyone who deeply desires to know God. All who live under the sway of *maya*, or cosmic delusion, and who live centered, therefore, in ego-consciousness, *must*, in order to know God, have at least one physical contact in their present incarnation with a God-realized guru. This was a teaching my Guru addressed to me personally.

Jesus himself, in passages we quoted earlier, told his disciples in effect, "Make the best use of this time you have with me, for I won't be here to protect you in the same way after I am gone." Though he was still a young man, the hints he gave that he would die early were plentiful, even if they remained largely unrecognized until *after* the Crucifixion.

Jesus said to them also:

"When ye have lifted up the Son of man, then shall ye know that I am he, and that I do nothing of myself; but as my Father hath taught me, I speak these things.

"And he that sent me is with me: the Father hath not left me alone; for I do always those things that please him." (John 8:28)

It must be strictly understood that Jesus was not urging personal devotion to himself.

"God is a Spirit," he said, **"and they that worship him must worship him in spirit and in truth."** (John 4:24) This same passage continues:

"The woman [of Samaria] saith unto him, I know that Messias cometh, which is called Christ: when he is come, he will tell us all things.

"Jesus saith unto her, I that speak unto thee am he." (John 4:25,26)

Elsewhere, he said also:

"My doctrine is not mine, but his that sent me.

"If any man will do his will, he shall know of the doctrine, whether it be of God, or whether I speak of myself.

"He that speaketh of himself seeketh his own glory: but he that seeketh his glory that sent him, the same is true, and no unrighteousness is in him." (John 7:16–18)

A few verses later he added:

"Ye both know me, and ye know whence I am: and I am not come of myself, but he that sent me is true, whom ye know not.

"But I know him: for I am from him, and he hath sent me." (John 7:28,29)

Impersonality is the essence of all true teaching.

You yourself don't exist, individually, except in idea; I don't exist; no one and no thing *can* exist except the One, Universal, Supreme Spirit, whose individual emanations all of us are. Our divinely assigned duty through eternity is to dissolve our separate self-awareness in the consciousness of that Eternal Self, which is infinite not in the sense of vast, but rather of having no finite boundaries at all. Jesus therefore said (again, in paraphrase), "God, who sent me, is the sole Reality, but you yourselves have yet to realize him. That is why He sent me, that I might guide those of you to Him who deeply desire to know Him."

Jesus, although so often constrained to use the first person pronoun, did so only because he had to emphasize that *he himself*, through people's attunement with his consciousness, could serve them as a doorway to Infinity. His words accomplished the particular purpose of discouraging people from going to the stream of lesser teachers who spring up constantly whenever people in general deeply desire to know Truth.

It is commonly believed among Christians that the disciples of Jesus were very much "of the people," and socially quite common. Yogananda stated definitely that such was not at all the case. "Christ's disciples," he said, "were already highly advanced spiritually." Fishermen and others of similarly "low caste" they may have been, and relatively low on the social scale, but they had, in former lives, attained high levels of spiritual refinement. Jesus saw their divine potential. It was on that basis that he selected them. Their social status had no meaning for him at all.

It has become a flaw in Christian thinking to insist, "We have our faults, all of us." I remember being slightly put off, during my mother's funeral, by a remark the minister made during his eulogy: "Of course," he said, "Gertrude had her faults." No doubt she had a few, but whatever they were, they were, in my opinion, very slight, whereas this man, I suspected, didn't know her well enough to name even one of them. His statement struck me as simply a concession to the common insistence on human sinfulness, "We're all sinners." Yogananda, moreover, taught us rather to see everyone in terms of his or her divine potential.

As regards Judas, I have already related the interesting discussion I had with my Guru, following his remark to me that Judas was a prophet.

"*Was* he!" I exclaimed in astonishment.

"Oh yes," he replied. "He would have had to be, to be one of the twelve."

Even advanced disciples, however, can still fall spiritually all the way until they reach the final stage—*Nirbikalpa Samadhi*, as it is called in India—when at last they attain full awareness that only the Infinite Self, God, exists. Thus, Yogananda explained that Judas still had some bad karma also, which he could have, but failed to, overcome. It was not his own absolute destiny to betray Jesus. There was, however, a definite destiny in the betrayal itself. It would have come about in one way or another. For it must be understood that the karma belonged not only to Judas, but to the Jewish people as a whole, to whom, as Jesus said, he had been sent. It was, in other words, a mass karma, not an individual one. Judas had to suffer personally the consequences of the part he'd played in that drama. Nevertheless, he was a great soul—far greater, indeed, than the many peripheral disciples who had come to the Master more recently in their divine search. It is better, in other words, to seek God and fail in the attempt—and even to fail greatly—than to be a lukewarm seeker—or, worse still, not even to seek Him at all. Judas Iscariot was, spiritually speaking, far ahead of the most successful materialistic businessman.

Nevertheless Jesus said, and Yogananda often reiterated, **"It were better for him [Yogananda's reference was to the betrayal by Judas] that a millstone were hanged about his neck, and that he were drowned in the depths of the sea.**

"Woe unto the world because of offenses! for it must needs be that offenses come; but woe to that man *by whom* the offense cometh!" (Matt. 18:6,7)

Jesus was referring at the time to those true disciples of his who were humble (**"as little children"**). He was saying also that others who received those disciples in Christ's name—not only as *his* disciples, but as instruments of the Christ consciousness—would in fact be receiving him, whereas those who hurt them would be committing an offense against the Christ consciousness itself, which ever resides within us all, but which is more openly manifested in those who love God. In the case of offense against saints who have achieved Self-realization, the offense is greatest, and the punishment, also, is more immediate, because, Yogananda explained, they have overcome "the thwarting crosscurrents of ego."

The greatest sin, of course, was Judas's betrayal of Jesus. This was a "sin against the Holy Ghost," with whom Judas had already been blessed to commune. To experience God's presence, and then, subsequently, to turn away from it can finally be forgiven only by the seeker himself, by turning back to the beatitude of which he has deprived himself. The return is not so easy, for that one "unforgivable" sin—unforgivable, that is, by anyone but one's self—sets up an inner vibration of restlessness, or uneasiness with one's self that can only be overcome by great personal effort.

People also sinned, however, and greatly, in persecuting the disciples of Jesus.

Yogananda said something similar regarding his own disciples. "The Divine Mother told me," he declared after a special ecstasy he'd been vouchsafed during the summer of 1948, "'In the beginning I sent you a few bad ones to test your love for Me. But now I am sending you angels, and whoever smites them, I [Myself] will smite.'"

Yet that disciple of Yogananda's who betrayed him most greatly was, for all that, a great soul, and (Yogananda stated firmly) will be liberated before very many more incarnations.

Sadhu Haridas (I've mentioned him twice already) fell from the spiritual path even though he was highly advanced. Yet, my Guru said, he achieved full liberation in that same lifetime. A student of Yogananda's, who was present when Yogananda related this story, objected, "How can that be? Isn't the punishment far greater for one who, though knowing the law, breaks it?"

"Mm-mm," replied the Master, shaking his head. "God is no tyrant. When you have eaten good cheese, then resume eating stale cheese again, you soon realize your mistake. If, then, you once again want only the good cheese, God won't deny you."

Judas, he told me, "was liberated in this lifetime." Yogananda said, "I myself knew him." Other disciples of Jesus must have achieved their freedom sooner, but I remember him saying that Mary Magdalene was born in the twentieth century as the Catholic stigmatist Therese Neumann of Konnersreuth, in Germany, and had not even yet achieved final liberation. He met this great saint in 1936.

The karma accrued by Judas for his act of betrayal was not only personal. It was a mass karma, and had to be borne by the entire Jewish people. As they—the **"chief priests, and elders,"** and **"the multitudes,"** speaking deliberately for all their people—cried out, prior to the Crucifixion, **"His blood be on us, and on our children."** (Matt. 27:25) Yogananda didn't often speak about this particular karma, for his concern, like that of Jesus, was people's spiritual upliftment and salvation. Nevertheless, he did often refer to the suffering that follows upon wrong karmic actions.

In the context of the Jewish people, although Yogananda under-emphasized this subject, I would interpolate from what he did say about karmic law that their subsequent suffering was primarily a consequence of that one great act of betrayal.

Karma is almost always mixed, however. Judas, for example, could not have betrayed Jesus had he not had the good karma to be born as a direct, close disciple. He suffered greatly for that betrayal, but his good karma stood him in good stead also, and flowered at last by taking him to divine liberation.

Yogananda often said, "God chooses those who choose Him." The Jewish people had chosen to walk in the ways of God. They could not have incurred the bad karma of betraying Christ had they not also had the good karma to attract him in the first place.

When a broken bone heals, it develops a hardness greater than the bone surrounding it. Similarly, the bad karma incurred by the Jewish people was due to the good karma, also, which they incurred in the first place by their intrinsic spiritual nobility. It was that good karma which had attracted the birth of the Christ among them. It will surely flower, someday, in spiritual greatness. For, as Yogananda said, "God is no tyrant." Jesus himself stated the way out of their karmic dilemma:

"O Jerusalem, Jerusalem, thou that killest the prophets, and stonest them which are sent unto thee, how often would I have gathered thy children together, even as a hen gathereth her chickens under her wings, and ye would not!

"Behold, your house is left unto you desolate.

"For I say unto you, Ye shall not see me henceforth, till ye shall say, Blessed is he that cometh in the name of the Lord." (Matt. 23:37–39)

The Jewish people must understand that God, who is indeed One God as they themselves declare daily in the prayer, "Hear O Israel, the Lord our God, the Lord is One," can come also to men "in the name of the Lord." God, being One, is the only reality in existence. Humility before Him, rather than arrogance (even when justified), will be, for them as a people, their ultimate salvation.

The following speculations may seem to be an intrusion on our theme. Nevertheless, they touch on the lives of so many people that I offer them in all humility for whatever they may be worth.

Was the formation of the modern state of Israel consequent upon a full expiation of the bad karma the Jewish people had incurred? This would, I believe, have been the case had that nation been formed in a spirit of humble and divine dedication to the One Lord. Because the basic ethos, however, behind the modern state of Israel is political, and not spiritual, I think this new country will find it has much still to learn about the spiritual law and its own role in fulfilling that law.

The Jews in Israel today describe themselves as basically atheistic, and as devoted to a purely political dream. How can such a self-definition help them to recapture their original and very real spirituality? It doesn't seem likely that the Jews will ever convert *en masse* to Christianity, particularly as the teachings of Christ are being taught in the churches today. There was, however, implanted deeply in their first faith—though later it became misunderstood—the concept of the Christ, or Christ consciousness. This concept needs to be understood as a universal truth.

These days, many Jews—the younger ones perhaps particularly—are turning to the yoga teachings of India. If, through this interest, they can recognize and accept once more the Eternal Religion, they too will be able to embrace also the teachings of Jesus Christ as a true expression of that religion, and will discover in them the universal truth in his teachings.

Yogananda predicted that the religion of all the world would be, in future, the concept of Self-realization.

The followers of Jesus Christ have erred greatly

also, in their intensely personal attitude toward him as the merely human Son of God, and in their inability to perceive his reality as the impersonal Divinity reflected in the entire created universe. Once that wrong twist in the road became fixed as dogma, many errors ensued as a natural consequence.

Thus, one thing that Jesus said has become a cornerstone of erroneous teaching in the Christian religion. We touched on this episode earlier.

"When Jesus came into the coasts of Caesarea Philippi, he asked his disciples, saying, Whom do men say that I the Son of man am?

"And they said, Some say that thou art John the Baptist: some Elias; and others, Jeremias, or one of the prophets.

"He saith unto them, But whom say ye that I am?

"And Simon Peter answered and said, Thou art the Christ, the son of the living God.

"And Jesus answered and said unto him, Blessed art thou, Simon Bar-Jona: for flesh and blood hath not revealed it unto thee, but my Father which is in heaven.

"And I say also unto thee, That thou art Peter [meaning *rock*], and upon this rock [*petra*, in Greek] I will build my church; and the gates of hell shall not prevail against it.

"And I will give unto thee the keys of the kingdom of heaven: and whatsoever thou shalt bind on earth shall be bound in heaven: and

**whatsoever thou shalt loose on earth shall be
loosed in heaven.**

**"Then charged he his disciples that they
should tell no man that he was Jesus the
Christ."** (Matt. 16:13–20)

First—as an aside, merely—Why did Jesus
"charge his disciples" not to tell anyone that he
was Jesus *the Christ*, since this fact was central to
the very validity of his mission? Never, in fact, did
he emphasize his human personality as possessing any intrinsic importance. **"My doctrine,"** he
said, **"is not mine, but his that sent me."** (John
7:16) So why, at the end of that last (and very important) passage, did he express the wish for this
truth not to be revealed?

Humanity, during the time of Jesus Christ, was
passing through a period, which was destined to
last several centuries more, of spiritual darkness.
I must explain this esoteric truth at some length in
this book, but for now the explanation will have to
be deferred since it would constitute a detour, and
would be too long to fit into the present chapter.

Still, it must be said here that people's understanding in those days was so matter-bound that
few could comprehend that Jesus, when he used
the pronoun "I," was not speaking of himself as a
man—not even as a great spiritual teacher—but of
the infinite Christ, with which his own consciousness was identified. He was like an explorer landing on the shores of a backward country, perhaps
on a Pacific island, and trying to tell them about

his own highly advanced civilization.

During World War II, the Allied forces created military bases on certain of those South Sea islands. Along with planes, ships, and advanced weaponry they brought food and unheard-of prosperity. Several decades later, according to my reading, someone returned to one of those islands and found the natives there worshiping before a reconstructed facsimile of an airplane, "propitiating" it and asking for a renewal of the amazing benefits they'd enjoyed for a time.

Jesus Christ was, in effect, teaching people not unlike those "primitive natives." Descending from the Supreme Spirit, he could give his listeners only as much as they were capable of absorbing, lest his message give them "spiritual indigestion."

Back, now, to the essence of the above passage. We've already pointed out, in support of our argument for reincarnation, that if there had not been Jews in those days who believed in reincarnation, the disciples would not have answered, "some say that thou art one of the [ancient] prophets." And if reincarnation was a false doctrine, Jesus would not have omitted to correct them after their reference to it.

Jesus continued, "But what about you, my direct disciples?" In effect he was asking, "What has been *your own* experience of me?" Peter alone answered, saying that Jesus was "the Christ, the son of the living God." From these words it is evident that Jesus had already spoken to the disciples about the Christ, as distinct from his own human personality. This manifestation of Christ was the Messiah who was "for to come": who manifested, through his little human persona, the infinite divine consciousness.

Presumably, other disciples had understood this teaching at least somewhat. Only Peter, however, demonstrated rock-firm spiritual perception in his expression of faith, which was born of the irrefragable insight of deep intuition. Jesus himself, Peter declared, was a full manifestation of that supreme, eternal truth.

Thus, when Jesus complimented him on the "rocklike" nature of his perception, he was speaking to Peter alone, even though other disciples were present.

Roman Catholics have persuaded themselves that Jesus was speaking of all futurity also: of a physical "church" founded on the "rock" of Peter's faith. This dogma is loaded with so many spiritual misconceptions that one wonders how even to shake each of them loose from the pile before casting it into the bonfire of discarded doctrines where it belongs. "Faith," for example: It wasn't mere belief that Peter manifested, in the ordinary sense of an intellectual hypothesis. Faith and belief are quite distinct from one another. Belief is provisional, whereas true faith comes only after that provisional belief has been tested and found true. If some of the spiritually advanced disciples of Jesus had not yet acquired such firm faith, how

could hundreds of millions of unenlightened, orthodox believers in future centuries pretend to
have acquired it? And how could this faith be preserved even for the long line of popes, many of
whom—so history declares—actually lived dis-
solute lives?

The word, "church" (in the sentence, "upon this
rock I will build my church") must be understood
deeply. A church signifies two things: a place
where people congregate to worship God; and also
a holy place, or "house of God." Paramhansa Yogananda declared this second meaning to be the
true one here. Jesus was saying, "On your firm
'rock' of inner Self-realization, Peter, I will be able
to establish my 'church' of cosmic consciousness."

Yogananda once said to me, "You will not be safe
[from delusion] until you have attained *nirbikalpa
samadhi*"—which is the highest state of perfect divine union. When Jesus said "the gates of hell
shall not prevail against it," he was speaking of
this absolute union. No lower state, wherein the
consciousness persists of having a separate, egoic
reality, can guarantee complete and final spiritual
victory.

All the teachings of Jesus were directed essentially toward helping the individual to attain his
own spiritual salvation. Jesus came, however,
with a particular *expression* of the eternal truths.
It was necessary for him to focus people's high
spiritual aspirations in himself as an instrument
of divine grace. Otherwise, the many schools of

thought that were rampant in his day would have diluted his message and made it seem merely another "school of philosophy," from whose teachings people could select as they chose.

Indeed, one of the great heresies in the early Church was launched by Arius, a fourth-century ecclesiastic and theologian who reasoned that Jesus can only have been a man, rather than the "only begotten Son of God." Arius stated his reason thus: If Jesus was God's son, there must have been a time when he didn't exist. The problem the church faced in those days was that, if Arius was right, and if Jesus was in fact only a man, then Jesus was at best only a wise man, but not one to promise divine salvation on his own personal reassurance.

In truth, both Arius and the Church Fathers were right. Christ (as distinct from Jesus the man) *is*, eternally, the Son of God. That manifestation of God does come into being, moreover, with the manifestation of Cosmic Creation. It is reabsorbed into the Spirit at the end of that manifestation, which appears cyclically.

A single appearance of Cosmic Creation is known, in *Sanaatan Dharma*, as a "Day of Brahma." It lasts for billions of years. At the end of that period it is dissolved in cosmic *Pralaya*, or "Dissolution," to be succeeded by what is known as the "Night of Brahma."

These grand, overarching cycles of Cosmic Time are repeated endlessly. It can rightly be said that

Christ, too, during the long Night of Brahma, is withdrawn into the "Father," or Supreme Spirit, and therefore ceases, in a sense, to exist. Thus, the Son does, in this way, come into being again and again with every re-manifestation of Cosmic Creation.

Arius, however, can hardly have had anything remotely similar to a literal understanding of this deep truth. His reasoning may have pointed in that direction, but it forced the false conclusion that Jesus Christ was, therefore, only a man and not the Son of God.

This teaching needs to be pursued, however, one step further. For even as Jesus was no *mere* man, so also no human being is *merely* human. Our potential is divine. Everything is a manifestation of God's consciousness—humanity even more so by virtue of having already attained, with ego-consciousness, a measure of *self*-consciousness.

Therefore it was that, when the Jews accused Jesus of blasphemy for his statement, **"I and my Father are one,"** his answer to them was, **"Is it not written in your law, I said, Ye are gods? If he called them gods, unto whom the word of God came, and the scripture cannot be broken [gainsaid]; Say ye of him, whom the Father hath sanctified, and sent into the world, Thou blasphemest; because I said, I am the Son of God?"** (John 10:34–36)

His divinity was a truth, in the last analysis, because cosmic consciousness is the destiny, and is *even now the potential,* of every human being!

What about the words Jesus spoke in that earlier quotation, **"And whatsoever thou shalt bind on earth shall be bound in heaven: and whatsoever thou shalt loose on earth shall be loosed in heaven"**? According to Roman Catholic dogma, these words mean that every ordained Roman Catholic priest has the power, after hearing a penitent's confession, to forgive him his sins. Paramhansa Yogananda, however, challenged this statement. "Test that belief," he said. "See what happens, for example, if you go to a priest and ask him to absolve you of the 'sin' of having overeaten the night before. Will your resulting stomach ache disappear? If so, *but only* if so, you might say that at least this particular priest has some power to forgive sins."

Paramhansa Yogananda often said that the simple word of a true master is "binding on the universe." A master's words, because they proceed from the realization of oneness with Him who created the whole universe, have great power. Only such a one can say to an ill person with true conviction, "You are well!" and that person must, indeed, become well. For his words must inevitably come true. Whatever he states with deep concentration will *have* to manifest itself in time in the realm of objective reality.

The ancient Indian sage Patanjali wrote, indeed, in his *Yoga Sutras* (Yoga aphorisms), that anyone who always speaks the strict truth develops the power to manifest outwardly whatsoever he declares with deep concentration.

We saw in an earlier chapter that Jesus, in referring to the "keys of the kingdom of heaven," alluded to the techniques of meditation—especially, Yogananda said, to the technique of Kriya Yoga—which "open the doors, or *chakras*, of the spine" and allow all the body's energy to rise toward the highest centers in the brain, where, truly, "the kingdom of God" exists in man.

A pundit (scriptural scholar) named Dinanath, whom I knew in New Delhi in the early 1960s, told me he had made a deep study of the ancient Christian writings. "In one of the old Hesychast writings," he said, "it is stated that when you repeat the traditional prayer, 'Lord Jesus Christ, have mercy upon me,' you should feel a coolness rising up the spine with those first words; and, with the second part ('have mercy upon me'), you should feel a warm sensation going down the spine." *Kriyabans*—practitioners, that is to say, of Kriya Yoga—will understand the inward meaning of those words.

The Way of the Pilgrim, a Christian classic well known in Russia and in countries westward from there as well, states, further, that the above prayer should be coordinated with the breath, inhaling as one utters "Lord Jesus Christ," and exhaling with the words, "have mercy upon me." *Kriyabans*, again, will find this counsel familiar.

Finally, Jesus spoke of these techniques as

"keys of the kingdom of heaven." What did he mean by "heaven"? We discussed this concept earlier. As for "kingdom," the term was familiar to the people of those days; it was something they could relate to and understand. In fact, much of what we might call "Christian mythology" springs from concepts that, in our own day, are out of date: a royal kingdom, with a Royal Personage ruling over it; a royal court complete with courtiers, crown, and a throne; hierarchies of power ascending pyramid-like to culminate in one, Supreme Ruler, God, enthroned high above all others with Jesus Christ at his right side and a host of angels below them in various postures of adoration. These static images possess a certain quaint charm, but for all that their existence in the scheme of things we now know must be classed with fairy tales. (Yes, Hinduism too is replete with comparably mythical images.)

All images like these were conceived during a relatively dark era, spiritually speaking. Modern Science has served mankind, in this case, as a divine broom; it has swept away the accumulated dust and cobwebs of uncounted centuries, and the litter of countless archaic concepts. Religiously inclined people should be grateful to science, therefore, even if most scientists themselves, after opening our mental windows onto vast and glorious vistas of reality, have allowed new dust to settle onto the scene. (The worst of this "new dust"—which I contrast here with "new wine"—is its materialistic belief that consciousness is something that must be *produced*, rather than being that which produces not only thoughts, but all material existence.)

Because science observes, it thinks that consciousness, too, must be observed, for scientists try conscientiously to remove the observer from everything observed. God, however, simply *is* Consciousness itself. The Indian scripture put it beautifully in describing God as Knowing, Knower, Known, as one.

"God's Kingdom" is infinite, of course, and embraces much more even than this physical universe. Indeed, scientists tell us that the material universe is *not* actually infinite, for, vast as it is, it is complete and self-contained. If one asks the obvious question, "What's outside of it?" science replies, "Nothing. You are applying finite ways of thinking to a level of reality where they no longer apply."

Only one thing can possibly be only as large as it is: that "thing" is thought itself! The thoughts formed by consciousness are what set their own limits. Beyond those limits, it may truly be said that nothing exists. The only way to expand that thought would be to push the thoughts outward by asking, "What lies outside?" That question would force the thought itself to expand and embrace a wider perspective.

We come now at last to the central theme of the present chapter: "New Wine." Jesus gave a new emphasis to *Sanaatan Dharma*, as it had been expressed through Judaism. The "old wine" of orthodox Judaism was a valid perception of Truth itself, but people's understanding of it had grown archaic and encrusted with layers of excessive reasoning. The Pharisees had banished God to a dry realm of carefully reasoned, man-made laws, and had burdened God Himself (their own concept of Him, that is to say) with characteristics that were altogether too human. Their concept of Him was of a jealous, angry, and vindictive Yahweh (Jehovah). Indeed, the old scriptures themselves described God as having these characteristics, though the descriptions were also taken out of context, and their truth, distorted.

Yes, God is indeed a "jealous God" in this important sense at least: His condition for revealing Himself to His children is that we be pure in heart, and that we have no other God, or idols of material, or outward-moving desires, before Him. God is not vindictive, moreover, but karmic law is very exacting—far more so than most people realize. And though emotions of any kind, including anger, have simply no place in the "kingdom" of divine consciousness, man does need sometimes to be "shaken up" by fear-inspiring images of the wrath of God. The search for God often, indeed, owes its initial energy to the "fear of God." (I remember Yogananda once scolding a disciple, and adding these surprising words: "God is angry with you for what you have done.")

God is, however, the supreme goal of life for everyone. He is infinitely loving, infinitely blissful, and radiates to infinity the "peace which passeth all understanding." In this sense, Jesus came on earth to humanize God by showing Him to be infinitely lovable.

At the same time, this was "new wine" for the "old wineskins," whose mind-set was to adhere strictly to the ancient dogmas. The new concepts Jesus proclaimed would spill out through many cracks in their brittle understanding. As Yogananda often put it, "Most people are psychological antiques. Their thinking, like old furniture, splits when it is exposed to the fresh air of new ideas."

I mentioned in the last chapter that Jesus did not die to save the whole human race from sin. He himself declared that he had come "for the lost sheep of the house of Israel." Even these "sheep," moreover, had to pay greatly for rejecting and betraying the gift God had sent them, which was His divine response to their good karma and to their prayers to be brought out of bondage. (They failed to understand that the real bondage is only one thing: to ego-consciousness!)

Even the disciples of Jesus did not become suddenly and completely free from sin. And Judas, who, in the end, deeply and bitterly regretted his sin of betrayal, and who (according to Christian dogma) ought to have been saved as much as anyone else by Christ's sacrifice from the consequences of his sin, had to pay the price of suffering for nearly two thousand years.

God is infinitely compassionate. At the same time, as human parents well know, a child needs sometimes to accept the painful consequences of its mistakes, lest it grow up spoiled, fretful, and emotionally immature. It would not even have been in mankind's highest interest for Jesus to have taken away all of its sins—or, say rather, the consequences for having committed them.

Finally, history itself shows that mankind became, on the whole, if anything even *worse* during the centuries immediately following the Crucifixion.

What Jesus accomplished through his divine self-sacrifice on the cross was the upliftment—but not, be it noted, the spiritual perfection—of his faithful disciples, that they might continue, on his behalf, his redemptive work after the death of his body.

Saint Simeon the New Theologian (who lived, as we stated earlier, all of a thousand years ago), asked the following question of his readers in one of his writings: Is a person really baptized if he is unaware, either at the time or later on, of any change in his consciousness? St. Simeon's answer to that question was resoundingly in the negative.

St. Paul, St. Simeon reminded his readers, in the epistle to the Galatians wrote, **"For as many of you as have been baptized into Christ *have put on Christ."*** (Gal. 3:27) "When you put on

clothes," continued St. Simeon, "aren't you perfectly aware that you have put on *something*? If
anyone is not so aware, what can it mean except
that he himself is either a corpse, or still naked?

"Verily," the saint concluded, "those who claim
to have been baptized, but who admit to having
experienced no inner spiritual awakening from
their baptism, can only be considered spiritual
corpses!" (Some of those old writers could be brac-
ingly caustic!)

Christians today, especially in the Western
churches, take everything, including baptism and
so-called new birth into the Christian life, completely (as they call it) "on faith." That "faith," however, is really nothing but blind belief.

Jesus spoke also of the need for a personal Savior. This need, too, must be fulfilled by some actual experience—by some kind of inner upliftment. The supposed fulfillment of that need must
not be left to any affirmation of mere dogma. I
have said that the true Savior is the guru, who
himself, or herself, knows God. I submit here
my own testimony: Living with a true guru
(Paramhansa Yogananda) under his personal
guidance, and tuning my consciousness to his
consciousness, have changed and uplifted me in
ways that I know I could never have accomplished
on my own.

Jesus said that his physical presence among his
disciples was a great help to them, spiritually.
What happened, then, after the Crucifixion? His

death did help them enormously, in relieving them of some of the burden of their own past karma. The impact on the whole world, however, was definitely to a lesser degree. Water always flows downhill, and if it issues out of the mountains onto a desert, it soon expends itself on those sands. Similarly, the karmic penance of Christ's crucifixion, being a single act and not renewed again and again in compensation for man's further and uninterrupted sinning, cannot have fully relieved the sins of all mankind. A finite cause, as I stated earlier, cannot have an infinite effect, for even though Jesus Christ's consciousness was infinite, the crucifixion of his body was a finite event. Wishful thinking, we should remind ourselves, is not "binding on the universe." Indeed, when we read the statement, "He died to save the whole world," we should bear in mind the peculiarities of human speech itself. In French, the expression, "*tout le monde*" (literally, "the whole world"), simply means, much more generally, "everybody."

What has kept Christ's true teachings alive has been the living presence of true saints among his followers. When their sainthood is ignored, discouraged, or persecuted, the effectiveness of his religion becomes proportionately diminished.

Sad to say, the situation in Christendom today has reached crisis proportions. Christianity, opposed on all sides by scientific arrogance; diluted by intellectual (but spiritually unenlightened) scholarship; filtered down through an ever-increasing admixture of egotism and worldliness, and distorted by claims like, "We're *all* saints!": The marvel is only that the teachings of Jesus Christ have survived at all! That they have done so is an indication of their true greatness. As Mahatma Gandhi said, in order to emphasize the reality of God: "In the midst of death, life persists."

Christianity today, however, has become a wilting plant. It is denied the "living water" of direct, inner, *personal* experience of God. Religion needs to be continuously renewed by the living presence of true saints, who have deeply practiced the high teachings *and realized their truth in themselves.* Most Christians today are like "old wineskins," incapable of accepting and containing the ever-fresh, dynamic "new wine" of Truth.

My fervent prayer is that this book, and its proclamation of Paramhansa Yogananda's *renewed revelation* of Christ's revelation, will initiate a renewal of dynamic, original faith in Jesus Christ.

Yogananda himself called his mission to the West, "The Second Coming of Christ."

CHAPTER TWENTY-ONE

GOD ALONE SAVES

ITOLD THIS STORY EARLIER, AT GREATER LENGTH. ON the occasion when Paramhansa Yogananda, traveling by train, was challenged by a fundamentalist Christian preacher, the preacher demanded, "Do you accept Jesus Christ as your only savior?" Yogananda answered, "I accept God as my Savior, and I believe that He has effected His salvation through many of His awakened sons, not only through Jesus Christ."

Christians as a whole have failed fully to understand how very impersonal Jesus was in all his references to himself. When, by contrast, he seemed quite self-assertive, it was always while speaking of the divine Self—as, for instance, when he said, **"I am the way, the truth, and the life: no man cometh unto the Father, but by me."** (John 14:6) His meaning, in such statements, was cosmic. His reference was to the omnipresent Christ consciousness, which alone was truly manifested through him. On the other hand, he never accepted personal praise. Rigidly, rather, he turned it away from himself toward God, as the sole Reality.

I saw this in my own Guru. Whenever people, Indian fashion, touched his feet as a gesture of respect and devotion, he always raised his right hand, with the fingers pointing straight upward, to indicate that he offered that gesture up to God where, he reminded us, it really belonged.

"And, behold, one came and said unto him, Good Master, what good thing shall I do, that I may have eternal life?

"And he said unto him, Why callest thou me good? there is none good but one, that is, God." (Matt. 19:16,17)

What we have here is a theme so grand that it makes me almost tremble as I place these words on paper in my poor efforts to explain the truths it propounds. The glory of Jesus Christ's divine essence was cosmic. By no means was it particular only to the time when he himself lived on the stage of human history in that little, human form. In a sense it is true that Jesus Christ died for all mankind— even as do all great, liberated masters. For although each of them incarnates on earth with a specific mission, yet also, in the divine effulgence and bliss-consciousness all of them radiate to the world, they bring blessings to the whole of mankind.

Sir Edwin Arnold, in his beautiful poem *The Light of Asia*, recounts the life of the Buddha. That epic-length poem describes thrillingly the moment when Lord Gautama achieved enlightenment and became the Buddha. The whole world, so that account states, experienced fleetingly, in that instant, a wave of upliftment. The wave passed wondrously through the hearts of all creatures, touching their consciousness with a breath of divine bliss. So does it happen in truth, when any soul on earth attains oneness with the Supreme Spirit. It happens even more so later on, when any soul, having finally worked out all the karma of its many past lives, attains final liberation. The blessing, in Buddha's case, was indeed of the latter, and still greater, kind, for he had been born already free. He, too, was an *avatar*, or incarnation of God.

When a soul attains final liberation (so my Guru averred), his earthly family for seven generations, forward and backward, are blessed with spiritual freedom. What degree of freedom they attain is, of course, relative and not absolute, for all beings must work hard to achieve final liberation. Nevertheless, what they receive—depending, each one, on his or her own receptivity—is a very great blessing. Perhaps they attain freedom from the need, at least, to be reborn on this material plane, sodden as it is with the heavy mud of delusion.

Dr. Lewis, Yogananda's first Kriya Yoga disciple in America, once asked him, "If a master's direct family are granted spiritual freedom, what about the disciples?"

"Oh, they come first!" was the reply.

Suppose one asks, "What about the whole world?" I feel safe in answering for him: "The world, too, is blessed with a degree of upliftment, though certainly it is not wholly saved."

The power of one ascended master—a soul, that is to say, that has finally attained complete liberation—is less than the power of a divine incarnation who has descended from the state of final union, and brings a divine dispensation to all men who will receive it.

How then, given this eternal truth, could the incarnation of Jesus Christ, a full incarnation of God, be less than a blessing on the whole of humanity? Were mankind never to be visited by such incarnations, the clouds of *maya* might easily close in forever upon the human race. No one, perhaps, would ever be inspired to strive for enlightenment.

People are born on earth as men and women. They grow up with the thought, "I am incomplete. I need a mate." And so, searching anxiously, they encounter someone who seems a likely candidate for bringing them that fulfillment. Rarely, alas, do they find the one, right person. They marry, produce progeny, and become wholly engrossed in their little families. Sexual union, instead of bringing them fulfillment, only depletes their energy— that of men, especially; women's depletion comes more through emotional attachment, and through the process of giving birth. Thus, human beings become bound more and more firmly to ego-consciousness.

And then, with time, they begin to "live again" through their children. This they do, however, not selflessly. Their ruling thought is, "*My* sons; *my* daughters." They dream of achieving, through those children, a more complete self-fulfillment. And then, as those children grow up and have children of their own, the first couple—grandparents, now—keep dreaming still of progeny, on and on through future generations. They project their dream of earthly perfection ever outward, farther and farther away from themselves.

After death, worldly attachments and desires still linger in their consciousness and, as Cosmic Creation was produced in the first place by consciousness, so those people's consciousness of worldly desires brings them back again and again—perhaps even to be reborn into the same family. Thus they hope, by means of constant "return engagements," to keep their private dream continuously alive and exciting.

People dream of eventually finding the perfect mate. Perhaps for a time they think that dream has been fulfilled. Again and again they are disappointed, however, and die with their dream of a perfect marriage still intact. Thus, they return to the material plane again and again. Like children engaged in an Easter egg hunt, they run from "bush to bush" seeking their one, true "other." If indeed every human being has a soul mate—and even electrons, it has been found, have their "twins" which work together with them in tandem, no matter how far apart they are located—how vast is the universe of conscious beings through which one's soul mate may need to be sought!

Yogananda, in his Bible commentaries, stated that one's soul mate may even be living on another planet. Final union with that other half may occur in vision. It *must* not, however—indeed, it *cannot*—be a sexual union, for in sexual union people's consciousness is drawn downward in the spine, away from their own higher, spiritual centers.

This teaching is touched on only lightly, if at all, by great masters, for they certainly don't want people seeking their soul mates on every street corner! The Gospel of St. Matthew states,

"The Pharisees also [along with "the multitudes"] came unto him, tempting him, and saying unto him, Is it lawful for a man to put away his wife for every cause?

"And he answered and said unto them, Have ye not read, that he which made them at the beginning made them male and female,

"And said, For this cause shall a man leave father and mother, and shall cleave to his wife: and they twain shall be one flesh?

"Wherefore they are no more twain, but one flesh. What therefore God hath joined together,

let not man put asunder.

"They [the Pharisees] say unto him, Why did Moses then command to give a writing of divorcement, and to put her away?

"He saith unto them, Moses because of the hardness of your hearts suffered you to put away your wives: but from the beginning it was not so.

"And I say unto you, Whosoever shall put away his wife, except it be for fornication [except, that is, if she be unfaithful sexually], and shall marry another, committeth adultery: and whoso marrieth her which is put away doth commit adultery." (Matt. 19:3–9)

Fornication for its own sake, moreover, is (Yogananda said) adulterous even in marriage, if it is without mutual love. For what adultery means is to adulterate: to admix with something pure an element of impurity.

The desire for a soul-mate is deeply embedded in human nature. Its roots lie deeper than the ego itself. God ultimately, however, is our true Soul Mate. In this case too, therefore, these words of Jesus remain eternally true:

"Seek ye the first the kingdom of God, and his righteousness; and all these things shall be added unto you." (Matt. 6:33)

If indeed every human being must eventually find his soul mate, this fulfillment, too, is one that "shall be added unto you" if you seek God first. The thing is, whether married or single, above all to make Him, eternally, your priority.

The passage on divorce continues:

"His disciples say unto him, If the case of the man be so with his wife [uncertain and insecure], [perhaps] it is not good to marry.

"But he said unto them, All men cannot receive this saying, save they to whom it is given.

"For there are some eunuchs, which were so born from their mother's womb: and there are some eunuchs which were made eunuchs of men: and there be eunuchs [people who abstain from sex], which have made themselves eunuchs [chaste] for the kingdom of heaven's sake. He that is able to receive it, let him receive it." (Matt. 19:10–12)

The words I quoted earlier, **"What therefore God hath joined together, let not man put asunder,"** must, Yogananda said, be understood as true soul-union in God, and not merely as the dedication to one another of a man and a woman, even if their union is consecrated in a church. Therefore Jesus said, **"He which made them *at the beginning*, made them male and female."** There is a divine, not merely a biological, truth in these words. Many marriages are based on a superficial, fleeting attraction—as Yogananda wryly observed: "on a union between a well-tied bow tie and an attractive shade of lipstick!" He himself, perhaps in concession to the times in which we live, went further than Jesus did in stating when divorce might be permissible. If a person's spouse is foolish, worldly, and above all if he or she exerts a downward pull on the consciousness of one who is trying to rise spiritually, divorce is spiritually justified. A teaching in the Indian scriptures is, "If a duty conflicts with a higher duty, it ceases to be a duty."

Yogananda sometimes told the story of a famous opera singer, Amelita Galli-Curci, who had later become his disciple. She first married a man who became, in time, a drunkard. One evening, in a drunken fit, he raised a chair to strike her. This time, she looked him straight in the eye, and with firm and deep concentration said, "Don't you dare touch me!" She walked out of the house forthwith. Years later she met someone else, whom in time she married. This man became to her, Yogananda stated, a true spiritual partner.

Divorce, in this case, was justified both morally and spiritually. Her first marriage had not been a "marriage in God," even though (considering that she was both Roman Catholic and Italian) it had probably been solemnized in a church by an ordained priest.

Again, there was a couple who lived for some years in Yogananda's seaside community in Encinitas, California. The man decided to leave the Master. Entering their house, he announced to his wife, "Let's pack up. We're getting out of here."

"Oh no," she replied. "You leave if you want to. I remain with my Guru."

Yogananda, speaking later with me (and, perhaps, with a few others) of this episode, quoted
the woman's words with approval.

He also told me of how his own family, during
his youth, had tried three times to get him married. Each time, he'd simply refused. On their
third attempt, he offered the girl to a cousin of his.
The young man was delighted to get her, for she
was exceptionally beautiful.

Yogananda returned to India in 1935, and
stayed in their home briefly. During that visit he
observed the wife nagging her husband unremit-
tingly. "I saw the poor man tiptoeing about," our
Guru told us, "like a mouse, forever in dread of
another tongue-lashing."

The Master took her aside and said to her, "You
know, I have some right to speak to you on these
matters, for you were promised first to me. What
I want to say to you is that, had we been married,
and had you treated me as I see you treating him,
I'd have given our marriage only one week. From
then on I'd have been in the Himalayas, devoting
my life to seeking God in meditation!" She heard
him, and—as much as was possible for her rather
aggressive nature—reformed.

It is permissible for one to leave his spouse for
God in cases where the spouse is trying to pull
him (or her) away from the spiritual life. Otherwise, as Yogananda frequently commented, "Loyalty is the first law of God."

Back, then, to our original theme: Mate, money,

fame, power, worldly position, children, a growing family tree of grandchildren and great grandchildren, and an accompanying sense of one's own importance—all these are *maya*'s ways of keeping people unendingly bound to the wheel of *samsara* (worldly involvement). Were it not for those few who become saints, and above all for the incarnations of God who appear on earth (though alas! from the human point of view too rarely), people might *never* even think of seeking a way to emerge at last from the swirling mists of delusion into the clear light of true understanding.

An *avatar*, or incarnation of God, has the power to lift innumerable souls out of delusion. As Lahiri Mahasaya predicted to Yogananda's mother on the day she brought her baby to him for a blessing, "Little mother, thy son will be a yogi. As a spiritual engine, he will carry many souls to God's kingdom." One imagines those powerful locomotives, God's direct incarnations, pulling lengthy trains behind them. Those masters who, by contrast, have ascended only in the present life, even though they reach the same level of divine realization, have not, flowing through them, the same spiritual power to uplift an innumerable throng of seekers.

Everyone, if he would find God, must first free at least a few others. I once asked my Guru, "How many must an ascending master save?"

"At least six," he replied.

That Jesus was a divine incarnation is hinted at

from the very beginning of his life. It was the three wise men who announced they had "seen his star in the east." That statement had a deeply esoteric meaning: Jesus, they were saying, had descended through the star which appears at the center of the spiritual eye, and which is the doorway to the inner kingdom of God.

Jesus brought a special dispensation to mankind. I remarked earlier that religiously minded people owe a great debt to science for having opened the windows of men's minds onto the vast realities in the material universe. Science deserves our gratitude. Scientists themselves, unfortunately, rarely have the humility to understand what a treasure they have brought: the gift of increased knowledge regarding the workings of God's creation. Most scientists lack superconscious intuition. They are like the artist who, on beholding a beautiful sunset, boasted, "I could paint a better sunset than that!" (And what could his colored daubs accomplish? At best they would be only smears of pigment on a little canvas, to be enjoyed only when the canvas is so placed as to reflect light! He wouldn't have even sunlight to illuminate his scene *from within*.) Scientists pride themselves on having discovered what was there, simply, already long before their very science was even a dream in anyone's mind!

Several months ago, I was the main speaker at a conference in Milan, Italy. The topic was, "Science and Religion." Ervin Laszlo, a great and wise scientist, had been invited to speak. At the last minute, however, he had been forced to cancel because of illness. Another scientist was accordingly invited to speak in his place. This replacement, proudly assured that science alone has all the answers, showed little respect for the subject of the conference, and began his talk by lurching (as it seemed to me) into the words, "Religion tries to instill blind belief in people, whereas science deals only with facts. Once a scientific fact has been proved, scientists everywhere in the world accept it without hesitation." (I've been exposed to that tired mantra all my life!)

He reminded me of a statement made by Max Planck, the famous German physicist, in his *Scientific Autobiography*: "A new scientific truth does not triumph by convincing its opponents and making them see the light, but rather because its opponents eventually die, and a new generation grows up that is familiar with it." Scientists, after all, are only human. Not many of them are wise. Many of them, as human beings, might almost be called small-minded, for they've blinded themselves, by exclusive focus on the power of reasoning, to the point where, often enough, they seem to lack even common sense!

It was purely delicious, for me, when this man, barely five minutes into his speech, began to squabble with other scientists on the platform, right before the whole audience, concerning some supposed scientific "fact" that he was championing!

Arrogance has been the undoing of many scientists, perhaps, who speak as though they considered the very universe their own personal responsibility! I remember my Guru once saying, "Pride is the death of wisdom."

Nevertheless, a humble view of the realities science has opened up for us should make us deeply grateful to science itself. It has provided us with what could be an ego-freeing awareness of cosmic realities. For the cosmic scheme is, fundamentally, completely impersonal. The thought springs naturally to our minds when we gaze up at night into the heavens, and contemplate the infinity of space and time: "How insignificant, in the cosmic order, am I!" To those whose thoughts penetrate even more deeply, a further thought may occur: "The cosmos, though an incontrovertible fact, can be understood only to the extent that our probing begins with *us, ourselves.*" Expanding beyond the petty little self—and even rejoicing in the comparison of our littleness to that vastness—we come at last to realize that, although the vast empyrean appears to have no actual center, it *does*, in fact, *have a center* in ourselves. The universe, Yogananda stated, is "center everywhere, circumference nowhere." Every human being is, as far as he himself is concerned, the center of everything in existence!

God dwells in the heart, moreover. Because of

Him, our souls have divine importance in the great scheme of things. In our egos we are not especially significant, but in our souls, and in the fact that God alone must first be found *within* each one of us, our importance is cosmic!

Science is, of course, self-condemned to viewing everything from the outside. It will never succeed, therefore, in prying from even the tiny electron its deepest secrets. *Sanaatan Dharma*, however, the Eternal Religion, offers truths by which everyone can come to know the one indwelling, divine Self. Beside this supernal discovery, all the knowledge with which science has provided us amounts to little more than rummaging around in the cosmic pantry, looking for something worthwhile to nibble on.

To get out of the ego, and to realize ourselves as that conscious essence from which all things were manifested, is simply not possible so long as man seeks release by egoic effort alone. Reason cannot supply him with the key he needs to unlock that door, for reason is already infected with delusion, which is the very disease it would cure. Wise is the scientist—alas, he is also rare—who doesn't preen *himself* on the findings of science. For, as I stated earlier, all that science can do is find what was there already. Rarely do scientists have the humility of George Washington Carver, the great Negro scientist, whose absence of pride drew the inspiration from God to find hundreds of uses for the humble peanut.

To get out of ego-consciousness, it is first necessary to tune in to someone who has already, himself, overcome the ego: a true guru, in other words. Few people are born so highly advanced that they no longer need the help of a guru, being in themselves already free enough from ego to be able to draw their help directly from God.

A few Christian saints have been born with this high state, and therefore have not needed a guru. Such persons have served as gurus, in their turn, to their own disciples. An example springs to mind: St. Francs of Assisi, to whom Jesus Christ often appeared physically. Jesus, on the other hand, so as to emphasize this eternal truth, went himself to John the Baptist for baptism. John had been, Yogananda explained, the guru of Jesus from ancient times. Jesus had outstripped his guru in spiritual advancement (something that does happen, sometimes). Therefore John demurred, saying:

"I have need to be baptized of thee, and comest thou to me?

"And Jesus answering said unto him, Suffer it to be so now: for thus it becometh us to fulfill all righteousness." (Matt. 3:14,15)

Paramhansa Yogananda explained that John had been one of the great olden prophets: Elijah. Jesus in that lifetime (so Yogananda said) had been his disciple Elisha (on whom Elijah cast his mantle). Therefore, when Jesus was transfigured before three of his disciples on Mount Tabor, they beheld him with Moses and Elias (the Greek version of the Hebrew name, Elijah). The Bible goes on to relate:

"And his disciples asked him, saying, Why then say the scribes that Elias must first come?

"And Jesus answered and said unto them, Elias truly shall come, and restore all things.

"But I say unto you, That Elias is come already, and they knew him not, but have done unto him whatsoever they listed. Likewise shall also the Son of man suffer of them.

"Then the disciples understood that he spake unto them of John the Baptist." (Matt. 17:10–13)

Jesus had no need of baptism from John; in fact, John said as much. Jesus, however, requested this grace of him in order to show to all "the world" the fact that this is, usually, the need of every true seeker.

Therefore said Jesus to Nicodemus, **"Verily, verily, I say unto thee, Except a man be born again, he cannot see the kingdom of God."** This account continues:

"Nicodemus saith unto him, How can a man be born when he is old? can he enter the second time into his mother's womb, and be born?

"Jesus answered, Verily, verily, I say unto thee, Except a man be born of water and of the Spirit, he cannot enter into the kingdom of God." (John 3:3–5)

To be born of water is to be born into a human

body. To be born of the spirit is to receive new birth into the Divine Spirit of God, from the guru.

The concept of our need for a guru was preserved in the Eastern Church, with its tradition of the *staretz* or personal spiritual teacher. In the West, unfortunately, this concept was lost sight of long ago, owing to the supreme importance the church claimed for itself as the soul's only channel to God (apart from Jesus Christ himself). This belief, though institutionally convenient, is in fact not valid. It has given rise, moreover, (as I said earlier) to numerous other fallacies. In consequence, few Christians nowadays who deeply yearn to know God have any recourse outside the numerous churches, each of which claims some degree of infallibility. The notion of having a guru has, therefore, among orthodox Christians been virtually forgotten.

The fallacy has been taken, in Protestant churches, to the extreme of insisting that one can get everything he needs by simply reading the Bible. Many even protest self-righteously, as I stated earlier, "Why, we're *all* saints!" (What a perfect way of keeping religion utterly mediocre!) Yogananda said to me, "If you argue with a scripture, it can't answer you. A true guru, however, can correct your misunderstandings."

The message Jesus brought from God was, as it would have had to be, *Sanaatan Dharma*, the Eternal Religion. His message was also special and particular, however, as truth often is when it is taught by a divine incarnation. It would not have been appropriate for Jesus to tell his followers to look for guidance to any other representative of the ancient truths. Even so, a time occurred when he qualified this fact also. The disciples came to him with news of someone who was of another following, but was casting out devils in his name.

"Master," the disciples said to him, **"we saw one casting out devils in thy name, and he followeth not us: and we forbad him, because he followeth not us.**

"But Jesus said, Forbid him not: for there is no man which shall do a miracle in my name, that can lightly speak evil of me.

"For he that is not against us is on our part." (Mark 9:38–40)

Jesus nevertheless, both in what he taught and in his divine presence, opened up new vistas onto Infinity. It behooved all those who followed him, and behooves all those even today who would follow in his footsteps, to honor him and to seek salvation in his name. Those, indeed, who teach in his name are right to make clear the truth that they represent him, above all. For although *Sanaatan Dharma* is eternal and the only true religion in the universe, many are the windows that open out onto it. The Eternal Religion cannot be understood except through one of the actual "openings" onto the cosmic verities.

Thus, Paramhansa Yogananda, whose coming

had been at the request of Jesus Christ, declared also that he himself was the last in his particular line of gurus. He placed Jesus Christ first in that sequence because it was Jesus who, by his request to Babaji, had started this mission. When Yogananda said that he himself was the last in that line, he did so because these were the five who, so charged by God, had initiated this divine dispensation. He never stated that there would be no other gurus *in* his work. Had he done so, it would have meant that his teaching was not valid.

I once asked him, "Is your mission a new religion?"

"It is a new *expression*," he replied, giving special emphasis to that last word. A new expression was what Jesus, too, brought to mankind.

To me, particularly while I've labored to fulfill my Guru's commission to me that I edit his writings, it has often seemed that Yogananda is himself the "*avatar*" of this new age of energy. The concept that there are different historical ages is something I shall do my best to clarify in the next chapter.

The message Yogananda was sent to deliver to Christians was one that he himself called the Second Coming of Christ. His teachings, though wholly Christian in content, opened up *new "windows"* onto the eternal truth of Christ's teachings. Yogananda showed the people living in this scientific age how, without diminishing their religious faith, to embrace the vast panorama that science has revealed to mankind. He showed, as science has also done, that reality is both infinite and infinitesimal. He declared—again, as science has done also—that matter has no existence except as countless different vibrations of energy.

What Yogananda taught was far in advance, however, of modern science, for he declared man's need to recognize *consciousness itself* as the supreme cause, and not as merely the effect of brain activity. He helped Westerners, schooled as they are in the "either . . . or" methods of Aristotelian logic, to discover that truth can often be stated in many ways: that the relativity of values is a fact, for the only thing absolute is the Supreme Spirit. (Thus, he resolved a great modern dilemma: absolute, versus relative, truth.)*

Jesus did the same. He said, for example, in his "Sermon on the Mount":

"Let your light so shine before men, that they may see your good works, and glorify your Father which is in heaven." (Matt. 5:16)

Only a little later, however, he said, **"And when thou prayest, thou shalt not be as the hypocrites . . . standing . . . in the corners of the streets, that they may be seen of men. . . . But thou, when thou prayest, enter into thy closet, and when thou hast shut thy door, pray to thy Father which is in secret; and thy Father which**

*See my book, *Out of the Labyrinth*, Crystal Clarity Publishers, 2001.

seeth in secret shall reward thee openly."
(Matt. 6:5,6)

A literal mind, addicted to the "either . . . or" consciousness of Western logic, might object, "Couldn't he make up his mind? If I declare my devotion in public, how can I at the same time keep it a secret?" There are many subtle nuances in life's truths, however. A great master's teaching must be viewed with intuitive, rather than with literal, understanding.

This fact is something I myself—raised as I'd been on Western methods of reasoning—had to learn from my Guru. A divine truth must be taken inside and understood in its own, specific context. In the example I just gave, the seeker needs to share with others the graces he receives, in meditation, of peace, light, and joy, for by selfishness his capacity for empathy would only shrink. He must receive these graces *from God*, however, in the secrecy of inner, meditative silence.

Yogananda appealed, as did Jesus also, to the deepest reality in all beings, whose universal desire is always the same: the soul's longing for perfect bliss. Based on this realization, Paramhansa Yogananda, like Jesus Christ, saw everyone, regardless of his outward form, as his brother or sister in God.

These truths need a new expression, however, in our new age. That we actually do live in a new age, into which science has heralded us, is something most people understand and accept, even though many of them also resist the concept. The ramifications of the conflict that is raging, in consequence, throughout the thinking world will be explored in the next chapter.

CHAPTER TWENTY-TWO

THE AGES OF HISTORY

Human nature hasn't changed much since the days of Jesus Christ, but our *under-standing* of it has certainly become more sophisticated. Most intelligent people today know that a person's conscious beliefs don't wholly define him as he is. Human nature is much more complex than anything suggested by superficial beliefs. A person can believe one thing consciously, yet *behave* in such a way as to contradict that belief and to show that his *real* beliefs are quite different. Our knowledge of human nature includes, now, an awareness of the subconscious. We know, therefore, that our human motivations can spring from depths we don't even consciously recognize.

Finally, there is some recognition nowadays that there may be spiritual dimensions in life, and in every human being, that are not generally known, but of which it is now possible to speak without being dismissed as a complete fool. When people present that old fundamentalist challenge, "Are you saved?" it is easier, now, to ask in return, "Saved from *what*?" And the usual answer, "Saved from eternal hell," can at least be contested by cool reasoning—as indeed I have tried to do in this book. For it is unthinkable to any fair-minded person that a loving God would so condemn his own children for actions they've committed—and committed, moreover, in ignorance—as to spurn them for all eternity! A finite cause, as I pointed out earlier, cannot have an infinite effect.

People have, in other words, become more open to common sense, and are less easily swayed by unreasonable and merely dogmatic pronouncements.

Jesus had to adjust his teaching to the general level of consciousness in his times. Again and again we find him saying, **"He that hath ears to hear, let him hear."**

"Take heed," he said once to his disciples, **"and beware of the leaven of the Pharisees and the Sadducees.**

"And [reading on] they reasoned among themselves, saying, It is because we have taken no bread.

"Which when Jesus perceived, he said unto them, O ye of little faith, why reason ye among yourselves, because ye have brought no bread?

"Do ye not yet understand, neither remember the five loaves of the five thousand, and how many baskets ye took up?

"Neither the seven loaves of the four thousand, and how many baskets ye took up? [He is referring here to the miracles of divine providence he'd performed.]

"How is it that ye do not understand that I spake it not to you concerning bread, that ye should beware of the leaven of the Pharisees and the Sadducees?

"Then understood they how that he bade them not beware of the leaven of bread, but of the doctrine of the Pharisees and of the Sadducees." (Matt. 16:6–12)

Many times his disciples took him literally, when he spoke only metaphorically. As another example, during his visit to Samaria, when they urged him to eat something and he answered saying, "I have meat to eat that ye know not of" (John 4:32), they thought he must have eaten already. All the answer he gave them on that occasion, however (vouchsafing no further explanation), was, "My meat is to do the will of him that sent me, and to finish his work." (John 4:34) His answer was not really quite adequate, in itself, for although it may satisfy the soul to do God's will, actions alone will not ordinarily fill anyone's stomach.

Jesus explained himself more fully on this point when he said to "the tempter" (Satan), "It

is written, Man shall not live by bread alone, but by every word that proceedeth out of the mouth of God." (Matt. 4:4) The people of his times, however, and to some extent even his own disciples, were not ready for teachings that were too far ahead of the general knowledge of their day.

A good example of present-day advancement is something everyone knows about now: energy. How could Jesus speak of energy, when the people of his day were not even aware that energy exists? Indeed, the whole world was dim on this point. In the yoga teachings of India, for example, energy (*prana*) had come to be thought of only in connection with the breath. Refinement of understanding has been increasing all over the world in the centuries since then, and not only in Western civilization.

Paramhansa Yogananda explained (as I stated in Chapter Sixteen) that man possesses another "mouth" besides the one through which he ingests food. This "mouth of God," as Jesus called it, is not physically visible, but it receives energy directly from the surrounding atmosphere rather than by the indirect method of introducing sustenance into the body by the physical mouth: food which the body must then convert into energy. The portal of entrance for this direct flow of energy is the medulla oblongata at the base of the brain. It is through this "*chakra*," or subtle center, that energy enters the body. This "mouth of God," so called, is also the seat of the ego. (The divine sense of Self, by contrast, is located in the heart.)

We all live to some extent by this energy. Without it, indeed, we would die. We can draw on it consciously, moreover, by a combination of awareness of it, and will power. Saints have been known even not to eat anything at all for years, living entirely by the inner, direct source of energy. One such saint was Therese Neumann, to whom I've alluded before in these pages.

For practical application of this knowledge, Yogananda taught a system of "energization exercises," as he called them, which enable the practitioner actually to energize his body at will. Thus, he helped us to make these truths more dynamic to our consciousness.

Jesus evidently did not feel he could stretch people's minds—not even those of his own disciples—so far as to speak of the cosmic energy. It is only in the last hundred years or so that humanity has come to some understanding of energy. During this time, science has proved that matter is, in fact, without substance at all: It consists simply of vibrations of energy.

In other ways, too, Jesus went along with the understanding of his times. For example, he ate meat, though many spiritual teachers nowadays recommend against it, and medical science is coming more and more widely to recognize that meat eating can actually cause many diseases. Yogananda also explained—something people nowadays are at least ready to consider—that meat eating exerts a downward pull on the mind, because mammals, whose consciousness is relatively highly developed compared to vegetables and even to fish, experience intense emotions when they are slaughtered: especially emotions of fear and anger. These feelings leave gross vibrations in the meat, which are absorbed by anyone who eats it. (No one two thousand years ago would have even understood that word, "vibrations.")

Many were the truths Jesus taught that could not be explained in those days but that, today, seem at least not so outrageous. One teaching of his to which Paramhansa Yogananda often referred was the following:

"And if thy right eye offend thee, pluck it out, and cast it from thee: for it is profitable for thee that one of thy members should perish, and not that thy whole body should be cast into hell.

"And if thy right hand offend thee, cut it off, and cast it from thee. . . ." He concluded by repeating the same words as those in the verse before. (Matt. 5:29,30)

Jesus, later in the same chapter, made it a point to state specifically that he was changing some of the ancient rules: those which, to him, were not essential to the teachings of *Sanaatan Dharma* since they were simply ways of helping people to absorb the Eternal Truth. The alterations he made showed how great incarnations of God do sometimes make changes in the way the eternal truths should be applied to the shifting temporal scenes of life. (Ordinary human beings, it should be added, must not presume to make such changes. Only great masters have the right, and indeed the duty, to do so, for their inspiration comes to them directly from God.)

In the above verses, however, one must ask: Did Jesus *literally* mean that one should pluck out his right eye and cut off his right hand if these "offend" him? What, for that matter, did he mean by that word, "offend"?

How can the eye offend us? Well, obviously— since Jesus was speaking spiritually—it offends against our higher nature if we gaze *pleasurably* on anything that is spiritually unclean or unholy. Such sights are best avoided, especially if, to us, they are attractive. The sight, then, becomes an offense—in the sense of being sinful—to the souls of those who revel in it.

Why—we then ask—did he specify the *right* eye? What both our eyes see is, after all, the same, so why blame only the right one? The answer is that the right is the positive side of the body. In ancient tradition, the right side of the body indicates energy that is given with full consent of the will. What Jesus meant, so Yogananda explained, was that seeing becomes an offense when we give the consent of our will power to what we see. We should withdraw our *attention* from anything that feeds thoughts of illicit, because impure, pleasure.

Yogananda went farther, however. He said that

what Jesus really meant, but was not in a position in those times to say, was that we should withdraw not only our attention, but above all our *energy*. For our energy can flow out toward sense objects even after our conscious attention has been withdrawn. This is the bane that subconscious influences can exert on the mind. (Those influences can also be a blessing, when they reinforce a wholesome direction of the will.) What we must do, then, is wholesomely redirect our *energy*. Only in this way can we change influences that, otherwise, keep rising into the mind from the subconscious, like bubbles in a glass of champagne.

Imagine a woman "baring all" seductively, so to speak, on a television screen. A sincere seeker of God and of higher truth might notice that scene fleetingly, but his normal and proper reaction would be simply to look away, or to close his eyes, or (if he could control the situation) to change the channel. If he finds himself drawn to gaze at the scene by the consent of his will, however, this exemplifies what Jesus meant by "thy right eye." In such a case, he must throw the thought out of his mind with a strong effort of the will ("pluck it out").

It is better ("more profitable" was the way Jesus expressed it) to live with fleeting regret for having refused to enjoy that scene than to let lascivious thoughts draw one's entire consciousness down into a pit from which there is, finally, no exit but to climb laboriously out again.

Merely to tell one's self, however, "I just won't think about it," is almost never adequate. Often, the more one tries not to think about something, the more he finds himself drawn irresistibly to thinking about it. The solution, then, is to direct *energy with will power* toward some other, more wholesome thought or activity. Don't merely try not to dwell on thoughts that you want to avoid: *Vigorously* divert the mind, *with energy*, in a new direction.

"Habits," my Guru once told me, "can be overcome in a day. They are only concentration of the mind. Concentrate differently, and a wrong habit can be banished in an instant." He also said that this new direction of concentrated thought must be accompanied by a vigorous, new, and creative flow of energy. "The greater the will," was his maxim, "the greater the flow of energy."

I have several times, over the years, tested the validity of this counsel, and have found it to work infallibly. It is like a story I once read of an alcoholic who wanted to overcome his addiction to liquor. One day he found himself drawn forcibly, because of long habit, to open a new bottle of whiskey. All at once, furious with himself, he grabbed every bottle of alcoholic drink from his liquor cabinet, carried the lot out of doors, and hurled them fiercely onto the sidewalk, shattering them completely. So vigorous was his determined renunciation at that moment that he found, later,

his habit patterns had been newly redirected—
completely so. Never again did he feel the desire
for liquor.

The Bhagavad Gita states, "To meditate on
sense objects, while outwardly abstaining from
them, is hypocrisy." Throughout the world, religious followers, not knowing the subtle key to self-
mastery, have lacked this secret: energy. They
haven't realized that transcendence requires a
withdrawal and redirection, not only of thoughts,
but of *energy* from every false attraction. This is
what Jesus Christ meant (but couldn't say, in his
cultural context). Yogananda *could* say it, however, for today we live in an age when everyone
knows of the existence of energy.

Yogananda told us of having once read an account in a newspaper of a woman who, deeply re-
morseful for having stolen, and wanting to obey
the commandment of Jesus, had cut off her right
hand. Alas, her penitential act brought her no
cure. The *impulse* to steal remained with her, and
she stole again—this time, with her *left* hand!

I have noticed in life that people with strong personalities often express themselves colorfully.
Jesus Christ, though he had long since overcome
all sense of having a separate ego of his own, still
possessed a strong personality. Far from being
self-effacing (the "gentle Jesus, meek and mild" of
sentimental tradition), he had, and indeed *needed*
to have, enormous strength of will to face the wilful opposition of a strong people, whom he'd been

sent to help. Therefore it was that he used such expressions as, **"And there be eunuchs, which have made themselves eunuchs for the kingdom of heaven's sake."** (Matt. 19:12) He didn't say, "Some people prefer to be chaste and celibate, for this practice helps them to direct all their thoughts upward in the recollection of God." He wanted to shock people, to seize their attention and make them remember his message.

In the foregoing commandment, too, he didn't say gently, "If your right eye takes pleasure in viewing wrongful images (whether sexual, or in other ways worldly), it would better for you if you looked away, or if you at least lowered your gaze." That would have been a sensible caution, and would have raised no eyebrows. Instead, however, what he stated, as strongly and colorfully as possible, was (in essence), "Pluck that image out of your eye and throw it onto a dungheap!" Be vigorous, in other words, in your resolution not to entertain for even a moment the slightest thought of delusion.

The mind likes, instead, to play with wrong thoughts. Perhaps it justifies itself with the rationalization that it only wants to understand what makes the forbidden scene attractive, and why. Never go down that path: it has led many a human being into a mire of delusive involvement. Instead, then, declare forcefully: "NO!" You don't need to understand the delusion. Understanding will come later, when your mind is calm, clear, and uplifted. It will never come if you try gently to puff away the clouds of delusion in the hope that they'll accommodate you by vanishing.

"The first thought of delusion," my Guru said to me: "*that* is the moment to catch it."

The important thing is to bring *energy*, also, into play. Reject delusion *with energy*. Had Jesus said those things, people would not have understood him.

Therefore I say that Yogananda, though he called his mission "The Second Coming of Christ," added new dimensions to Christ's teachings that accord well with man's expanded understanding in this new age. And therefore, also, I speak of Yogananda as the *avatar*, or divine incarnation, for this age of energy. His mission was to show people how completely compatible Christ's teachings were with the expanded, and self-expanding, knowledge of our times.

Jesus was not only, at the beginning of our Christian era, the messiah to the Jews. He said also, **"Other sheep I have that are not of this fold: them also I must bring, and they shall hear my voice; and there shall be one fold, and one shepherd."** (John 10:16) "One fold," indeed, and the one recognized, eternal religion, which Yogananda explained as Self-realization. Jesus Christ, too, will be a living messiah for all time.

The age Jesus lived in was, religiously speaking, rigidly dogmatic. His fellow Jews criticized him again and again for not "measuring up" to their ideas of what a teacher to the Jews ought to be and to teach. His own followers continued, through the centuries that followed, to be as dogmatic about their own traditions as the Jews had been about theirs. Moreover, as Christianity entered into, and became absorbed by, the Greco-Roman world, it adopted the rigid disciplines of Greek reasoning to bolster the dogmas it was formulating. Thus it shunned the more fluid perceptions that come with soul-intuition.

Times have changed. Mankind is now more advanced—clearly so—not only in objective and subjective knowledge, but also in empathetic awareness, human being for human being.

What explanation can be advanced for such a great change? Only two thousand years have passed: not so very much time, surely, despite the Christian dream of a millennium as being a very long time.

Many ancient cultures,* interestingly, believed that there had been a successive series of ages— of recurring cycles, some of them said. The Egyptians spoke of a gradual descent from a much higher age. It is interesting to note that many scholars have commented that Egyptian history seems to have begun at its height, and thereafter only declined. The Greeks spoke of a downward

*As evidenced by more than 200 myths and folk stories from over thirty cultures, according to Giorgio de Santillana, former professor of history at M.I.T. (Massachusetts Institute of Technology), and co-author of the book, *Hamlet's Mill.*

succession of ages also: gold, silver, copper, and iron. The Hopi of the American Southwest speak even today of four "worlds," or epochs of time. So also did the Aztecs of Mexico. The Scandinavian countries (Norsemen) also believed in four declining ages. The four descending ages were, again, a part of Celtic tradition. In Asia, the Sumerians believed there had been higher ages in the past. The Persians, like the Greeks, spoke of four descending ages: gold, silver, steel, and iron. There is also some suggestion of this knowledge among the ancient Hebrews, in the Book of Daniel.

In ancient India, the tradition existed of a *cycle* of four ages, or *yugas*: *Satya* (spiritual) yuga; *Treta* (a predominantly mental age); *Dwapara*, an age of energy; and *Kali yuga*, a dark age of widespread ignorance.

In India, and perhaps elsewhere as well, the tradition was that the great cycles of time recurred regularly, in unceasing repetition.

In all of these cultures, the belief was held that mankind, at the time when those traditions (according to present knowledge) were recorded, had reached the lowest age. Modern historians have of course treated those traditions with the condescension of "wise old age" for the "fairy tales" of childhood, or, equally, as the nostalgia people generally feel for "the good old days." It is interesting, however, that those traditions were so widespread. They seem, indeed, to have been almost universal.

Science today has opened our eyes to the vastness of the universe, and also to its subtlety. At
the same time, however, science has had an eye
only for material realities. It *is* developing ever-
greater sophistication in its understanding, but it
still seems far from perceiving the universe in
terms of cosmic *influences*.

One such influence was described in ancient
times (especially in India) as the great cycles of
cosmic time.

What was taught more specifically by other ancient civilizations, beyond that of India, has been
obscured by the fact that, over time, all those civilizations have crumbled and disappeared. The
only culture still functioning—and some of its old
traditions, it must be admitted, have reached a
somewhat tottering old age—is the culture of
India. India's basic spirituality has preserved its
traditions, wobbling but still upright, from the
natural disintegrations of time.

In that tradition, most—and perhaps all—of the
discoveries of modern science were anticipated.
The vastness of the universe was known. Also
known was the fact that energy is the basis of
matter. Indeed, their knowledge went much further, for it claimed that will-directed thought is
what generated energy in the first place. It also
claimed that unmoving consciousness (inconceivable to the modern mind) predated thought, and
was the very foundation of universal Creation.

It is an astonishing legacy, one that science has

only succeeded in confirming—albeit its confirmation is rather like stating that the base of that tall mountain over there does, in fact, exist.

Paramhansa Yogananda's guru, Swami Sri Yukteswar, said that there is definitely truth to the declaration of the ancients that the vast cycles of time exist; that the universe, having been conceived first by consciousness, and projected out of consciousness by thought (idea forms), and then energy, is far more conscious than the mind of man has imagined. Cosmic influences do exist. They flow, indeed, like streams and rivers through the entire universe, influencing even the consciousness of mankind.

It sounds "far out." Most people, indeed, will probably dismiss the whole concept as "poppycock." Very well, let us take it as such. Still, it does answer certain questions very well that have never before come under consideration. Those who have made these assertions, moreover—not only Swami Sri Yukteswar, who was a great modern sage, but also great *rishis* (sages) of olden times—have not been the sort of persons whom any sensible human being would dismiss blithely as stupid.

Sri Yukteswar corrected modern Hindu traditions, and presented a timetable regarding our own earth and solar system that is easier to grasp. Hinduism is a very old tree, and is in present need of pruning to rid it of growths like those which have appeared also on the much younger tree of original Christianity. In Hinduism, indeed, the case is worse owing to the extreme antiquity of that ancient religion. According to modern Hindu tradition, we now live in a descending *Kali Yuga*, or dark age, which is destined to last another four hundred thirty thousand years.

According to that same tradition, the days of Rama (during *Treta Yuga*) in the *Ramayana*, and of *Krishna* (toward the end of descending *Dwapara Yuga*) in the *Mahabharata*—both of them stated, therefore, to have lived in higher ages— would have to have been impossibly distant in the past, too long a span of time for mankind to have remembered, especially considering how prominent a place those two figures hold in *modern* memory.

Another tradition in modern (as well as in less recent) India is that, at the end of *Kali Yuga*, *Satya Yuga* (the Golden, or Spiritual, Age) will immediately begin again. Nothing in Nature endorses such a sudden shift. Day fades to twilight before it becomes night; night always fades to predawn light before becoming day again. Summer fades to autumn before it becomes Winter; Winter changes to Spring before Summer returns. Nothing in the universe moves by sudden jerks. Even supernovas, sudden as they seem, take time to develop, and then, again, to fade away. All this is perfectly obvious; I state it only to point out that ancient traditions must be pruned regularly of fallacies, which grow up owing to human misunderstanding.

Swami Sri Yukteswar declared that certain errors of reckoning had crept into the ancient traditions. When a great master takes the trouble, moreover, to make such a strong declaration (as opposed merely to going along affably with tradition), it is idle to speculate that he may only be stating an opinion. If there is a place in human thinking for dogmatism, I think it must begin with accepting statements made by those who, alone among mankind, have demonstrated true wisdom. A human being without any firm convictions deserves to be classified among the invertebrates. A strong corroboration for this particular dogma (if that is what it is) may be seen in the fact that the truly wise are always in deep agreement with one another. All the arguments in religion have been fomented by lesser men. As my Guru said, "Fools argue; wise men discuss." The wise, in their discussions, always agree on fundamental points of truth.

According to Swami Sri Yukteswar, our planet and solar system are affected by a Cosmic Year, or complete cycle of ages, lasting 24,000 years: 12,000 ascending, 12,000 descending.

The nadir of that descent, he said, was reached in the year 500 A.D. From then on there has been, as he pointed out, a gradual ascent toward ever-greater understanding and enlightenment.

History does, in fact, show a gradual decline in ancient times (ancient, that is, relative to our present time sense). Egyptian history seems to have sprung out of nothing, so to speak, at a peak from which it descended to final disintegration. Egyptologists, eager for acceptance by other scientists as scientists themselves, have denied this claim. The claim has nevertheless been made again and again, and by serious scholars.

I wish I could take the time to explore this subject of ancient civilizations in depth, for it has always fascinated me. The theme of this book, however, prevents me from making such a foray. I must content myself, therefore, with saying that the years prior to 500 A.D. do indeed seem to have been accompanied by a gradual descent into what has been called, in the West, a dark age.

Interestingly, knowledge that was lost in the descending arc seems to have reappeared at comparable points on the re-ascending arc. The ancient Greeks knew that the world is round. They knew that it is not the center of the universe. They even knew about the atom—a very recent discovery in modern times. That knowledge was subsequently lost, however. In the Christian era, the cosmology of Ptolemy became accepted so dogmatically by the Church that Copernicus, a great, trail-blazing scientist, dared not, for much of his life, announce his findings, which proved that the earth is not at the center of everything. Galileo faced persecution by the Church for stating that the earth moves. (And Galileo was only "forgiven" by the Catholic Church in the second half of the twentieth century—after four hundred years!)

According to Sri Yukteswar, we came out of *Kali Yuga* (the Dark Age) only in 1700 A.D. Since that time, there has been a great surge of awakening. A 200-year bridge (or *sandhya*) to the succeeding age of energy, which ancient Indian tradition called *Dwapara Yuga*, brings us to 1900 A.D., the beginning of Dwapara proper. Since then we have seen a virtual explosion in human progress.

I need hardly recount more than a handful of the inventions that have come to light in our own times through men like Edison, Tesla, Marconi, and countless others: alternate-current electricity; electronic engineering; widespread telephonic communication; radio; television; airplane travel; travel to outer space and the exploration of the moon and Mars; mobile telephones; computers. I need hardly speak, moreover, of the contributions made by Albert Einstein, especially with his Law of Relativity.

We are, in fact (and not in some hippie, hallucinogenic fancy) living in a new age: an age of energy.

We are also seeing the less fortunate consequences of transition from one age to another: a global struggle between old, restrictive ways of thinking and of doing things, and newer, evermore expansive ways. Personally, I do not see how this struggle can resolve itself peacefully, though we all, of course, hope that it will do so.

There is, alas! violence in the air. Terrorists pretend they have the solution: Blow up everything!

create a world-wide "brotherhood" of everyone who is in agreement with them, and blow all the rest to smithereens. People who favor violence, however, will never be at peace with anyone until they've found peace in themselves. The sort of "peace" they envision, if they could indeed bring it about, would turn out to be a boiling cauldron of hatred, discord, and self-righteous back-and-forth denunciations, all of them ending finally in—well, a play I wrote when I was fifteen said it perfectly: a huge explosion, greater than all the rest. And then—Silence.

We must seek a peaceful way of resolving our differences. We must become solution-conscious, and give up our traditional problem-consciousness.

How—I have asked myself—will this book be received: With open minded gratitude for the common sense it expresses? or with dogmatic blame, outrage, and persecution? Or will it, perhaps, encounter a mixture of both? The first reception is what I would greatly prefer. The second would be a great pity for mankind itself, never mind what happens to me. The third, I am sorry to say, is the most likely outcome. I don't think what I have written will be ignored, though there is always that possibility. If it leads to personal hardship for me, however—well, I am prepared for it. My God is Truth. I have no other.

In time, the contest cannot but resolve itself. I myself believe in Paramhansa Yogananda's prediction of "a new world of peace, harmony, and prosperity for all," when people give up fighting the inevitable and learn to accept, and even to love, one another, and then to work together for the common weal.

Then will the Second Coming of Christ become a reality: not necessarily the return of Jesus the man, but of the principles for which he stood bravely and, eventually, died on the cross.

CHAPTER TWENTY-THREE

THE MISSING YEARS

"Now his parents went to Jerusalem every year at the feast of the passover.

"And when he was twelve years old, they went up to Jerusalem after the custom of the feast.

"And when they had fulfilled the days, as they returned, the child Jesus tarried behind in Jerusalem; and Joseph and his mother knew not of it.

"But they, supposing him to have been in the company, went a day's journey; and they sought him among their kinsfolk and acquaintance.

"And when they found him not, they turned back again to Jerusalem, seeking him.

"And it came to pass, that after three days they found him in the temple, sitting in the midst of the doctors, both hearing them, and asking them questions.

"And all that heard him were astonished at his understanding and answers.

"And when they saw him, they were amazed: and his mother said unto him, Son, why hast thou thus dealt with us? behold, thy father and I have sought thee sorrowing.

"And he said unto them, How is it that ye sought me? wist ye not that I must be about my Father's business?

"And they understood not the saying which he spake unto them.

"And he went down with them, and came to Nazareth, and was subject unto them: but his mother kept all these sayings in her heart.

"And Jesus increased in wisdom and stature, and in favor with God and man." (Luke 2:41–52)

SO ENDS THE LAST BIBLICAL ACCOUNT OF THE childhood of Jesus. From then on nothing more appears until his apparently sudden arrival on the scene at the age of thirty. Often and often people have asked the question: What transpired during those missing eighteen years? The life of someone so very important as Jesus Christ must surely have been combed over again and again, its every episode discussed and analyzed. Instead of which . . . *nothing*? It seems more than strange: It seems quite impossible.

Many have suggested that those "lost years"

must have been excised from the Bible. The scribes who recorded his story—assuming they did remove that account—didn't dare to substitute for it something of their own creation. Assuming that what we do find is true—that "he went down with them, and came to Nazareth, and was subject unto them"—his "subjection" to them can hardly have lasted for eighteen years considering the "declaration of independence" he made to them at the age of twelve.

It would have been easy for the account to continue, "And he grew to manhood, and worked with his father as a carpenter." Whoever the scribes were, they didn't dare say even that much.

Christian tradition does have him working as a carpenter. Jesus, however, seems flatly to contradict that tradition, for his own words were, **"Wist ye not that I must be about my Father's business?"** After this strong statement, it is unthinkable that he would have simply gone home, remained there for eighteen years, and become a common apprentice and journeyman carpenter under Joseph until the age of thirty, and *only then* commenced his life's mission. At twelve he had already told his parents he had God's work to do. And, as he strongly implied, *he had begun that mission already*.

Westerners are likely to object, "But twelve is too young for any boy to begin a life mission!" His parents evidently held the same view. It is obvious, however, that Jesus did not hold it, for we find him *telling them* in no uncertain words—words very different, moreover, from what one would expect of any child of twelve—what he must do. Under comparable circumstances, wouldn't any other child have been overwhelmed with joy to see his parents again—after three long days? Jesus reacted as no one could have expected. He didn't cry, "Mommy! Mommy! You're here! I'm coming! I'm coming!" and rush to her, flinging his arms emotionally around her knees. In fact, his response seems very suggestive of the answer he gave on another occasion, many years later:

"While he yet talked to the people, behold, his mother and his brethren stood without, desiring to speak with him.

"Then one said unto him, Behold, thy mother and thy brethren stand without, desiring to speak with thee.

"But he answered and said unto him that told him, Who is my mother? and who are my brethren?

"And he stretched forth his hand toward his disciples, and said, Behold my mother and my brethren!

"For whosoever shall do the will of my Father which is in heaven, the same is my brother, and sister, and mother." (Matt. 12:46–50)

I am not familiar with Judaic traditions, but from everything I've heard about "Jewish mothers" I imagine it would be unthinkable in that tradition for a twelve-year-old child—especially one with a heart so full of love—coolly to declare his independence from his parents. In that first account he seems almost to have scolded them for finding him. Visualize the scene, and reflect that it occurred after *three whole* days. Surely the event was extraordinary.

I remember a time when I myself was separated from my parents for only one hour. It was on a ship which was steaming into New York Harbor. I wasn't twelve, but nevertheless, how differently I reacted: I was *panic-stricken!* Crowds of grown-ups towered all around me, hemming me in. I had no idea where my parents were. Images formed in my mind of landing all alone in a strange city, inexperienced, and utterly helpless. I freely confess I sobbed desperately. And what a relief it was to find them at last!

The only episodes I know that were comparable to this story about Jesus, who was virtually renouncing every blood tie to his family, have occurred in the lives of great reincarnated masters.

Swami Shankara, in south India, told his mother at the age of six that he had decided to renounce the world for God. When she tried, quite naturally, to hold him, he jumped into a river and allowed himself—so the story goes—to be caught by a crocodile.

"Look, Mother!" he cried. "Either you give me your consent, or I will let this crocodile take me. Whatever happens, you won't have me anymore!"

Hastily she gave her permission. And the child,

who had been born with divine power, made the crocodile release him, whereupon his life mission began. That mission, interestingly enough, ended also at the age of thirty-three.

My Guru recounted this story to me as a historic fact. For those who don't believe it, here is another one which occurred more recently:

Swami Pranabananda, a disciple of Lahiri Mahasaya—Pranabananda, my Guru told me, attained full liberation in that life—left his body.* "In his next incarnation," my Guru said, "he left home at the age of six. His purpose, he declared, was to join Babaji in the Himalayas." After a brief pause, my Guru continued with a smile, "It caused a lot of commotion in that village at the time!"

Paramhansa Yogananda himself ran away from home at a young age. His older brother succeeded in bringing him back, but the seeds of world-renunciation, which had been sprouting from the very beginning of this life, lay deeply buried in his nature.

In the light of spiritual tradition—especially in India, where the lamp of spirituality has burned brightly for centuries—that declaration by Jesus at the age of twelve, that he must "be about his Father's business," was not unique. That he had, moreover, a karmic tie with India had already been indicated by the visit, soon after his birth, of

*The account appears in *Autobiography of a Yogi.*

the three wise men of the East.

Clearly then, to start with, those eighteen years must have been deliberately omitted from the official account of Christ's life. For some reason, which we must explore, people felt it prudent to do so. Evidently, however, as I said, no one dared to insert even one sentence to replace what had been removed.

Two vital questions forcibly intrude themselves on this picture: *What* was omitted? And, *What was the reason* for that omission?

In 1958, I had an interesting conversation with a prominent spiritual leader in India: Swami Bharati Krishna Tirtha, the Shankaracharya of Gowardhan Math. He was at that time the senior representative of the ancient Shankara Order of Swamis. Throughout the land people respected him highly as a man of truth and honor. My own experience with him, which covered many months, supports that reputation. (I mention these credits to say that what he told me, though I cannot prove it, had the ring of authenticity. I myself accepted it as true.)

That much said, let me quote something he told me, as exactly in his own words as I can remember them.

"Some years ago [he said] I came into possession of one of only three copies of an ancient document which purported to be an account of the proceedings of one of the early Councils of Constantinople. [The swami told me the date of that council, but I forget which one it was.] In that council, the question was raised as to how the Church should deal with the record, which still existed, of the missing eighteen years of Jesus Christ's life.

"The problem raised was that the account might unsettle the faith of devout Christians. The Bible stated that Jesus had spent at least a number of those 'lost' years with great masters in India, to which land he had gone to study with them. The question raised in the council was whether Christians might not be shaken in their faith if they thought that Jesus Christ, the Son of God, had studied under anyone. The general feeling of the prelates was that the account should be removed in order to protect the devotion of the faithful.

"At that point," Bharati Krishna Tirtha continued, "someone in the audience got up and stated, 'I am a layman, not a priest, and am aware that it is not customary for such as I to speak at these councils. However, I feel I must speak out. What I have to say is, If the apostles themselves were not shaken in their faith by this revelation, why should we who truly believe, all of us, that Jesus was the Son of God, have less trust then they? Surely the simple truth will not in any way diminish his stature in people's eyes!' The man's objection was not considered, however, and the account of those eighteen years was removed forthwith from the Bible."

I cannot vouch for the truth of the above statement. I know that there are records in India which support the claim that Jesus lived in that country for several years. Accounts have been published describing documents that still exist in the ancient Tibetan monastery of Himis, in Leh, a province of Ladakh in northern Kashmir. I will return to these records later in this chapter. Eyewitness accounts by people who have seen them have increased in number ever since 1887, when they were first discovered.

Let me first submit, however, what to me is the strongest testimony of all: the fact that Paramhansa Yogananda himself declared many times, as a definite fact, that Jesus Christ did visit India, and that he lived there for some years.

I had been with my Guru for just a month when he invited me to his desert retreat at Twenty-Nine Palms, California, where he was dictating his revised correspondence-course lessons. During one evening's session he stated during dictation: "The three wise men who came to honor the Christ Child after his birth in Bethlehem were the line of gurus who later sent me to the West: Babaji, Lahiri Mahasaya, and Swami Sri Yukteswar." This was heady stuff, especially for a young neophyte! I'd learned for the first time about yoga, gurus, karma, etc., only a week before traveling across America to meet him. That meeting had taken place, as I said, hardly a month earlier. At our meeting I'd begged him to accept me as a disciple, and—unprecedentedly, as I later learned—was accepted on the spot. Suddenly, now, I found myself plunged into a completely new way of life. And here, only one month later, I was listening to this stunning revelation!

I think that perhaps acceptance of this book may depend somewhat on my own credibility. Let me add, therefore, that this seemingly abrupt change in my life was by no means so sudden as it appeared to others—especially to my parents, who were at that time far away in Egypt, where my father had been transferred to a new post. I had been seeking truth in secret, however, almost desperately for years. Reading *Autobiography of a Yogi* had changed my life completely forever thereafter. So utter was my faith in this new—but anciently familiar—teacher in my life that, whenever someone represented some teaching to me as being his, even if it seemed strange to me, the only question I asked was, "Did our Guru say that?" If the answer was yes, I posed no further questions.

So, yes, it was startling to hear that the three wise men had identities which could actually be named in our own age. Yet there was something about Paramhansa Yogananda that convinced me, as no one else had ever come close to doing, that he knew the Truth. He fitted exactly something that was said about Jesus: **"Never man spake like this man."** (John 7:46) Yogananda's words held more than conviction: they rang with divine wisdom. Unaccountably, when I was with him, I often felt that I was in the presence of God Himself. There was about him a certain divine aura. And though some of my readers may dismiss my words as proof of my simplicity and gullibility, I was in fact, when I was young, something of a rebel against intellectual authority. I refused to believe anyone unless I was convinced, first, that he knew what he was talking about.

Yogananda announced to us also, "Jesus, in his youth, paid a return visit to India to study under the 'wise men' who had come to honor him as a baby."

People may wonder, as those prelates did at the Council of Constantinople of which the Jagadguru Shankaracharya spoke, why an Incarnation of God needed to learn from anybody. The truth is, as Jesus put it to John the Baptist, **"Suffer it to be so now: for thus it becometh us to fulfill all righteousness."** (Matt. 3:15)

Even though Jesus was indeed one with the true Son of God (the Christ consciousness)—though not, be it noted, the *only* such Son—he went by that way which would "fulfill all righteousness." God is not miserly about sending his awakened Sons, who have become one with Him, to help His fallen children. Even incarnations of God, however, have to pass through the usual stages of infancy, childhood, adolescence, and maturity. If Jesus spoke in the temple in such a way that others were **"astonished at his understanding and answers,"** we must add that his parents, too, were amazed. In other words, he had been until then, in their eyes, a growing child—precocious no doubt, but hardly omniscient!

A liberated master, whose mission it is to mix with the public, must comport himself in such a way as not to *impose* his wisdom on those who hear him. He must, for their sake, seem down to earth and, in that sense, perfectly normal. It would be no help to them were he to overwhelm them with his omniscience in everything. My own Guru often expressed himself, when I knew him, in such a way as to make us feel that he didn't mind disagreement. I often questioned him—more so, perhaps, than most others, for I've always had a questioning mind—and he replied graciously, though often he telescoped his answer as if to oblige me to meet him on his own level of intuitive insight. He also said to me, concerning his own guru, "My master would often end a statement with the words, 'Don't you think so?' as if to invite us to make an effort to understand him, rather than receiving his words passively."

Thus, it was perfectly normal for a great master—indeed, for an *avatar* like Jesus, which is to say an Incarnation of God—to assume for a time the slight veil of delusion, as well as the behavior of a normal human being, in order to help others, later.

I once asked my Guru, "Does an *avatar* always live in the consciousness of oneness with God?"

Yogananda replied, "He never loses, inwardly,

the consciousness of being free." Nothing, in other words, binds his consciousness. We see this freedom in Yogananda's autobiography, despite the lengths to which he went, in humility, to help the reader to identify with everything he himself went through.

Our Guru told a group of us toward the end of his life, "I went to all those saints as a child, hoping to learn from them, but I found they kept asking questions *of me.*" They called him, "*Chhoto Mahasaya,*" which translates not only as, "little sir" (as he himself translated the term in his book), but also as, "Little Saint."

In 1887, the Russian writer Nicolas Notovitch discovered in the monastery of Himis an ancient manuscript which detailed the life of Jesus (called Issa in that work). It recounts that Issa had traveled there as a young man, and had later "preached the holy doctrine in India and among the children of Israel." It tells how Jesus (Issa) left home to avoid pressure from his parents, Joseph and Mary, to take a wife. Legend has it that he traveled by camel caravan over the "Silk Road," which was the main passage between the East and the West.

Notovitch published a book which became famous in his time, called *The Unknown Life of Jesus Christ.* In it he described Issa (Jesus) spending time in Puri, Orissa, among the priests at the famous Jagannath Temple. According to that account, Jesus got into trouble with the Brahmin

pundits, or priests, for defying the customary pro-
scriptions against members of the lower castes,
whom he himself taught freely. I myself am somewhat inclined to doubt whether Jesus made so
much of an issue of the caste system, or that he
tried to reform it. He may indeed have criticized it,
and may thereby have offended those orthodox
Brahmins who served as priests in the great temple. As for himself, however, he later said, when he
began his mission, that that mission was to **"the
lost sheep of the house of Israel."** Still, it must
be added that it would not have been out of keeping with his nature (as we know it) had he stood up
boldly for the Eternal Truth, and therefore spoken
out fearlessly against any man-made aberration of
that truth.

A prominent disciple of the great Sri Ramakrishna, Swami Abhedananada, later (in 1922)
went to Ladakh in order to verify the account
by Notovitch, and actually succeeded in doing so.
Later still, the well-known Russian artist—
who was already well known as a veritable "Re-
naissance Man"—Nicholas Roerich (I believe
Paramhansa Yogananda got to meet him), wrote
in 1929 of the many legends he had heard in
Kashmir about the visit of Jesus Christ to that
land, and about the manuscripts at Himis
monastery.

Madam Elisabeth G. Caspari, a Swiss musi-
cian, and her husband visited the Himis
monastery during the summer of 1939. There the

couple also learned from the librarian, along with two other monks of that monastery, about the manuscripts, which were shown to them (but were not translated for them).

An interesting feature of Jesus' way of teaching was his doing so in the form of parables. This method has always been common in India, but it was not common, so far as I know, among the Jews.

It was the destiny of Jesus, as he himself declared, to fulfill his mission in Israel. Therefore he returned, and came for baptism to John the Baptist, his destined guru. Christ's teaching reflected, however, a much more cosmopolitan outlook than that of John, who (the Bible tells us) lived **"in the wilderness. . . . [and] had his raiment of camel's hair, and a leathern girdle about his loins; and his meat [diet] was locusts and wild honey,"** and who, in addressing some of the more learned of his listeners, would cry out, **"O generation of vipers."** (Matt. 3:3,4,7)

Do we see in Jesus Christ's words to Nicodemus, which we quoted earlier—**"Verily, verily, I say unto thee, Except a man be born again, he cannot see the kingdom of God"**—a hint of teachings to which he'd been exposed in India? I know of no tradition in Judaism of being born again in the same body. India, however, does have that tradition. Brahmins, if they are indeed *true* to their divine calling, *are* described as twice-born in just the sense that Jesus goes on to describe in his second answer to Nicodemus:

"Nicodemus saith unto him, How can a man be born when he is old? can he enter the second time into his mother's womb, and be born?

"Jesus answered, Verily, verily, I say unto thee, Except a man be born of water and of the Spirit, he cannot enter into the kingdom of God." (John 3:3–5) I've explained this inner meaning already: namely, that to be born of water means to be born into a body, whereas to be born of the Spirit means to be born into spiritual consciousness: to emerge from the chrysalis of ego-consciousness into divine consciousness—an emergence in which the guru acts as the "midwife."

Do we see, again, in Jesus Christ's parable of the Prodigal Son a hint of his own experience of traveling from Israel to India? He himself was no prodigal son, of course, but that beautiful story may have been suggested to him by his journeys. In one sense, the possibility that he may have paid a return visit to the three wise men, to study under them, could have been seen as a "coming home." Then again, his return to Israel to carry out his life mission, and his receiving formal baptism from his guru John the Baptist, would certainly have been a final homecoming. Of course, the story of the Prodigal Son is an allegory for the soul's departure from God into the land of delusion, and of its return to God after wandering long in the "land of" ignorance. Still, the story itself could have been suggested to the mind of Jesus by his own wanderings. (Obviously, I offer this suggestion with no hint of trying to prove anything. I find it merely interesting.)

The account of Jesus leaving home as a boy to avoid marriage is very much in keeping with ancient tradition in India. Marriage in Israel, too, was arranged in those days after a boy reached the age of thirteen.

The story is told in south India of the great *mauni*, or "silent saint," Sadasiva, who as a young man lived in his parents' house and spent his time in studying the scriptures and meditating. One day he emerged from his room to find an unusual commotion in the home. Inquiring as to the reason for all that hubbub, he was told, "We are preparing for the arrival of your bride." (Marriages in olden times, especially in India, were arranged by the parents.)

Sadasiva returned to his room and reflected, "If the mere prospect of her coming can so unsettle my routine, how much worse would her actual 'in house' residence here be!" He slipped out that very night, and never returned.

To the average person, such complete non-attachment to home and family seems extraordinary. Sooner or later, however, everyone, if he would find God, must disappoint his family's expectations of him. All of us came alone into the world, and will depart it alone. In the end, every soul, in its true essence, must "go on alone."

What, incidentally, of the family of Jesus? It says, **"While he yet talked to the people, behold, his mother, and his brethren stood without, desiring to speak with him."** The New Testament also describes James as being a brother of Jesus. Much has been made, especially in the Catholic Church, of his mother Mary having been always a virgin: conceived immaculately, and immaculate forever thereafter. The Catholic Church also encourages devotion to the Virgin Mary, whom it offers as a substitute for the Divine Mother aspect of God. I said earlier that the Cosmic Mother represents the *AUM* vibration, through which one must in fact pass in order to reach the unmoving, Christ consciousness which is present in each particle of creation.

It is true that, by Eastern tradition, one's so-called "brothers" may also be one's first cousins — "cousin brother" is an expression one often hears in India. Yet I, personally, see no real problem with praying to the Virgin Mary. I too believe she was a virgin when she conceived Jesus, even if she did subsequently have other children. Paramhansa Yogananda said once in a prayer to God, "Thou hast suckled me through many mothers. And this last one was Thyself." His mother had eight children, and gave birth to them all by normal means. It is not the mere act of procreation that introduces the element of delusion. It is *attachment* to that act. Yogananda's most highly advanced disciple, Sister Gyanamata, had been married and had had a son. Yet he stated at her funeral, "I have searched her life, and have found therein not *a single sin.*"

So it seems unnecessary, to me, to worry whether Jesus did or did not have actual brothers. That his mother was holy and, indeed, *truly* immaculate I think everyone who believes in Jesus Christ agrees. I certainly do.

There has always been a tie between Judaism and Hinduism. Strange as it may seem, that tie is strongest in the insistence of both religions on the existence of one God. In Judaism, the statement, "Hear O Israel, the Lord our God is One," is unequivocal. And in Hinduism, the concept of a Supreme Spirit, Brahman, admits of no other. Indeed, by a strange-seeming paradox, the concept of Brahman is even more absolute in India than in the Judaic concept of Yahweh, or Jehovah. For the Jews have always seen God as separate—even aloof—from themselves. Brahman, however, in Hinduism (and, indeed, in *Sanaatan Dharma* everywhere) is the only reality in existence.

From this concept arose the justification for the innumerable so-called "gods" of Hinduism, which Judaeo-Christian tradition unjustly condemns. Those "gods" are conceived of in India as aspects, only, of the Undefinable. They are intended as means of awakening devotion to the Supreme, and are far from being the "golden calf" so excoriated (justly so) in Judaism.

Idol worship, Yogananda explained, means worshiping anything other than God: money, sex, power, fame, sensory pleasures. *That* was what the golden calf represented, which those Jews worshiped who had fallen into delusion while Moses was up on the mountain, communing with God. The golden calf symbolized the Jewish fetish (which some say continues to this day) with money, wealth, and material security. Jesus himself said:

"He that loveth father or mother more than me is not worthy of me: and he that loveth son or daughter more than me is not worthy of me." (Matt. 10:37) He said also:

"All that ever came before me are thieves and robbers: but the sheep did not hear them." (John 10:8) Jesus obviously was not referring to the old prophets who came before him in time, for he said elsewhere also, **"Think not that I am come to destroy the law, or the prophets: I am not come to destroy, but to fulfill."** (Matt. 5:17) Yogananda explained that Jesus was speaking of himself, as he often did, in the impersonal sense as the Son of God, or Christ consciousness. Those spiritual teachers and teachers of religion, in other words, who try to draw people's devotion to themselves, instead of directing it to God where alone it belongs, are indeed "thieves and robbers."

It is the ego, more even than "gold" and other worldly and false fulfillments, that constitutes the idol most people worship. Christians should

understand idol worship in this fundamental
sense, and should be especially forgiving of devotional images, since they themselves keep images
of Jesus on the cross on their altars, and also
keep many other devotional pictures. Through the
centuries, moreover, Christianity has inspired
many glorious works of devotional art, depicting
sacred scenes.

Hinduism is a much older religion than Christianity, and, because it was not started by any individual but sprang into existence during a higher
age when many people actually communed with
God, it contains many devotional images. Of some
comfort to Christians may be the fact that Hindus, too, often squabble among themselves as to
the "one, true" image of God. As Yogananda used
to say, "Ignorance, East and West, is fifty-fifty." In
India, too, only true saints deserve consideration
as the custodians of religion. The competitive
spirit one sees in religion everywhere is a manifestation of *Kali Yuga*. It may still remain somewhat during ascending *Dwapara Yuga*, but it will
certainly die out as man becomes progressively
enlightened through higher ages.

The masters are not affected by the great cycles
of time. They abide ever in perfect wisdom. Jesus
Christ had one mission above all: to teach every-
one, and especially his own Jewish people, that
God is One, and that all men, being a part of that
Oneness, must seek their highest fulfillment in
His love.

CHAPTER TWENTY-FOUR

CONCLUSION

THIS IS THE FINAL CHAPTER OF OUR BOOK — WHICH I feel I've written *with* you, not *at* or even *for* you. I was praying, "What should I say, Lord, to finish off any last doubts that might be lingering in the reader's mind?" And then one of my favorite "spirituals" came to mind:

Nobody knows the trouble I've seen.
Nobody knows but Jesus.

And I realized that I've said so much about the *impersonal* aspect of Christ's life that you might feel robbed of that dear, *personal* side of him, with whom we can all share our moments of sorrow, our troubles, and our difficulties. If so, I should be very sorry, for that conclusion would be wrong in terms not only of human needs, but also of my own feelings, and of cosmic truth itself.

Here's an illustration Yogananda used: Think of a funnel, narrowing down to its small end in you; the other end widening out to infinity. Yes, that's not, in itself, a personal image: I realize that funnels have no feelings. (Well, I've said that everything is conscious, so I suppose one could still endow funnels with consciousness! Even so, I admit it's a stretch.) So let's just place it in the background of our mental picture, and think of Jesus, the man, talking to us, consoling us, smiling at us with sweet, loving sympathy, interest, and concern. Behind him, his consciousness, and also the love he expresses, widen outward to infinity. Nevertheless, they have also a narrow focus: in him as a man, and *in you and me*, as human beings.

God, I said, is both infinite and infinitesimal. What makes divine love and Jesus Christ's love impersonal is only this: God wants nothing *from* you or me. Our human feelings, however, our human needs, our joys and our griefs: **you and I** *as human beings* mean as much to Him as they mean to us! For, in Truth, *He is in us*!

God created everything *from within*. He *became* you! "He wants nothing from you," Yogananda used to say to us, "except your love." You are already as close to Him as the greatest saint and master that ever lived. In that sense, indeed, the Protestant boast, "We're *all* saints!" is valid. The only difference between you and Jesus Christ himself is that you are still—one supposes—a

Prodigal Son, wandering in the land of delusion. Your thoughts and energies roam still, far away from your true Self. *Within yourself,* however, dwells the living Christ. That is why Jesus said, **"Neither shall they say, Lo here! or, lo there! for, behold, the kingdom of God is within you."** (Luke 17:21)

Jesus didn't come on earth to show people how great *he* was. He came to show us how great *we ourselves* are, in our divine potential.

Many years ago, on a visit to Australia, a man came up to me after a lecture and said, "I heard you speaking quite a lot about God. Well, I'm an atheist. What have you got to say to me that would interest me?"

I paused hardly a second in silent prayer, then answered, "Why don't you think of God as the highest potential you can imagine for yourself?"

For a moment, he was surprised into silence. Then, with a rather pleased, though self-deprecating, grin he replied, "Yeah, well, I guess I can live with that!"

God cares, you see, *for you*—for your smallest thoughts and feelings. In that caring, however, He invites you to *look at yourself* also impersonally: to see those thoughts and feelings as windows onto infinity; to see yourself, as you are now, as also the tip of a funnel, which reaches upward and outward, and becomes lost in infinite skies. Those "skies" are impersonal only in the sense that they ask nothing of you. Their influence, however, would draw you out of your petty ego to the realization that love itself, *divine* love, cannot remain confined forever in your little cup of human consciousness.

St. Paul wrote to the Corinthians: **"When I was a child, I spake as a child, I understood as a child, I thought as a child: but when I became a man, I put away childish things."** (I Cor. 13:11)

He went on to speak of a future time when he would see God face to face: **"Then shall I know even as also I am known."** God knows us, and loves us, not only as we know ourselves, and as we are in ourselves, but also as we are in truth, in *our very own* divine potential.

I once read a story of a Catholic nun in Europe who escaped Communist persecution. It was a dramatic and beautiful account. My only clear memory of it, however, is that she kept a small picture of Jesus in her pocket, and kept patting that pocket lovingly for reassurance during every harrowing experience. Sweet, touching, and, yes, inspiring! To one who loves God, God becomes in a sense a lovingly prized possession, something we can hold in our hands; something, above all, we can hold in our hearts.

The impersonal side should be kept ever in mind, lest we trivialize God. To love Him personally, however, is nevertheless a good beginning.

I used, in the beginning of my spiritual journey, to pray silently to my Guru, "Teach me to love you as you love me."

One day he looked at me deeply and said, "How can the little cup hold the whole ocean?" I understood him. We must seek ever to enter and expand our consciousness into the great ocean of divine love. As Jesus said,

"He that findeth his life shall lose it: and he that loseth his life for my sake shall find it." (Matt. 10:39)

Most people, however, are not ready to think of dissolving their egos in God, and that weakness was what Jesus meant to address here. The wonderful thing about true spirituality, as opposed to formal religion, is that its teachings make no absolute demands of anyone. Wherever you are *right now*, whether geographically or on your own level of consciousness, that is where God will meet you, if you call to Him with a sincere heart.

I read a novel years ago about a man who gave his life to God, and "of course" (such was the author's shallow understanding) attained only disillusionment in the end. We live in an age of experimentation, so why not experiment on yourself? See whether God will not listen, *and also answer you.* He is with you every moment of your life—"Nearest of the near, Dearest of the dear," as my Guru used to put it. Just try the following experiment:

Think of God in the second person: *You*, not He. Don't look up formal prayers in a hymnal or prayer book. Talk to Him in the language of your own heart. Share with Him your every thought, your every feeling. Talk to Jesus in that way, and to Mary, and to the saints. Say, "This person has hurt me deeply, Lord. What shall I do about it?" Or say, "I'm off to work now, Jesus. Be with me today. Guide my thoughts, that they be pleasing to you." Say "You," not "Thou," which isn't any longer the way we speak in daily life. Talk to him as a Friend, a Father, a Mother, even as your Beloved.

One of the great mistakes people make is to think, when God answers them in some particular aspect, that that aspect defines Him entirely as He is. He is all things. He could come to you as a Sacred Crocodile if that happened to be how you loved Him (though I can't really imagine anyone really loving Him in that form!). To be serious, I think you might find some one person who inspires you, and imagine God in that form.

My own godfather's wife had a sweet, motherly expression which I used, first, to visualize as my Divine Mother, since no other image came to mind that inspired me. (My own mother's face might have done it for me, but I had known her in too many ordinary, familial circumstances, whereas I rarely saw my godfather's wife.) It served me well, for starters. Gradually my visualizations took me beyond human forms altogether, and I felt my Divine Mother everywhere, behind all outer forms.

Whatever form you choose, just see to it that you don't become narrow or fanatical. In India, many people have almost come to blows over whether God should be worshiped as Vishnu, Shiva, Kali, Durga, Krishna, or Rama, or as the non-dual Absolute. To climb a mountain—as their own sages have many times pointed out— you can ascend it from the south, the north, the east, or the west. The important thing is to get to the top.

Try, therefore, simply talking with God—not *to* Him, and not *at* Him, but *with* Him. Think, as you go for a walk, "Your energy is powering my legs." If you hear a dog barking in the distance, ask God, "Is there something You are trying to tell me through that bark?" A materialist would of course answer, "That dog is barking with its own interests in mind. Why take it personally?" But God is everywhere. He can speak to you consciously through all things, if you will listen not only with your mind, but with your heart.

God is in every person you meet. It would be a good practice, while walking down any city street, to look at every passerby and think of him or her as God in that form. Then tell yourself, "He (or she), too, wants what I want: happiness." He/she may visualize that fulfillment as a new job, or a raise in salary, or a wife or a husband, or children, or as any of the innumerable things people yearn for everywhere on earth, in the expectation that they'll find happiness through them. Look at them more deeply, however, and tell yourself, "What their souls *really* want is divine bliss, which is only masquerading as human happiness. In that yearning, they are all my brothers and sisters, even if their present intentions are misguided." Talk to God about them in your heart. Ask Him to bless them. In time, with this practice, you will come to think of all life as a great, glorious symphony, blending all creatures together in wonderful, flowing chords, rhythms, and melodies of divine aspiration.

Don't tell anyone about this practice, for if you do, that outward flow of energy will drain your inner treasure, and may dilute it with other people's cynicism, lack of comprehension, or prosaic matter-of-factness.

One challenge that people will fling at you is, "So what, exactly, do you mean when you say that God answers you? Are you suggesting He performs miracles? And are you really going to say that you believe in the miracles of Jesus Christ? Come off it! Things like that just don't happen!"

Don't they? I lived with a true man of God, and saw things many people would say were impossible. But I learned that these are not things to speak about openly. I learned my lesson one day, after a gathering in Beverly Hills. I had been invited there to perform yoga postures at a Jewish Bar Mitzvah. Afterward, a materialistic Jewish psychiatrist cornered me and challenged my beliefs. I defended them as reasonably as I could, and then, to clinch my argument, I spoke of certain miracles to which I'd been a witness. It did no good at all. In fact, I could see the thought in his mind, "Perhaps I could see this 'patient' at ten o'-clock next Wednesday morning."

A few days later, I served lunch for Yogananda and several guests, and followed the meal with a short demonstration of yoga postures. After the guests had departed, I sat alone at the table for a few minutes with my Guru. During our conversation he paused briefly, then commented, "By the way, when you are with atheists and materialists, don't speak to them of miracles."

"You knew!" I exclaimed.

Looking at me deeply, he replied, "I know every single thought you think." Often, during our time together, he demonstrated the truth of that statement.

Let me address rather the question, then: How are so-called miracles even possible? (I speak of them as "so-called," because nothing is miraculous, really, in the sense of naturally impossible. Were someone today able to travel backward in time, and appear to people four hundred years ago, and were he to tell them of the wonders of radio and television, he would probably be locked up as a lunatic.)

I have spoken of the scientifically proved fact that matter exists only as vibrations of energy. Yogananda's dictum, "The greater the will, the greater the flow of energy," provides a clue as to how that energy itself was brought into manifestation: It was by an act of divine will, outwardly projected.

God, the Supreme Spirit, willed creation into existence. First, what He manifested were thought forms—ideas for the further manifestation of creation. Those ideas might be compared to an architect's blueprint. When God saw "that it was good," He projected those ideas outward further (working through already-manifested beings) by His divine will, manifesting energy.

The astral world, which most people think of as heaven, is actually a universe of energy. It is, Swami Sri Yukteswar said, much larger than the material universe. Finally, God (again, through higher beings) vibrated that astral energy still more grossly, to produce the material universe.

Incidentally, Yogananda explained that the reason God said, **"Let us make man in our image, after our likeness."** (Gen. 1:26) was that God created man *through* actual, high beings.

Is there, or will there ever be, the prospect of some even-denser manifestation of the divine will than the material? In my understanding, there can never be, for that which conceals divine freedom in an appearance of complete inertia (that is to say, in matter) permits no further descent. Never mind about hell: In a sense we are living in hell already. This does not mean that there is no actual, astral hell, for indeed such a hell exists also.

When the thick walls of flesh are removed by death, human emotions and feelings are released from their narrow confinement in a body into the far less circumscribed essence which, if one's feelings are dark, can lead to suffering far more intense than people ever know on earth (though it brings a release into far greater joy, for those who ascend to the astral heavens). Fortunately, the experience of hell is not permanent, for the germ of divinity is centered ever in each soul, however much it may be covered over with the impurities of lust, avarice, passion, anger, jealousy, hatred, and other dark emotions. God condemns no one, even temporarily, to hell. People condemn themselves, by the violence of their own self-created thoughts and emotions.

Back, now, to the subject of miracles: Anyone who becomes even somewhat aware of the subtle energies within him can direct those energies in ways that, to most people, will seem miraculous. These are really only workings of Natural Law; nothing about them is really miraculous. Nevertheless, when one has become fully conscious of the upward flow of that energy within him, he can effortlessly perform feats which, to the ordinary person, would seem impossible.

When the energy flows upward with *kundalini* from the sacral center in the spine, the *Swadisthan,* which controls the water "element" or elemental stage of manifestation (described as "water" because the energy in that center manifests fluidity), the yogi who has "opened" this center can walk on water. That was what Sadhu Haridas did in that boat with the Christian missionary.

When the energy flows upward from the heart or dorsal center (the *Anahat chakra*, which is also the "air" center), he can levitate—as St. Theresa of Avila did, much against her own will, anxious as she was not to make a spectacle of herself.

All the yoga teachings caution people never to display these powers unless they feel a divine sanction from within. The caution is given to protect the aspiring yogi from falling into spiritual pride. The great master Sri Ramakrishna cautioned his disciples on the subject of spiritual pride, saying, "Ordinary pride is relatively easy to dispose of, for in the realm of relativity no state of mind ever lasts for long. Pride is soon followed, therefore, by a fall, or by opposing forces which produce inner conflict and unhappiness. The foundation of worldly pride is no more substantial than a bubble. Spiritual pride, however, is founded on something real, and it can take the spiritual aspirant incarnations to come out of it."

Give back to God, therefore, everything He gives to you. Don't hug it to yourself—an act which would mean only affirming it as something possessed by your ego. Jesus said, indeed, in two combined verses that my Guru often quoted:

"Verily I say unto you, There is no man that hath left house, or brethren, or sisters, or father, or mother, or wife, or children, or lands, for my name's sake, and the gospel's, But he shall receive an hundredfold now in this time, houses, and brethren, and sisters, and mothers,

and children, and lands, with persecutions; and in the world to come eternal life." (Matt. 19:29 and Mark 10:29,30) Only Mark added that part about persecution, but Yogananda always stressed this word also, for, he said, "No one who gives his life wholly to God can escape Satan's displeasure." The real riches one receives from God are also, in part, the necessary riches of this world, for one does find himself sustained, and never abandoned, if he clings to God.

I must add to that word "persecution," however, that abandonment by God can sometimes *seem* total. God's tests can be very hard. Nevertheless, I say this with the conviction born of experience: *God does not abandon His own.* His own, moreover, are all those who place their lives unreservedly in His hands. As the Bhagavad Gita says, "O Arjuna, know this for a certainty: My devotee is never lost." Christ's promise of abundance is not limited to heavenly rewards. It is fulfilled also in this life. All one's earthly needs are fulfilled even to overflowing.

He added to the above verses in both gospels, **"But many that are first shall be last; and the last shall be first."** How many long-term devotees on the spiritual path claim precedence over newcomers with the smug statement, "Don't you think I ought to know better? I have been following these teachings much longer than you have!" Yogananda often quoted those words also to remind his disciples that what matters is not seniority, rank, or years on the spiritual path, but the intensity of one's own dedication. He added, "Hold nothing back from God. Give to Him everything you have, and everything you are."

Materialists, inevitably, will respond to the promise of God's abundance, "Oh, yeah?" and "How?" and, "What about all the starving poor in the world? What about their sufferings? What about the massive cataclysms, which impersonally claim both the virtuous and the sinful?"

Paramhansa Yogananda asks this question in his book, *The Rubaiyat of Omar Khayyam Explained*: "Is life so difficult to understand? Well, of course it is! If it were easy to grasp the drift and purpose of this spectacle, how well would that speak for the skill of the Dramatist? The Divine Playwright has concealed the nature of His plot— which is, in itself, straightforward—behind endless subplots and complexities. He has cloaked the wonderful ending of the play behind a network of confusing hints and plausible-seeming, but false, explanations for the events taking place. It is a story wrought with incalculable skill, its true purpose concealed with sublimest artistry behind myriads of tragic and comic secondary plots.

"The whole meaning of the story comes clear in the end. When the soul attains Self-realization and eternal freedom, it understands, and then, with clapping wings, it applauds enthusiastically.

"Someday God will lift for all of us—each one in turn—the heavy curtain of illusion, and play out for us the final scene of His Divine Drama. When this happens, the glorious ending that He had in mind from the beginning will be revealed to us at last."

Ah, what a sublime work Yogananda created with his explanation of that true scripture. Omar Khayyam's poem seems to be, on the surface, a mere love song. In truth, it is a timeless, great scripture.

Yes, God tests those who love Him. Look at Job —not for comfort, to be sure, but to stiffen your spine with divine courage! And yet, there is another truth to keep in mind always: Jesus promised to send "the Comforter." I'll discuss Yogananda's explanation of that meaning in a moment. First, let me point out an important truth: No one who has found God has ever cried in disappointment, "What a scam!" All who know Him have been overwhelmed with oceanic joy.

Sister Gyanamata, whom I mentioned toward the end of the last chapter, was on her deathbed, about to leave her body. The last words she uttered, ecstatically, were, "What joy! Too much joy!"

Such is the experience, in the end, of every soul. Moses was not allowed to enter the Promised Land. That prohibition applied, however, only to Moses the *man*. Though a fully enlightened soul, his human ego had to leave even itself behind before his soul could enter into the *true* Promised Land: the inner Kingdom of God. And only those who had been born out of bondage—soul qualities such as pure love, self-surrender to God, and universal compassion—were allowed to enter in. Every ego-born characteristic, on the other hand, no matter how noble, had first to die before the "chosen people"—those qualities of our nature which we raise wholly toward God—could fulfill their divine destiny.

People don't see beyond the veil. Someone dies, and his friends and loved ones cry, "Poor soul!" They've no idea what his present state is. Death is nothing, in itself. It is a matter of merely stepping out of one's costume when the play is over, and returning to one's other, more normal life.

Life is not the horror show they imagine it to be who "keep all their eggs in the one basket" of life on earth. The materialists want materialistic answers to their intellectual doubts and challenges. It doesn't always work that way. I speak with some experience on this point. God doesn't always give you what you want, but if you live for Him sincerely, you will find that God gives you something much better than you ever imagined. In other words, the system *works*. Why not try it?

Modern man believes in the value of experimentation. Very well, why not submit this truth to the test of *your own* experience. I challenge you! Yogananda challenged you! It is high time those materialists were driven, mumbling, into the cobwebbed corner where they belong!

The spiritual path, which is *true* Christianity, is endlessly satisfying. People imagine shriveled-up nuns and monks, "meek" priests and pastors, all of them forever deprecating themselves (to the point of causing universal exasperation), and emotionally starved "faithful"—like a certain classmate of mine in college with the appropriate name, Coffin, who would gaze at us lugubriously and ask, "Have you been saved?" People like that find "inspiration" in judging anyone dourly who doesn't see things just the way they do.

Let us consider that word, "meek." Jesus said in the Beatitudes, **"Blessed are the meek: for they shall inherit the earth."** (Matt. 5:5) Looking at the blessing that follows upon meekness, one sees that by "meek" Jesus couldn't have meant the somewhat hangdog expression so many Christians assume in their effort to be humble. Those people alone "inherit the earth" who work with it harmoniously, instead of trying to wrest from it the treasures they want. Blessed, then, are the *harmonious*. That *has to be* what Jesus meant.

True religion means to live a spiritual life. Living such a life, however, need not necessarily mean being religious. The outer trappings and ceremonies of formal religion serve a valid purpose if they help one in his search for an inner life. Spirituality, however, is the true and only goal offered in the highest teachings of every true scripture.

Jesus promised to send the Comforter. What did he mean? When the Comforter came, it was on the day of Pentecost. Let us read the account:

"And when the day of Pentecost was fully come, they were all with one accord in one place.

"And suddenly there came a sound from heaven as of a rushing mighty wind, and it filled all the house where they were sitting.

"And there appeared unto them cloven tongues like as of fire, and it sat upon each of them.

"And they were all filled with the Holy Ghost, and began to speak with other tongues, as the Spirit gave them utterance." (Acts 2:1–4)

The "rushing mighty wind" is a manifestation of the cosmic *AUM*, the Holy Ghost, or Holy Spirit. The sound of that Cosmic Vibration is supremely comforting. It plays on the harp strings, so to speak, of one's very being. Earthly sounds, even the most beautiful of them, become tiresome in time, and even irritating if we hear them for too long. When one hears the sound of *AUM*, however, he knows with utter certainty that he could never tire of it through all eternity, for it is the vibration of his very being. Many times, while writing this book, I have been entranced to hear that sound within and around me, as if in divine corroboration and approval of what I had written.

The tongues of fire have an esoteric meaning which I will suggest to the reader that he look up in the edition of Paramhansa Yogananda's book, *The Second Coming of Christ*. That volume, heavily edited as it is, and somewhat difficult to read, will bestow on the serious student great blessings, and he will find his efforts richly repaid.

The speaking in tongues comes indeed as a power bestowed in communion with the Holy Ghost. All languages are expressions of *AUM*. If sometime, in a foreign country, you find yourself up against an alien tongue, try to tune into it *from within* instead of worrying too anxiously, outwardly, about the complexities of a strange grammar. You will quickly find those complexities resolving themselves in a surprising simplicity.

My own efforts in this direction have not been accompanied consciously by inner communion with *AUM*, but I have tried to tune into those languages from within, and have found that they come with surprising ease. Natives of the countries I've been in have often thought I was their countryman. One day in Calcutta I was speaking on the street with my driver before going into a shop. A passerby, hearing me talk and seeing my white skin, later asked the driver in astonishment, "Is he *Bengali*?" No, I don't speak good Bengali, but at least I have the vibration of it down pretty well.

I have heard self-styled "Pentecostals" speaking in what they called "tongues." To anyone who knows languages it sounds like gibberish. No language on earth could be so starved of variety in its syllables! Yogananda spoke of "the unholy ghost of emotions." Really to commune with the Comforter is to listen calmly, in meditation, to

AUM. That sound, as one listens, gives supreme comfort to the soul. Doctor Lewis, Yogananda's first Kriya Yoga disciple in America, quoted the Guru to us in telling the following story:

"Master had said to me, 'When you are in *AUM,* nothing can touch you.'

"One day I was out sailing in a boat on the ocean when suddenly a great storm arose. It threatened to capsize our boat, and I thought we were goners. And then I remembered Master's words. I gazed up into the light, and then I knew we were safe. [The inner light is a primary manifestation of the Cosmic Vibration.]

"When I got home, and just as I walked in the door, the phone rang. Master was on the other end of the line. He said to me, 'You came near getting wet, Doctor, didn't you?'"

There is a technique for listening to the *AUM* sound. Although I am not free to include it in the pages of this book, I urge every reader to consider very seriously the thought of learning and practicing it.

Jesus said, **"I am the vine, ye are the branches: He that abideth in me, and I in him, the same bringeth forth much fruit: for without me ye can do nothing.**

"If a man abide not in me, he is cast forth as a branch, and is withered; and men gather them, and cast them into the fire, and they are burned.

"If ye abide in me, and my words abide in

you, ye shall ask what ye will, and it shall be done unto you." (John 15:5–7)

I have used elsewhere the illustration of the sounding board. This image, coupled with the Comforter, and with the image Jesus gives here of the vine and its branches, may help to clarify for everyone an eternal truth. *AUM*, the Holy Ghost, is the sounding board. The Christ consciousness is the vine of which all of us are a part. If one will act in the thought of being united to Cosmic Truth (the vine, the sounding board, the Eternal Comforter) he will know that God and Jesus Christ are always with him, and that he has no further need of anything else, anywhere.

Communion with the Holy Ghost is, above all, a means of entering into, and flowing with, the stream of divine love. Love God, therefore. As a true Christian, love Jesus as your divine friend, who came down to earth for *your* upliftment. The more you tune into his deep message, the more also you will know that only one thing matters in life: selfless, divine love, like that of an eternal child for his Heavenly Father, and for his Divine Friend.

LIST OF INDEXES

INDEX OF QUOTATIONS BY JESUS

INDEX OF QUOTATIONS FROM THE BIBLE

INDEX OF QUOTATIONS BY OTHERS

INDEX OF BIBLE VERSES

ABOUT THE AUTHOR

"As a bright light shining in the midst of darkness, so was Yogananda's presence in this world. Such a great soul comes on earth only rarely, when there is a real need among men."
—The Shankaracharya of Kanchipuram

PARAMHANSA YOGANANDA

Born in India in 1893, Paramhansa Yogananda was trained from his early years to bring India's ancient science of Self-realization to the West.

In 1920 he moved to the United States to begin what was to develop into a worldwide work touching millions of lives. Americans were hungry for India's spiritual teachings, and for the liberating techniques of yoga.

In 1946 he published what has become a spiritual classic and one of the best-loved books of the 20th century, *Autobiography of a Yogi*. In addition, Yogananda established headquarters for a worldwide work, wrote a number of books and study courses, gave lectures to thousands in most major cities across the United States, wrote music and poetry, and trained disciples. He was invited to the White House by Calvin Coolidge, and he initiated Mahatma Gandhi into Kriya Yoga, his most advanced technique of meditation.

Yogananda's message to the West highlighted the unity of all religions, and the importance of love for God combined with scientific techniques of meditation.

"*Swami Kriyananda is a man of wisdom and compassion in action, truly one of the leading lights in the spiritual world today.*"
—Lama Surya Das, Dzogchen Center, author of *Awakening The Buddha Within*

SWAMI KRIYANANDA

A prolific author, accomplished composer, playwright, and artist, and a world-renowned spiritual teacher, Swami Kriyananda refers to himself simply as "a humble disciple" of the great God-realized master, Paramhansa Yogananda. He met his guru at the young age of twenty-two, and served him during the last four years of the Master's life. And he has done so continuously ever since.

Kriyananda was born in Rumania of American parents, and educated in Europe, England, and the United States. Philosophically and artistically inclined from youth, he soon came to question life's meaning and society's values. During a period of intense inward reflection, he discovered Yogananda's *Autobiography of a Yogi*, and immediately traveled 3,000 miles from New York to

California to meet the Master, who accepted him as a monastic disciple. Yogananda appointed him as the head of the monastery, authorized him to teach in his name and to give initiation into Kriya Yoga, and entrusted him with the missions of writing and developing what he called "world brotherhood colonies."

Recognized as the "father of the spiritual communities movement" in the United States, Swami Kriyananda founded Ananda World Brotherhood Community in 1968. It has served as a model for a number of communities founded subsequently in the United States and Europe.

In 2003 Swami Kriyananda, then in his seventy-eighth year, moved to India with a small international group of disciples, to dedicate his remaining years to making his guru's teachings better known. To this end he appears daily on Indian national television with his program, A Way of Awakening. He has established Ananda Sangha, which publishes many of his eighty-six literary works and spreads the teachings of Kriya Yoga throughout India. His vision for the next years includes founding cooperative spiritual communities in India, a temple of all religions dedicated to Paramhansa Yogananda, a retreat center, a school system, and a monastery, as well as a university-level Yoga Institute of Living Wisdom.

About the Painter

Dana Lynne Andersen, M.A.

The cover illustration by Dana Lynne Andersen was commissioned for this book. The title "Pearl of

Great Price" refers to the parable in which Christ proclaimed that the kingdom of God was like a priceless pearl; *"Again, the kingdom of heaven is like unto a merchant man, seeking goodly pearls: who, when he had found one pearl of great price, went and sold all he had, and bought it."* (Matt. 13:45) In the painting the pearl represents the still point of awareness that calms the storm and from which the cosmic consciousness of Christ emerges. When we have found the 'pearl of great price' within us, all worldly needs are satisfied.

Dana Lynne Andersen is an international artist of growing renown, acclaimed for the insight she brings to the role of consciousness in the arts. She sends a clarion call to artists to produce work of elevated and expanded vision. In contrast to the idea of 'art for art's sake' she advocates 'art on purpose', referring to work that is deliberate in its intention to uplift humanity and serve as a vehicle of inspiration. Considering the watershed challenge and opportunity of our tumultuous times, she encourages artists of every kind (painters, sculptors, composers, musicians, writers and filmmakers) to join in using the power of art to awaken higher capacities and catalyze positive change. She is the founder of Awakening Arts Institute centered in Nevada City, California, a worldwide network of artists, patrons and friends dedicated to awakening higher consciousness through the arts. See www.awakeningarts.com.

FURTHER EXPLORATIONS

In addition to *Autobiography of a Yogi*, one of
Yogananda's other best-known and most
profound masterpieces is his commentary on
the Bhagavad Gita. Recently, Swami Kriyananda,
direct disciple of Yogananda, published an edition
of Yogananda's Gita commentaries:

The Essence of the Bhagavad Gita
Explained by Paramhansa Yogananda, As Remembered by His Disciple, Swami Kriyananda

Rarely in a lifetime does a new spiritual classic
appear that has the power to change people's lives
and transform future generations. This is such a
book. *The Essence of the Bhagavad Gita Explained
by Paramhansa Yogananda* shares the profound insights of Paramhansa Yogananda, as remembered

by one of his few remaining direct disciples, Swami Kriyananda.

This revelation of India's best-loved scripture approaches it from an entirely fresh perspective, showing its deep allegorical meaning and also its down-to-earth practicality. The themes presented are universal: how to achieve victory in life in union with the divine; how to prepare for life's "final exam," death, and what happens afterward; how to triumph over all pain and suffering.

Swami Kriyananda worked with Paramhansa Yogananda in 1950 while the Master completed his commentary. At that time Yogananda commissioned him to disseminate his teachings worldwide. Kriyananda declares, "Yogananda's insights into the Gita are the most amazing, thrilling, and helpful of any I have ever read."

"It is doubtful that there has been a more important spiritual writing in the past 50 years than this soul-stirring, monumental work. Through a mind blessed with special clarity, Swami Kriyananda has brought us his most vivid memories of the explanations by Paramhansa Yogananda of the Bhagavad Gita, allowing us to hear with greater vibrancy than ever before the Melodies of the Divine. At last the "Lord's Song" is not a mystery to our mind, but music to our ears! What a gift! What a treasure! My personal gratitude to Swami Kriyananda shall be everlasting."

—Neale Donald Walsch, author of
Conversations with God

Crystal Clarity publishes the original, unedited edition of Paramhansa Yogananda's spiritual masterpiece:

Autobiography of a Yogi
Paramhansa Yogananda

This is a new edition, featuring previously unavailable material, of a true spiritual classic, *Autobiography of a Yogi*: one of the best-selling Eastern philosophy titles of all-time, with millions of copies sold, named one of the best and most influential books of the 20th century.

This highly prized verbatim reprinting of the original 1946 edition is the ONLY one available free from textual changes made after Yogananda's death.

This updated edition contains bonus materials, including a last chapter that Yogananda himself wrote in 1951, five years after the publication of the first edition. It is the only version of this chapter available without posthumous changes.

Yogananda was the first yoga master of India whose mission it was to live and teach in the West. His first-hand account of his life experiences includes childhood revelations, stories of his visits to saints and masters in India, and long-secret teachings of Self-realization that he made available to the Western reader.

*"In the original edition, published during Yo-
gananda's life, one is more in contact with Yogananda himself. While Yogananda founded centers and organizations, his concern was more with
guiding individuals to direct communion with Divinity rather than with promoting any one church as
opposed to another. This spirit is easier to grasp in
the original edition of this great spiritual and yogic
classic."*

—David Frawley, Director, American
Institute of Vedic Studies

There are two different collections of the
sayings, stories, and wisdom of Yogananda, each
covering a diverse range of spiritual practices and
topics, presented in an enjoyable, easy-to-read
format.

Conversations with Yogananda
Edited with commentary by Swami Kriyananda

This is an unparalleled, first-hand account of
the teachings of Paramhansa Yogananda. Featuring nearly 500 never-before-released stories,
sayings, and insights, this is an extensive, yet
eminently accessible treasure trove of wisdom
from one of the 20th century's most famous yoga
masters. Compiled and edited with commentary,
by Swami Kriyananda, one of Yogananda's closest
direct disciples.

"Not many theologians can speak of Conscious bliss from a place of personal experience. Paramhansa Yogananda, a renowned twentieth-century spiritual teacher . . . can. His personal authority lends dramatic credibility to concepts and methods for spiritual aspirants from any tradition, from uncertain agnostics to fervent believers."

—*ForeWord* Magazine

The Essence of Self-Realization
Edited and compiled by Swami Kriyananda

A fantastic volume of the stories, sayings, and wisdom of Paramhansa Yogananda, this book covers more than 20 essential topics about the spiritual path and practices. Subjects covered include: the true purpose of life, the folly of materialism, the essential unity of all religions, the laws of karma and reincarnation, grace vs. self-effort, the need for a guru, how to pray effectively, meditation, and many more.

"A wonderful book! To find a previously unknown message from Yogananda now is an extraordinary spiritual gift. Essence is wonderful to read in bits and pieces, before bed or to open up at random for an encouraging word from one of this century's most beloved spiritual teachers."

—*Body, Mind, Spirit* Magazine

If you would like to learn more about Paramhansa Yogananda and his teachings, Crystal Clarity Publishers offers many additional resources to assist you.

The Wisdom of Yogananda series features writings of Paramhansa Yogananda not available elsewhere. These books capture the Master's expansive and compassionate wisdom, his sense of fun, and his practical spiritual guidance. The books include writings from his earliest years in America, in an approachable, easy-to-read format. The words of the Master are presented with minimal editing, to capture the fresh and original voice of one of the most highly regarded spiritual teachers of the 20th century.

How to Be Happy All the Time

The Wisdom of Yogananda Series, Volume 1
Paramhansa Yogananda

The human drive for happiness is one of our most far-reaching and fundamental needs. Yet, despite our desperate search for happiness, according to a recent Gallup Poll, only a minority of North Americans describe themselves as "very happy." It seems that very few of us have truly unlocked the secrets of lasting joy and inner peace.

In this volume of all-new, never-before-released material, Paramhansa Yogananda playfully and powerfully explains virtually everything needed to lead a happier, more fulfilling life. Topics covered include: looking for happiness in the right places;

choosing to be happy; tools and techniques for achieving happiness; sharing happiness with others; balancing success and happiness, and many more.

Karma and Reincarnation
The Wisdom of Yogananda Series, Volume 2
Paramhansa Yogananda

The interrelated ideas of karma and reincarnation have intrigued us for millennia. In today's post-modern culture, the idea of "karma" has become mainstream while belief in reincarnation is now at an all-time high in the West. Yet, for all of the burgeoning interest, very few of us truly understand what these terms mean and how these laws work.

In this volume of all-new material, Paramhansa Yogananda—one of the most respected spiritual teachers of the 20th century—definitively reveals the truth behind karma, death, reincarnation, and the afterlife. With clarity and simplicity, Yogananda makes the mysterious understandable. Topics covered include: how karma works; how we can change our karma; the relationship between karma and reincarnation; what we can learn from our past lives; how to overcome karmic obstacles; how to die with uplifted consciousness; what happens after death; the true purpose of life, and much more.

If you'd like a succinct, easy-to-understand overview of Yogananda's teachings and their place within ancient and contemporary spiritual thought and practices, we suggest:

God Is for Everyone

Inspired by Paramhansa Yogananda, written by Swami Kriyananda

This book outlines the core of Yogananda's teachings. *God Is for Everyone* presents a concept of God and spiritual meaning that will appeal to everyone, from the most uncertain agnostic to the most fervent believer. Clearly and simply written, thoroughly nonsectarian and non-dogmatic in its approach, with a strong emphasis on the underlying unity of all religions, this is the perfect introduction to the spiritual path.

"This book makes accessible the inspired pursuit of Bliss in simple, understandable ways. Written as an introduction for those just starting on the spiritual path, it is also a rejuvenating and inspiring boost for experienced seekers. Clear, practical techniques are offered to enhance personal spiritual practices. The author maintains that "everyone in the world is on the spiritual path" whether they know it or not, even if they are temporarily merely seeking pleasure and avoiding pain. Sooner or later, "They will want to experience Him (God)." Experiencing God—and specifically experiencing God as Bliss—is that underlying goal of this work,

based on the teachings of a self-realized teacher. It hits the mark for contemporary spirituality."
—*ForeWord* Magazine

During his lifetime, Yogananda was famous for being a powerful speaker and riveting personality, and an awe-inspiring presence. If you'd like to experience a taste of this, we suggest:

Paramhansa Yogananda: Rare Film Collection

This DVD contains three short film clips of the world-renowned spiritual teacher, Paramhansa Yogananda, recorded in the 1920s and 1930s. Thrilling and utterly fascinating, the unique combination of both seeing and hearing Yogananda is a life-changing experience. Also included is a video slideshow depicting many of the places that Yogananda himself wrote about in *Autobiography of a Yogi*. Narrated by his close disciple, Swami Kriyananda, this video retraces Yogananda's footsteps throughout India, recounting his visits with many great saints and sages. Filled with many rare and precious photographs. This is a must-have for anyone who has ever been touched by this great master.

Yogananda has many direct disciples, individuals that he personally trained to carry on various aspects of his mission after his passing. One of the best known of these disciples is Swami Kriyananda, the founder of Ananda and Crystal Clarity Publishers. Kriyananda's autobiography, a sequel of sorts to *Autobiography of a Yogi*, contains hundreds of stories about Yogananda, culled from the nearly four years that Kriyananda lived with and was trained by Yogananda. It offers the unique perspective of a disciple reflecting on his time with a great Master:

The Path
One Man's Quest on the Only Path There Is
Swami Kriyananda (J. Donald Walters)

The Path is the moving story of Kriyananda's years with Paramhansa Yogananda. *The Path* completes Yogananda's life story and includes more than 400 never-before-published stories about Yogananda, India's emissary to the West and the first yoga master to spend the greater part of his life in America.

"The Path *is a deeply moving revelation of one man's poignant search for truth. With this book, Walters provides us with a rarely seen portrait of the joys and the problems of the spiritual path. The* Path *is filled with profound insight and practical advice for the novice and the more advanced*

seeker. I cannot conceive of anyone not deriving value from reading Walters' life story."
—Michael Toms, Founder and President,New Dimensions Radio

"This book let me see inside the life and teaching of a great modern saint. Yogananda has found a worthy Boswell to convey not only the man but the spirit of the man."
—James Fadiman, author of *Unlimiting Your Life* and *Essential Suffism*

Crystal Clarity also offers two additional biographical resources about Swami Kriyananda. These are:

The Story Behind the Story
My Life of Service Through Writing
Swami Kriyananda

This is a warm, personal account of the inspirations which motivated seventy-two of Kriyananda's books, and the significance which he perceives in them. A delightful "behind-the-scenes" glimpse into the private world of an inspired author.

Faith Is My Armor
The Life of Swami Kriyananda
Devi Novak

Faith Is My Armor tells the complete story of

Swami Kriyananda's life: from his childhood in
Rumania, to his desperate search for meaning in
life, and to his training under his great Guru, the
Indian Master, Paramhansa Yogananda. As a
youth of 22, he first met and pledged his disciple-
ship to Yogananda, entering the monastery
Yogananda had founded in Southern California.

If you would like to learn more about the spiritual heritage of India, the highest meaning of
Hinduism, Yoga, and Christianity, including the
deeper, underlying unity between Eastern and
Western spirituality, you will enjoy reading:

The Hindu Way of Awakening

*Its Revelation, Its Symbols: An Essential View of
    Religion*
Swami Kriyananda

In a scholarly and thorough manner,
Kriyananda brings order to the seeming chaos of
the vast symbols and imagery one encounters in
Hinduism, and clearly communicates the underlying teachings from which these symbols arise.
Sure to deepen your understanding and appreciation of the Hindu religion, this book also helps
establish the transcendent unity of all religions.

*"Swami Kriyananda's inspired, entertaining,
energetic writing style makes this book delightful
reading for Hindus and non-Hindus alike. He*

brings order to the seeming chaos of the vast symbols and imagery one encounters in Hinduism and brings forth the under-lying teachings from which these symbols arise . . . Kriyananda does a superb job not only in deepening our understanding and appreciation of the Hindu religion, but of encouraging us to expand our awareness to include an appreciation of truth in all religions."

—Yoga International

The Promise of Immortality

The True Teaching of the Bible and the Bhagavad
J. Donald Walters (Swami Kriyananda)

Destined to become a classic, *The Promise of Immortality* is the most complete commentary available on the parallel passages in the Bible and the Bhagavad Gita, India's ancient scripture. Compellingly written, this groundbreaking book illuminates the similarities between these two great scriptures in a way that vibrantly brings them to life. Mr. Walters sheds light on famous passages from both texts, showing their practical relevance for the modern day, and their potential to help us achieve lasting spiritual transformation.

"While Walters' study speaks to an urgent need for understanding and compassion, his book also brings both the Bible and The Bhagavad Gita vibrantly to life. The Promise of Immortality is the

most complete commentary available on the parallel passages in these two texts."
—*Bodhi Tree Book Review*

If you would like to learn how to begin your own practice of yoga postures, meditation, Kriya Yoga, and more, as taught by Yogananda and Kriyananda, we strongly recommend the following:

The Art and Science of Raja Yoga
Swami Kriyananda

Contains fourteen lessons in which the original yoga science emerges in all its glory—a proven system for realizing one's spiritual destiny. This is the most comprehensive course available on yoga and meditation today. Over 450 pages of text and photos give you a complete and detailed presentation of yoga postures, yoga philosophy, affirmations, meditation instruction, and breathing techniques. Also included are suggestions for daily yoga routines, information on proper diet, recipes, and alternative healing techniques. The book also comes with an audio CD that contains: a guided yoga postures sessions, a guided meditation, and an inspiring talk on how you can use these techniques to solve many of the problems of daily life.

"It's tough to do a good yoga book, because a number of variables have to converge: substantive

integrity, clarity in how-to explanations and quality visuals. By those measures, this book succeeds. Walters' long teaching record shows his ability to discuss key yogic concepts and practices in simple terms. . . . This comprehensive guide has an extra medium to distinguish it on the crowded yoga bookshelf. . . . All things considered, it's superior to books that reduce yoga to a series of physical exercises taught by this year's guru."
—*Publishers Weekly*

Meditation for Starters
J. Donald Walters (Swami Kriyananda)

Meditation brings balance into our lives, providing an oasis of profound rest and renewal. Doctors are prescribing it for a variety of stress-related diseases. This award-winning book offers simple but powerful guidelines for attaining inner peace. Learn to prepare the body and mind for meditation with special breathing techniques and ways to focus and "let go"; develop superconscious awareness; strengthen your willpower; improve your intuition and increase your calmness.

Awaken to Superconsciousness
Meditation for Inner Peace, Intuitive Guidance, and Greater Awareness
Swami Kriyananda

This popular guide includes everything you need to know about the philosophy and practice of meditation, and how to apply the meditative mind to resolving common daily conflicts in uncommon, superconscious ways. Superconsciousness is the hidden mechanism at work behind intuition, spiritual and physical healing, successful problem solving, and finding deep, and lasting, joy.

"A brilliant, thoroughly enjoyable guide to the art and science of meditation. [Swami Kriyananda] entertains, informs, and inspires—his enthusiasm for the subject is contagious. This book is a joy to read from beginning to end."

—*Yoga International*

Ananda Yoga for Higher Awareness
Swami Kriyananda (J. Donald Walters)

Ananda Yoga is the system of postures that Kriyananda developed based on the training and instruction he personally received from Yogananda. This handy lay-flat reference book covers the basic principles of hatha yoga, including relaxation poses, spinal stretches, and inverted and sitting poses, all illustrated with photographs. Includes suggestions for routines of varying lengths for beginning to advanced study.

Affirmations for Self-Healing
J. Donald Walters (Swami Kriyananda)

This inspirational book contains 52 affirmations and prayers, each pair devoted to improving a quality in ourselves. Strengthen your will power; cultivate forgiveness, patience, health, and enthusiasm. A powerful tool for self-transformation.

Swami Kriyananda has also written extensively on philosophy, science, and the humanities:

Out of the Labyrinth

For Those Who Want to Believe, But Can't
Swami Kriyananda (J. Donald Walters)

Modern scientific and philosophical claims that life is meaningless and merely mechanistic are refuted by Kriyananda with his fresh approach to evolution and directional relativity. Hailed by scientists and religious leaders alike, this book is essential for everyone who is struggling to find answers to existential dilemmas.

Hope for a Better World!

The Small Communities Solution
Swami Kriyananda (J. Donald Walters)

In proposing what he calls "the small communities solution," the author expands Yogananda's vision of "world brotherhood colonies," which offer hope and promise for building a better world by example, rather than mere precept.

"Walters takes us on a fascinating journey backward in time in order to explore the future of human relationships. He guides us through the history of Western thought to arrive at a deep understanding of our evolutionary moment—the expansion of human consciousness. Like a good storyteller, Walters keeps us waiting breathlessly

to hear more, and how we can put ourselves on this path to a better world."
—Louise Diamond, Ph.D., author of *The Courage for Peace* and *The Peace Book*

Books by Swami Kriyananda on Arts and Education:

Art as a Hidden Message
Swami Kriyananda (J. Donald Walters)

With insightful commentary on the great musicians, artists, and creative thinkers of our time, this book offers a blueprint for the future of art, one that views both artistic expression and artistic appreciation as creative communication.

"Kriyananda's predictions for Art's future are enlightening. They include a return to simplicity and a renascence of beautiful melodies. This book is, I believe, the most important book of our time on this vitally important subject."
—Derek Bell

Space, Light, and Harmony
The Story of Crystal Hermitage
J. Donald Walters (Swami Kriyananda)

Space, Light, and Harmony—containing 70 beautiful color photographs—is an adventure in design, building, and living. It is the true story of the evolution of a home—from initial planning to interior decorating—that serves as a powerful metaphor for personal development.

Education for Life
Preparing Children to Meet the Challenges
Swami Kriyananda

This book offers a constructive and brilliant alternative to what has been called the disaster of modern education, which, according to the author, derives from an emphasis on technological competence at the expense of spiritual values. Based on the pioneering educational work in India by Paramhansa Yogananda, the *Education for Life* system has been tested and proven for over three decades at the many Living Wisdom schools located throughout the United States, and will provide the basis for The Yoga Institute of Living Wisdom in India.

"The author makes clear that 'education for life' begins in the home. The moment people become parents, they become the primary teachers. Through reading this book, parents will be learning more simple and effective methods of leading their children into becoming happier and more successful human beings. They will also be learning from their off-spring. The author's techniques will help produce a much less stressful home-life for all."

—Jim Doran, Education Consultant,
Joyful Child Journal

The Art of Supportive Leadership
*A Practical Guide for People in Positions of
    Responsibility*
Swami Kriyananda

Here is a new approach, one that views leadership in terms of shared accomplishment rather than personal advancement. Drawn from timeless Eastern wisdom, this book is clear, concise, and practical—designed from the start to quickly produce results even for those who don't have huge amounts of time to spare.

Used in training seminars in the United States, Europe, and India, this book gives practical advice for leaders and emerging leaders to help them increase effectiveness, creativity, and team building. Individual entrepreneurs, corporations such as Kellogg, military and police personnel, and non-profit organizations are using this approach.

"We've been looking for something like this for a long time. We use it in our Managers Training Workshop. This book is very practical, very readable, and concise. Highly recommended!"
—Kellogg Corporation

Money Magnetism
How to Attract What You Need When You Need It
Swami Kriyananda

This book can change your life by changing how you think and feel about money. According to the author, anyone can attract wealth: "There need be no limits to the flow of your abundance." Through numerous stories and examples from his own life and others', Swami Kriyananda vividly— sometimes humorously—shows you how and why the principles of money magnetism work, and how you can immediately start applying them to achieve greater success in your material and your spiritual life.

"A thoughtful, spiritual guide to financial and personal prosperity. This book has timeless wisdom and practical solutions."
—Maria Nemeth, author of *The Energy of Money*

Material Success Through Yoga Principles
A Twenty-six Lesson Study-at-home Program
Swami Kriyananda

This new course by Swami Kriyananda condenses the experience of nearly sixty years of work—organizing, building, and creating out of "thin air" seven of the largest, best-known, and most successful communities in the world today.

These lessons compellingly communicate that spirituality and material success are not separate, unrelated aspects of life. These two fields of endeavor can indeed help each other. By following yoga principles, you can have all the benefits of true success: happiness, inner peace, understanding, true friendships, and life's normal comforts without the suffocation of meaningless luxury.

Each of the twenty-six lessons is packed with

information, examples, stories, inspiration, and solutions to common problems that face every person seeking success.

By applying the principles and practices taught in this course, business, government, and educational leaders will be better prepared to guide our future directions with dignity, right-action, and success. It is also of immense help to the millions who suffer from symptoms of stressful business rhythms, and who seek a more balanced approach to personal satisfaction through their work.

"[This] is a significant contribution to the transformation of human awareness. . . . This course provides the platform on which ethics and practicality meet, each strengthening the other. I sincerely recommend that business and government leaders who want to be morally, psychologically, and practically prepared for the challenges that face our world study this course and apply its lessons with all due urgency, making it part of their training program for leaders of tomorrow."
—Professor Ervin Laszlo, Nobel Peace Prize Nominee, Founder and President, Club of Budapest

Crystal Clarity also makes available many music and spoken word audio resources. Here are some that you might find helpful:

Kriyananda Chants Yogananda
Swami Kriyananda

This CD offers a rare treat: hear Swami Kriyananda chant the spiritualized songs of his guru, Paramhansa Yogananda, in a unique and deeply inward way. Throughout the ages, chanting has been a means to achieve deeper meditation. Kriyananda's devotional chanting is certain to uplift your spirit.

AUM: Mantra of Eternity
Swami Kriyananda

This recording features nearly 70 minutes of continuous vocal chanting of AUM, the Sanskrit word meaning peace and oneness of spirit. AUM, the cosmic creative vibration, is extensively discussed by Yogananda in *Autobiography of a Yogi*. Chanted here by his disciple, Kriyananda, this recording is a stirring way to tune into this cosmic power.

Mantra
Swami Kriyananda

Discover the ancient healing chants of India. For millennia, the Gayatri Mantra and the Mahamrityunjaya Mantra have echoed down the banks of the holy river Ganges. These mantras express the heart's longing for peace, wisdom, and ultimate freedom from all earthly limitations, expressing the essence of every prayer. Both mantras are chanted in the traditional Sanskrit style, accompanied by the sound of 120 tambouras.

Metaphysical Meditations
Swami Kriyananda (J. Donald Walters)

Kriyananda's soothing voice leads you in thirteen guided meditations based on the soul-inspiring, mystical poetry of Paramhansa Yogananda. Each meditation is accompanied by beautiful classical music to help you quiet your thoughts and prepare you for deep states of meditation. Includes a full recitation of Yogananda's poem, Samadhi, which appears in *Autobiography of a Yogi*. A great aid to the serious meditator, as well as those just beginning their practice.

The original 1946 edition of *Autobiography of a Yogi* is also available as an audio book.

Autobiography of a Yogi

by Paramhansa Yogananda, read by Swami Kriyananda

audio book, selected chapters, 10 hours

This is a recording of the original, unedited 1946 edition of *Autobiography of a Yogi*, presented on six cassettes. Read by Swami Kriyananda, this is the only audio edition that is read by one of Yogananda's direct disciples—someone who both knew him and was directly trained by him. This abridged reading focuses on the key chapters and most thrilling sections of this spiritual classic.

Ananda Sangha

ANANDA SANGHA IS A FELLOWSHIP OF KINDRED souls following the teachings of Paramhansa Yogananda. The Sangha embraces the search for higher consciousness through the practice of meditation, and through the ideal of service to others in their quest for Self-realization. Approximately 10,000 spiritual seekers are affiliated with Ananda Sangha throughout the world.

Founded in 1968 by Swami Kriyananda, a direct disciple of Paramhansa Yogananda, Ananda includes seven communities in the United States and Europe, and an eighth community in India. Worldwide, about 1,000 devotees live in these spiritual communities, which are based on Yogananda's ideals of "plain living and high thinking."

"Thousands of youths must go north, south, east and west to cover the earth with little colonies, demonstrating that simplicity of living plus high thinking lead to the greatest happiness!"

After pronouncing these words at a garden party in Beverly Hills, California in 1949, Paramhansa Yogananda raised his arms, and chanting the sacred cosmic vibration AUM, he "registered in the ether" his blessings on what has become the spiritual communities movement. From that moment on, Swami Kriyananda dedicated himself to bringing this vision from inspiration to reality by establishing communities where home, job, school, worship, family, friends, and recreation could evolve together as part of the interwoven fabric of harmonious, balanced living. Yogananda predicted that these communities would "spread like wildfire," becoming the model lifestyle for the coming millennium.

Swami Kriyananda lived with his guru during the last four years of the Master's life, and continued to serve his organization for another ten years, bringing the teachings of Kriya Yoga and Self-realization to audiences in the United States, Europe, Australia, and, from 1958–1962, India. In 1968, together with a small group of close friends and students, he founded the first "world brotherhood community" in the foothills of the Sierra Nevada Mountains in northeastern California. Initially a meditation retreat center located on 67 acres of forested land, Ananda World Brotherhood Community today encompasses 1,000 acres where about 250 people live a dynamic, fulfilling life based on the principles and practices of spiritual, mental, and physical development, cooperation, respect, and divine friendship.

At this writing, after nearly forty years of existence, Ananda is one of the most successful networks of intentional communities in the world. Urban communities have been developed in Palo Alto and Sacramento, California; Portland, Oregon; Seattle, Washington; and Rhode Island. In Europe, near Assisi, Italy, a spiritual retreat and community was established in 1983, where today nearly one hundred residents from eight countries live. The Expanding Light, a guest retreat for spiritual studies visited by over 2,000 people each year, offers courses in Self-realization and related subjects.

Ananda Sangha Contact Information

mail:

14618 Tyler Foote Road
Nevada City, CA 95959

phone:

530. 478.7560

online:

www.ananda.org

email:

sanghainfo@ananda.org

CRYSTAL CLARITY PUBLISHERS

W HEN YOU'RE SEEKING A BOOK ON PRACTICAL spiritual living, you want to know it's based on an authentic tradition of timeless teachings and resonates with integrity.

This is the goal of Crystal Clarity Publishers: to offer you books of practical wisdom filled with true spiritual principles that have not only been tested through the ages but also through personal experience.

Started in 1968, Crystal Clarity is the publishing house of Ananda, a spiritual community dedicated to meditation and living by true values, as shared by Paramhansa Yogananda, and his direct disciple, Swami Kriyananda, the founder of Ananda. The members of our staff and each of our authors live by these principles. Our worldwide work touches thousands around the world whose lives have been enriched by these universal teachings.

We publish only books that combine creative thinking, universal principles, and a timeless message. Crystal Clarity books will open doors to help you discover more fulfillment and joy by living and acting from the center of peace within you.

To request a catalog, place an order for the above listed products, or to find out more information, please contact us:

mail:

    14618 Tyler Foote Road
    Nevada City, CA 95959

phone:

    800.424.1055 (toll free in USA and Canada)
    530.478.7600

fax:

    530.478.7610

email:

    clarity@crystalclarity.com

For our online catalog, complete with secure ordering, please visit us on the web at:

    www.crystalclarity.com